Spellbound
Festive Beading
Four

A Spellbound Bead Co Book
Copyright © Spellbound Bead Co Publishing 2019

First Published in the UK 2019

Julie Ashford has asserted her right to be identified as author of this work in accordance with the Copyright, Designs and Patents Act, 1988.

All rights reserved. No part of this publication may be reproduced, stored in a retrieval system, or transmitted in any form or by any means, by photocopying, recording or otherwise, without prior permission in writing from the publisher.

The designs in this book must not be reproduced for resale or financial gain.

The author and publisher have made every effort to ensure that all the instructions in the book are accurate and safe, and therefore cannot accept liability for any resulting injury, damage or loss to persons or property, however it may arise.

Names of manufacturers, bead ranges and other products are provided for the information of readers, with no intention to infringe copyright or trademarks.

Printed in the UK by WM Print
for the Spellbound Bead Co

ISBN - 978-0-9565030-9-1

10 9 8 7 6 5 4 3 2 1

Editor: Jean Hall
Pattern Testing and Sample Production: Edna Kedge and Vicky Pritchard
Additional designs - Vicky Pritchard and Jodie Garrington
Photography: Spellbound Bead Co

Visit our website at www.spellboundbead.co.uk

Spellbound Bead Co
47 Tamworth Street
Lichfield
Staffordshire
WS13 6JW
England

Call 01543 417650 for direct sales
or your local wholesale distributor

Also available in this series:

Spellbound Festive Beading
ISBN 978-0-9565030-2-2

Spellbound Festive Beading Two
ISBN 978-0-9565030-5-3

Spellbound Festive Beading Three
ISBN 978-0-9565030-8-4

Acknowledgements

Thank you to everyone who has contributed to this book - the eagle-eyed pattern testers and an editor par-excellence; the oh-so-patient bead counters, tea-makers and the photography assistants who hold branches very still and tweak robins' beaks.

Also a big thank you to all of our customers who show boundless enthusiasm for beading and baubles.
This book is dedicated to them and to everyone who has a passion for beads, colour and all things that sparkle.

Contents

Introduction	4
Essential Ingredients	6
Tools & Useful Extras	7
Tips & Techniques	8
Beadwork Stitches for Beginners	10

The Projects

Candy Canes	12
Snowdrop Bauble	16
Robin Bauble	20
Finlandia Tree	28
Heavenly Bauble	34
Comet Bauble	40
Candle Decoration	48
Lotus Bauble	56
Anastasia Bauble	64
Peacock Bauble	72
Nutcracker Soldier	88
Tin Drum	98
Sugar Plum Fairy	102
Index & Suppliers	112

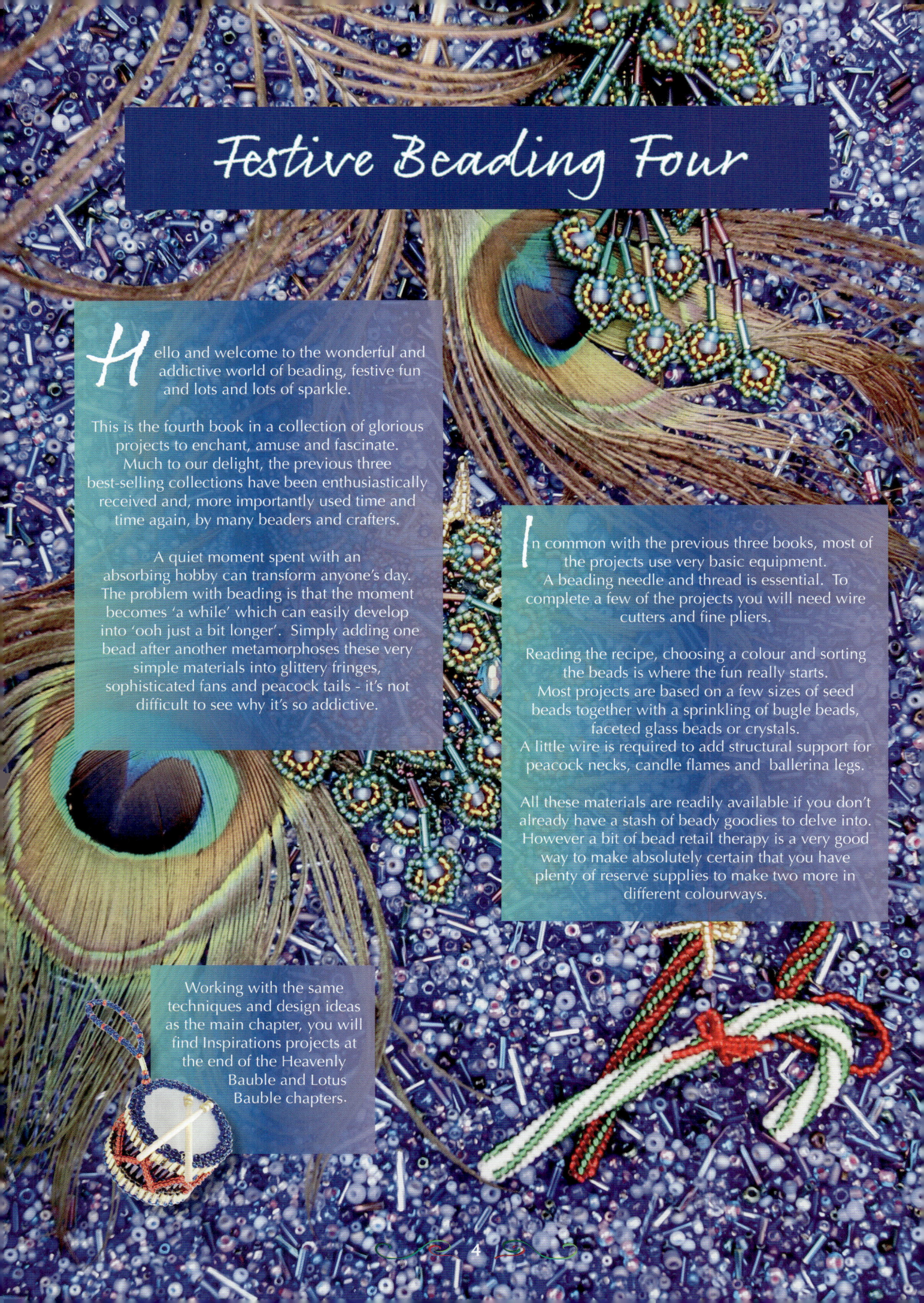

Festive Beading Four

Hello and welcome to the wonderful and addictive world of beading, festive fun and lots and lots of sparkle.

This is the fourth book in a collection of glorious projects to enchant, amuse and fascinate. Much to our delight, the previous three best-selling collections have been enthusiastically received and, more importantly used time and time again, by many beaders and crafters.

A quiet moment spent with an absorbing hobby can transform anyone's day. The problem with beading is that the moment becomes 'a while' which can easily develop into 'ooh just a bit longer'. Simply adding one bead after another metamorphoses these very simple materials into glittery fringes, sophisticated fans and peacock tails - it's not difficult to see why it's so addictive.

In common with the previous three books, most of the projects use very basic equipment. A beading needle and thread is essential. To complete a few of the projects you will need wire cutters and fine pliers.

Reading the recipe, choosing a colour and sorting the beads is where the fun really starts. Most projects are based on a few sizes of seed beads together with a sprinkling of bugle beads, faceted glass beads or crystals. A little wire is required to add structural support for peacock necks, candle flames and ballerina legs.

All these materials are readily available if you don't already have a stash of beady goodies to delve into. However a bit of bead retail therapy is a very good way to make absolutely certain that you have plenty of reserve supplies to make two more in different colourways.

Working with the same techniques and design ideas as the main chapter, you will find Inspirations projects at the end of the Heavenly Bauble and Lotus Bauble chapters.

Choose a Project to Suit Your Beading Experience

One Star - very easy - this project will be quick to make.

Two Stars - simple techniques - this project will take a little more time to complete.

Three Stars - getting a little more complex but manageable for a beginner with patience.

Four Stars - several stages building on top of one another using a variety of stitches. These are projects for someone with a bit of beading experience.

Choosing what to make is probably the most difficult aspect of beading. And soon you will discover side projects developing as you work...a feather motif from the Lotus Bauble will become a fern leaf or an ear of wheat; or perhaps the wings on a fairy will turn into a butterfly.

Making candles could become addictive as they look even better en masse, as do the calorie-free Candy Canes; and a line of snow-sprinkled Finlandia Trees is fabulous dotted along a branch from the garden.

For baroque splendour the Anastasia Bauble with its encrusted crystal rivoli swags is the height of luxury, or there's the Art Deco drama of the Luxor design.

And of course for a real Christmas treat, there's a trip to the ballet where you can create a handsome Honour Guard of Nutcracker soldiers and twinkling Sugar Plum Fairies that will delight everyone.

Look out for the Extra Info boxes. They contain hints and tips on the techniques and materials you will be using in the projects.

It's time to get started. Put those boring everyday routines to one side, get your beads out and indulge in some real colour therapy.

Happy Beading !

Julie
July 2019

Essential Ingredients

The projects in this book all use a very simple selection of beads. For a lot of the designs you will need just two or three colours or sizes of seed beads, one size of bugle beads and a selection of fire polished faceted beads. This quick guide will give you an introduction to these basic supplies and the few extra items you might need for some of the patterns.

Seed Beads

These are the small glass beads used for weaving and stringing intricate patterns, tassels and fringes.

Seed beads are available in many sizes. These sizes are quoted on an inverse scale so size 6/0 is larger than a size 10/0.

These projects use sizes 6/0, 8/0, 10/0 and 15/0 seed beads. If preferred you can substitute size 11/0 for size 10/0 seed beads in most of the designs.

Seed beads are manufactured in the Czech Republic or Japan. Czech seeds tend to be more rounded than the Japanese seeds so it is better not to mix the two types of the same size in the same project.

Bugle Beads

Bugles are small glass tubes which are available in several lengths. Most of these projects use size 3 bugle beads which are 6-7mm long, or a size 2 bugle which measures 4-5mm in length.

Nib-Bit Beads

Two-holed beads resembling sweetcorn kernels. Made by Matubo in the Czech Republic.

Twin Beads

Twin beads have an eliptical 2.5 x 5mm profile and have two parallel holes. They are manufactured by Preciosa in the Czech Republic. Please also see Tips & Techniques.

Fire Polished Faceted Glass

These hand-faceted beads are heated in a kiln to give the glass a glossy finish.

Crystal Beads

Precision-cut faceted lead crystal glass beads have maximum sparkle.

Delica Beads

These tiny, cylinder-shaped glass beads are used for accurate weaving as they will sit close together like bricks in a wall. They are available in several sizes and hundreds of colours. This book uses only size 11/0 Delicas.

Rivoli Stones
These are sunray-cut stones without holes. A setting is created using seed beads and Delica beads in the Anastasia project.

Wire & Findings
Half-hard 1.2mm and 0.8mm diameter wire is used to make armatures in several projects. Half-hard wire bends easily with hand tools but is stiff enough to retain the form required.

Filigree Bead Cups make epaulettes for soldiers and skirts and halos for angels.

Beading Thread
Sold under many brand names such as Nymo and Superlon, beading thread is available in several thicknesses and many colours.

These projects all use a size D thread.

Fishhook Earwires are comfortable to wear but you can substitute post & ball or clip earfittings if you prefer.

Czech glass wing beads make creating angels easy on the Heavenly Bauble.

Spring clips for tree decorations are available from specialist suppliers. Choose one with a single spur for the Christmas Candle chapter.

Tools & Useful Extras

Threading Necessities

Beading Needles

Beading needles have a very narrow eye so they can pass through beads that have a small hole.

Size 10 Beading is a general beading needle that is suitable for most of the projects.

Size 12 Beading is a little finer to allow multiple passes of the thread through the bead holes.

Sharp Scissors to trim the threads close to the work are essential.

A Thread Conditioner such as Thread Magic helps to smooth the kinks in the thread if you get into a knot or tangle.

A Fleecy Beading Mat with a slight pile will stop the beads from rolling around and make it easy to pick up small beads using the point of the needle.

Pliers
A tool set is required to construct the simple wire armatures underlying several designs

Round-Nosed Pliers for turning loops.

Cutters for trimming wire to length.

Chain-Nosed or Flat-Nosed Pliers for gripping, and opening and closing jump rings.

Tips & Techniques

There are a few basic techniques that you will need to know in order to work through the projects in this book. If you need a special technique for a particular project it will be explained within that chapter, but for the techniques that apply to most of the designs this is what you need to read.

Using a Keeper Bead

Before you start a piece of beadwork you will need to put a stopper at the end of the thread. The easiest stopper to use is a keeper bead.

A keeper bead is a spare bead, ideally of a different colour to the work, that is held on a temporary knot close to the end of the thread. Once the beading is completed the keeper bead is removed. That end of the thread is then knotted securely and finished neatly within the beadwork.

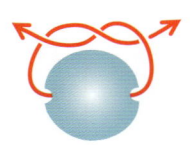

fig 1

To Add a Keeper Bead - Position the keeper bead 15cm from the end of the thread (unless instructed otherwise) and tie a simple overhand knot around the bead (fig 1). When you thread on the first beads of the pattern push them right up to the keeper bead - the tension in the thread will prevent the keeper bead from slipping.

When the work is complete, untie the knot and remove the keeper bead. Attach the needle to this end of the thread and secure as shown opposite.

Correcting a Mistake

If you make a mistake whilst you are following a pattern remove the needle and pull the thread back until you have undone the work sufficiently. Do not turn the needle and try to pass it back through the holes in the beads - the needle tip will certainly catch another thread inside the beads and make a filamentous knot that is almost impossible to undo successfully.

If you are working with a double thread, carefully pull on the thread to bring the blunt end of the needle backwards through the beading. Take your time and the needle will be guided back through the exact path it had taken previously and you will not cause a knot.

Making A Wire Loop With Pliers

Hold the cut end of the wire in a pair of round-nosed pliers. With your other hand, grip the wire 8mm below the plier jaws to give firm support. Roll the wrist holding the pliers to form the loop. Make sure it is properly closed and centralise the loop above the beads with the tips of the pliers.

A Note About Baubles

Baubles are made by many different manufacturers – some are hand-blown, paper-thin glass and others are machine-made in both glass and plastic.

Hand-blown baubles can vary a little in size from the stated diameter so you may need to adjust the bead count slightly if you are making a closely-fitted design. The variety of neck sizes across all diameters of baubles, both hand-made and machine-made, is quite marked.

The bauble designs in this book require a close-fitted ring of beads around the neck so you may need to adjust your bead count accordingly. Guidance is given where necessary if you need to make adjustments.

Adding in a New Thread

On occasion you will need to add a new thread to the work.

Work the old thread until you have no less than 15cm of thread remaining. Remove the needle from this thread end and leave the end hanging loose.

Prepare the needle with a new thread and tie a keeper bead 5cm from the end.

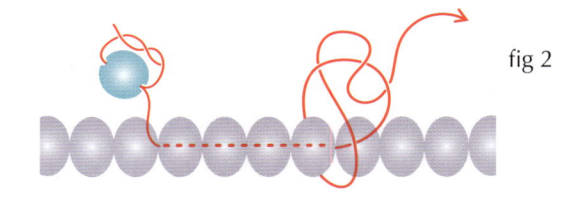

fig 2

Starting about 15 beads back from the old thread end pass the needle through 3 or 4 beads towards the old thread end.

Make a double knot here (fig 2). Pass the needle through a further 4 or 5 beads and repeat the knot. Pass the needle through to emerge alongside the old thread end and continue the beading.

When you have worked on a little, trim away the tail of thread and the keeper bead as close as possible to the beads for a neat finish.

A note of caution - before you make the knots, make sure that the needle does not have to pass through these beads again. If it does, add the new thread using a keeper bead with a 15cm thread tail and do not tie any knots around the existing thread. You can return to the keeper bead later, remove it and attach the needle to this thread end. Secure as in 'Finishing Off a Thread End' opposite.

Finishing off a Thread End

You will need to finish off a thread end neatly and securely.

Pass the needle through a few beads of the pattern. At that position pick up the thread between the beads with the point of the needle. Pull the needle through to leave a loop of thread 2cm in diameter. Pass the needle through the loop twice (fig 3) and gently pull down to form a double knot between the beads.

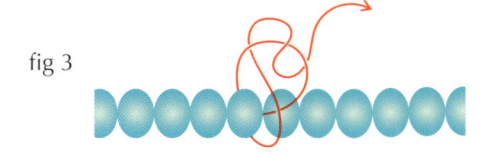

fig 3

Pass through five or six beads of the work and repeat the double knot. Pass through five or six more beads before trimming the thread end as close as possible to the work.

Do not finish off any thread ends until instructed to do so - you might need that thread end again or the needle might have to pass past that position again. See 'Knotty Problems' below.

Knotty Problems

Knots as Obstacles

Be careful where you tie your knots when adding a new thread to your work or finishing off an old thread end. Do not position the knots adjacent to, or inside beads that you have to pass the needle through again, because it will not fit through a hole blocked with thread. Sometimes it is better to leave an old thread end hanging loose and return to it later, than to place a knot where it might cause an obstruction.

Preventing Unwanted Knots

It can be very frustrating to get a knot in your working thread - especially if it keeps happening. There are a few things you can try that might help to prevent these annoying knots.

Don't work with a thread that is too long for you – if the stated 1.8m is too much for you to manage, use a shorter length and add a new thread if necessary.

If you get a knot, undo it carefully and condition the thread, with a suitable product such as Thread Magic, to remove the distortions in the fibres. The thread will be less likely to re-knot in the same place.

Towards the end of a reel, the thread can be very curly. Cut a slightly shorter length of thread, pulling it between your fingers to help to release the curls, before you prepare the needle. An application of thread conditioner can help too. If it is very distorted be prepared to throw away the last metre or so, rather than spoil your project.

Twin Beads

Twin beads have two parallel holes (fig 4). It is important to thread through the right hole in the correct direction.

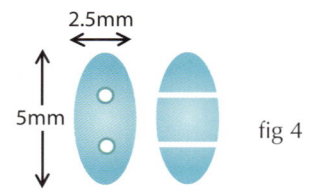

2.5mm
5mm
fig 4

Having an eliptical profile, the Twin beads will form a curve if threaded one against the other through the hole at one end (fig 5).

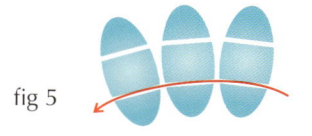

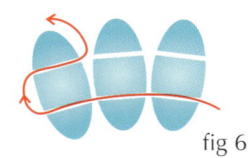

fig 5

fig 6

If you are instructed to pass through the second hole in a Twin bead you must ensure that the needle passes through this hole in the opposite direction creating a strap of thread on the side of the Twin bead (fig 6). This reverses the direction of the needle and gives you access to the outer row of holes on the Twin beads of the previous row.

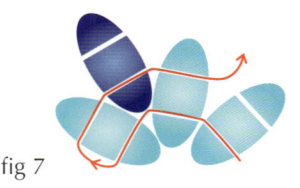

fig 7

Adding a new Twin bead into the gap between the second, or outer holes, on the new row fills in the gap between the outer holes on the first row of Twin beads (fig 7).

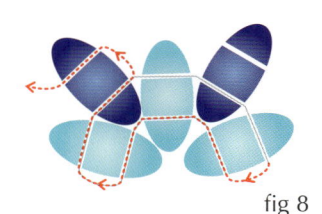

You may have to take a long route back to reposition the needle.
Make sure it is pointing in the correct direction for the next row (fig 8).

fig 8

Beadwork Stitches for Beginners

There are five basic beadwork stitches used in this book - Ladder stitch, Brick stitch, Square stitch, Peyote stitch and Tubular Herringbone stitch. Ladder stitch can be used to form a foundation row for both Brick stitch and Tubular Herringbone stitch so a simple guide to this is given first. If you have not used these techniques before you may find these extra notes useful.

Ladder Stitch

Ladder stitch lines up the bead holes in each new stitch parallel to the holes in the previous stitch.

1 Prepare the needle with 1m of single thread and tie a keeper bead 15cm from the end. Thread on two beads. Pass the needle back up through the first bead and down through the second to bring the two beads alongside one another (fig 1).

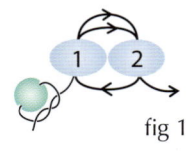

fig 1 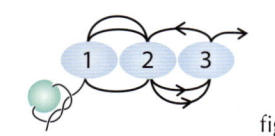   fig 2 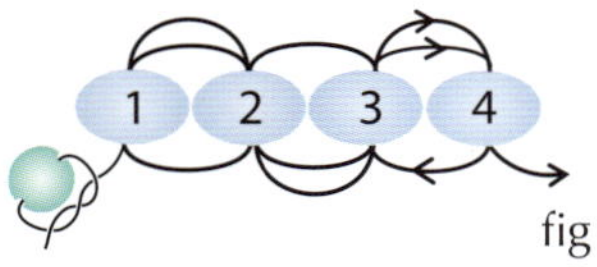   fig 3

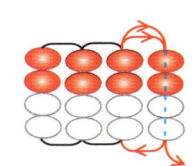

When making the hat in the Robin Bauble chapter the beads are added in groups of four. The ladder effect shows clearly as each stitch of four beads adds one rung to the Ladder stitch row.

2 Thread on a third bead; pass the needle down bead 2 and back up bead 3 bringing bead 3 to sit alongside beads 1 and 2 (fig 2).
Repeat to add a fourth bead (fig 3). Notice that the thread path alternates up and down with each new stitch. This is Ladder stitch.

Brick Stitch

Brick stitch is so called because of the pattern the beads form as they line up, in staggered rows, giving the impression of a brick wall. It requires a starter row or 'foundation row' onto which the first row of Brick stitch is worked.

3 **The Ladder Stitch Foundation Row** - Make a row of ten Ladder-stitched beads as in Steps 1 and 2 (fig 4). The Brick stitches attach to the loops of thread along the edge of the Ladder-stitched row.

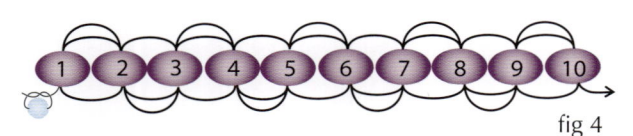

fig 4

4 **Starting Brick Stitch** - Thread on two beads (11 & 12). Pick up the loop of thread between beads 10 and 9 and pass back up through bead 12 in the opposite direction (fig 5). This should bring the two new beads to sit alongside one another with bead 11 slightly overhanging the previous row.

fig 5   fig 6

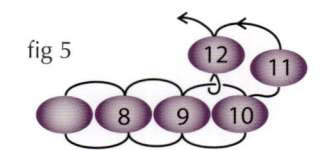

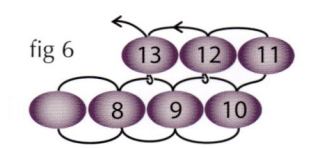

5 Thread on bead 13. Pick up the loop of thread between beads 9 and 8 and pass back up bead 13 (fig 6). Repeat, adding one bead at a time, to the end of the row (ten beads in total).

6 Thread on beads 21 and 22 to start the next row (fig 7) and work to the end of the row.

fig 7

This is Brick stitch.

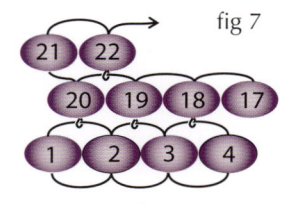

Each row starts with a two-bead stitch followed by a series of single-bead stitches. The beads of each row should sit alongside one another, with the holes parallel and the rows should sit closely on top of one another. You should not be able to see the thread except at the top and bottom of the work.

The Nutcracker's face is made using Brick Stitch.

It is then embellished using a combination of Square stitches and fringe strands to add the nose, moustache, beard and hair.

10

Tubular Herringbone

Tubular Herringbone stitch is used in this book to create slim flexible ropes.

The thread path pulls each two-bead stitch into a shallow V and as the rows build you start to see a Herringbone (chevron) pattern emerge. A length of Tubular Herringbone stitch needs a foundation row – this is normally made in Ladder stitch.

7 The Ladder Stitch Foundation - Make a row of six Ladder-stitched beads (as in Steps 1 and 2).
Link the first bead to the last with a Ladder stitch to make a ring (or drum) (fig 8).

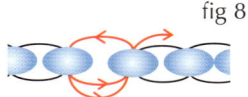

fig 8

To make the first row of Tubular Herringbone stitch the needle passes up and down through the holes of the foundation row.

8 Tubular Herringbone Stitch - Thread on two beads. Pass down the next bead around the foundation row and up the following bead (fig 9).
Repeat to the end of the row.

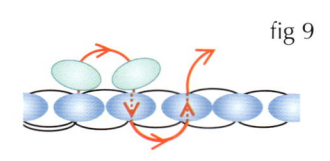

fig 9

Reposition the needle for the next row by passing up through the first bead of the row just completed (fig 10).

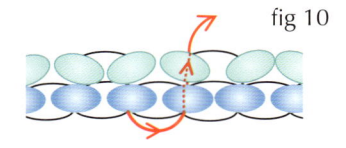

fig 10

9 Thread on two beads to start a new row.
Pass down through the adjacent bead of the previous row and up through the next bead along (fig 11).
Repeat to the end of the row.

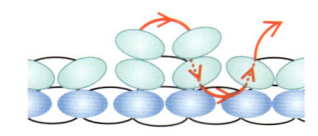

fig 11

Square Stitch

In Square stitch the needle makes a square-shaped path through a newly-added bead and the adjacent bead on the previous row. Square stitches are often used to link adjacent beads from separate rows or to secure a seam.

To begin a block of Square stitch you need a starter row of beads (fig 12).

fig 12

Thread on the first bead of the second row.
Pass the needle through the last bead of the starter row and back through the new bead to bring the two beads together with the holes parallel (fig 13).

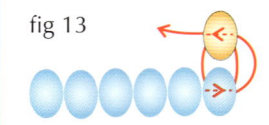

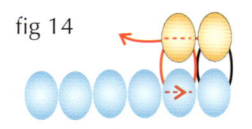

fig 13   fig 14

Thread on a new bead and pass the needle through the next bead along the starter row and back through the new bead (fig 14) – note the square path of the thread.

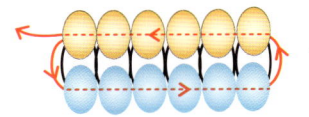

fig 15

At the end of a row, pass the needle through the previous row and back along the new row to bring all of the beads into line (fig 15).

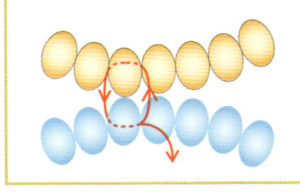

A single Square stitch can be used to link two adjacent rows. These stitches are often reinforced with another pass of thread.

Even-Count Peyote Stitch

Even-Count Peyote stitch starts with an even number of beads. Alternate beads are added on the next row to produce a key and keyhole profile. On the following row the needle weaves through the key beads adding new beads into the keyholes.

fig 16

Thread on ten beads (an even number) for the starter row (fig 16).

Thread on one bead and pass back through bead nine of the starter row (fig 17).

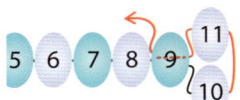

fig 17

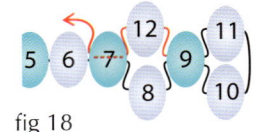

fig 18

Thread on one bead and pass through bead seven (fig 18).
Repeat to the end of the row.

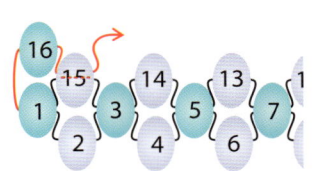

fig 19

Thread on one bead to start the new row. Pass through the first key bead along to pull the new bead into the first keyhole (fig 19).

Repeat to add a bead into the next keyhole (fig 20).
Repeat to the end of the row.

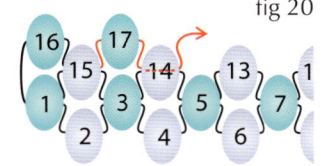

fig 20

11

Candy Canes

You Will Need

Materials

to Make a Red & White Candy Cane

5g of size 10 ceylon white seed beads A
5g of size 10 silver lined red seed beads B
2g of size 10 silver lined green seed beads C
15cm of 1.2mm half-hard silver plated wire
White size D beading thread

to Make a Green & White Candy Cane

Swap the colours of B and C
Use a white beading thread

to Make a Red & Green Candy Cane

Swap the colours of A and C
Use a red or green beading thread

Tools

A size 10 beading needle
A pair of scissors to trim the threads
Flat-nosed pliers and wire cutters

a completed Candy Cane Decoration measures approximately 8.0 x 3.5cm

Traditional sweetie treats usually don't last until Twelfth Night. These jolly candy canes are dentist-friendly, easy to make & will sparkle year after year.

The Decoration is Made in Three Stages

A length of Twisted Tubular Herringbone stitch is used to create a hollow rope.

A length of wire is threaded down the centre of the rope. This wire is bent into shape and the ends of the rope are sealed.

The bow and hanging loop are added to complete the decoration.

Extra Info....
The Candy Canes are made in Twisted Tubular Herringbone stitch.

To make the tube twist, the needle is repositioned for the start of the next stitch through the beads of the previous two rows (rather than through just one row, as in the standard technique). This adjustment tilts the completed stitch.

By tilting all the stitches, the tube appears to twist. Working a candy cane stripe makes the twist effect more noticable.

1 Tubular Twisted Herringbone stitch - Prepare the needle with 1.5m of single thread and tie a keeper bead 20cm from the end.

2 A Ladder stitch foundation row is required to support the first row of Herringbone stitch.

Thread on 2A and 2B. Pass the needle up the 2A and down the 2B to make two columns (fig 1). Pass through the beads again to make the stitch firm.

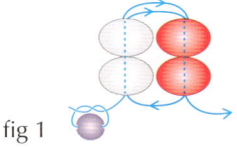

fig 1

Thread on 2A and pass down the 2B and up the new 2A to make a new column (fig 2).
Pass the needle through the beads again to make the stitch firm.

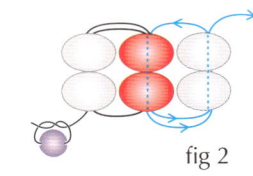

fig 2

Thread on 2B and pass up the previous 2A and down the new 2B (fig 3).
Pass the needle through the beads again to make the stitch firm.

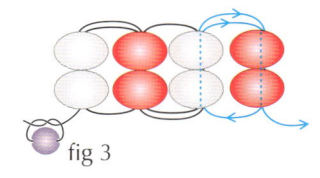

fig 3

This is Ladder stitch.

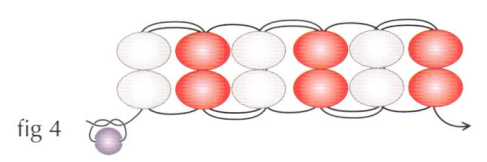

fig 4

Repeat to add another column of 2A and one column of 2B (fig 4).

3 Pass the needle up the first column of 2A, down the last column of 2B and up the first 2A once more to form a small cylinder (fig 5).

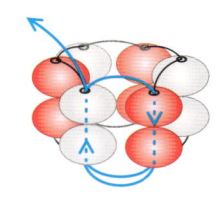

Pass the needle through these four beads again to make the stitch firm.

fig 5

4 One row of plain Herringbone stitch is required before starting the twist. There will be three stitches in this row.

The needle is emerging at the top of the cylinder from an A bead.

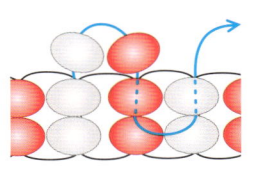

Stitch One - Thread on 1A and 1B. Pass down the next B bead along the top edge of the cylinder and up the following 1A (fig 6).

fig 6

Stitch Two - Repeat to add one stitch of 1A and 1B (fig 7).

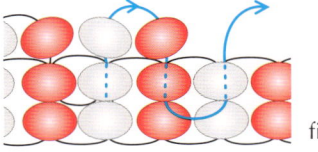

fig 7

Stitch Three - Thread on 1A and 1B. Pass down the next 1B along the top edge of the cylinder, up the following 1A of the cylinder and the first 1A of this row (fig 8).

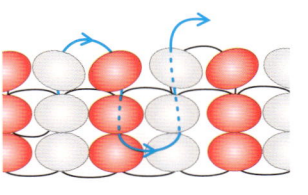

fig 8

The third stitch both completes the row and repositions the needle for the new row.

5 Making the Twist - On the previous row of plain Herringbone stitch the needle passed down the next 1B along and up the following 1A.

To make the rope twist, the needle passes down the next 1B and up the top 2A of the next column - at the end of the row it passes up the top 3A (to finish the stitch and reposition the needle for the new row).

There will be three stitches in this row.

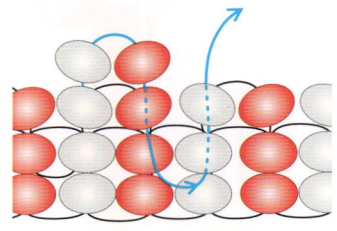

fig 9

Stitch One - Thread on 1A and 1B. Pass down the following 1B and up the top 2A of the next column around (fig 9).

Stitch Two - Repeat Stitch One.

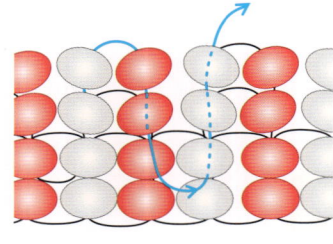

Stitch Three - Thread on 1A and 1B. Pass down the following 1B and up the top 3A of the next column (fig 10).

fig 10

After five rows of these three stitches, the twist will start to be quite noticeable.

Repeat until the rope measures 10.5cm in length.

6 The end of the rope needs to be closed in a little.

Thread on 1A. Pass down the next 1B bead and up the following 1A (fig 11). Repeat twice to complete the row.

Pass through the first 1A of this row to reposition the needle for the next row.

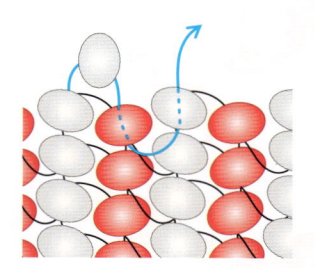

fig 11

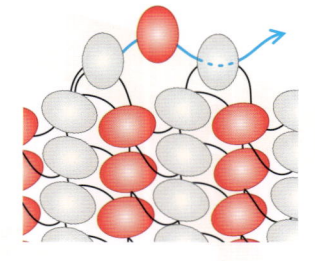

Thread on 1B and pass through the next A bead along (fig 12). Repeat this stitch twice.

fig 12

Pass through the first 1B of the row just made but do not pull the thread tight - leave a channel down the centre to allow the wire to pass through.

Remove the needle and leave the thread hanging loose.

7 Remove the keeper bead from the start of the foundation row and attach the needle to this thread end.

This end of the rope needs to be closed tight.

Thread on 1A. Working along the lower edge of the foundation row, Pass up the next B bead around and down the following 1A (fig 13).

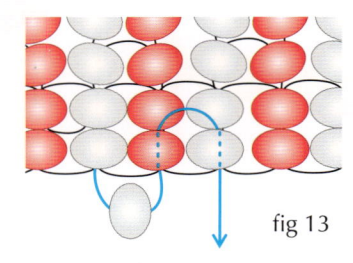

Repeat twice to add 3A in total.

fig 13

Pass the needle through the 3A just added and pull the thread tight to draw the beads into the centre of the space.

Pass the needle through the 3A beads twice more to make sure the closure is neat and firm.
Finish off this thread end neatly and securely.

Reattach the needle to the thread end at the other end of the rope.

8 Wiring and Bending the Cane - Fold the last 6mm of the 15cm wire over and flatten to make a smooth, neat bend at the end (fig 14).

Pass this neatened end of the wire through the hole at the top of the rope and down the centre of the work so it pushes up to the closed end made in Step 7.

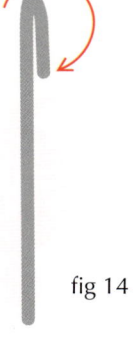

fig 14

Stretch the rope gently so it is at its fullest extent and trim the excess wire flush with the open end of the rope.

Pull the wire out of the rope just a little so you can bend this end into a flat loop as fig 14.

Push the wire back inside the rope so the newly-folded end just disappears and the other end is tight against the inside of the closed end.

Pull the thread tight on the open end of the the rope to close up the gap. Pass the needle through the last 3B beads and pull firmly. Repeat.

Make sure that the wire cannot poke back through any gap and finish off the thread end neatly and securely.

9 The top of the cane needs to be bent over into a hook. The top of this bend should be approximately 2.5cm from the top end of the rope.

You can make the bend quite easily with your fingers, but wrapping the work over a 1.0 – 1.5cm cylindrical mould makes it a little easier - try using a wooden spoon handle or a marker pen.

Make your bend and adjust the rope so the twist sits evenly along the length.

10 **The Bow and Hanging Loop** - Prepare the needle with 1.2m of single thread and tie a keeper bead 15cm from the end.

Decide which side of the cane you want to face forwards (to be decorated with the bow). On the reverse side, 5.5 – 6.0cm from the bottom of the cane, pass the needle through one of the A or B beads so the keeper bead pulls up snug to the work.

Thread on sufficient C beads to make a complete band around the cane at this position (approximately 18C).

Pass the needle through the first C bead again to close up the band (fig 15).

Pass through all the beads of the band again to make it firm.

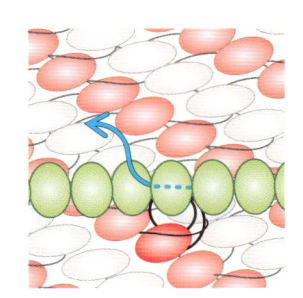

fig 15

Pass through half the band beads to emerge from the C bead closest to the centre front of the cane, ready to make the bow.

11 Thread on 7C. Leaving aside the last 1C to anchor the strand, pass back through the previous 6C and the C bead on the band in the opposite direction (fig 16).

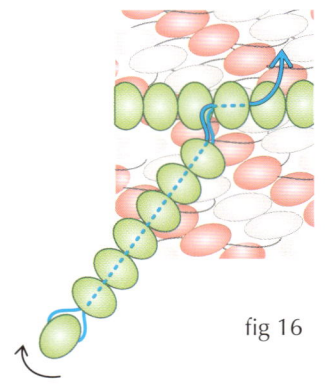

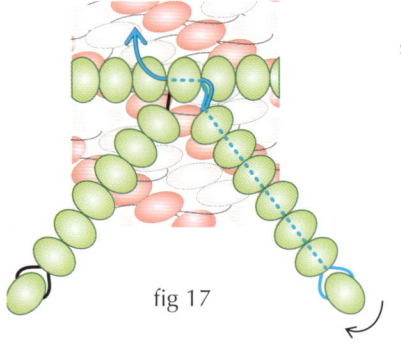

fig 16

Repeat to add a 7C strand to this side of the C bead on the band (fig 17).

Pull both these strands into position below the band to form the tails of the bow.

fig 17

12 Thread on 9C and pass back through the same C bead on the band to make a bow loop (fig 18).

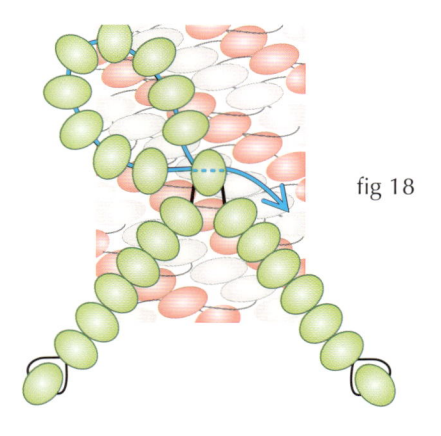

fig 18

Repeat to make a bow loop on this side of the C bead.

Pass the needle through the second half of the band to emerge at the keeper bead.

13 The Hanging Loop - Make a firm stitch through two beads of the Herringbone rope at this position so the start of the hanging loop has a strong connection to the cane.

Thread on 50C. Pass through the same two beads on the rope to close up the loop at the back of the cane.

Pass the needle through the 50C beads of the loop again to strengthen. Reinforce the connection to the back of the cane with two firm stitches through the most appropriately placed beads on the Herringbone rope.

Pass the needle through the beads of the band to emerge behind the bow. Make a stitch through the closest bead or beads of the twist to hold the band firm. If necessary make a few stitches to hold the bow loops and tails neatly in place.

Finish off all the remaining thread ends neatly and securely.

Snowdrop Bauble

You Will Need

Materials

One 40mm frosted white glass bauble
12g of size 10 silver lined crystal seed beads A
6g of size 8 silver lined crystal seed beads B
15g of ceylon white Twin beads C
4g of size 3 silver lined crystal bugle beads D
Twenty-five 4mm crystal AB fire polished glass beads E
Sixteen 9x7mm crystal AB fire polished glass drops F
One 8mm crystal AB fire polished glass bead G
White size D beading thread

Tools

A size 10 beading needle
A pair of scissors to trim the threads

A classic demonstration of beautiful beaded fringing, and reminiscent of delicate Art Nouveau lamp shades, Twin bead snowdrop motifs support long twinkling strands of seed beads and sparkling faceted drops.

The Decoration is Made in Four Stages

A foundation row is fitted around the neck of the bauble.

Three rows of netted beadwork are added to cover the main body of the bauble.

Sixteen dangling fringe strands are attached to the lower edge of the netting.

The hanging loop is added to the top of the bauble.

This design uses two-hole Twin beads. If you have not used Twin beads before see page 9 (Tips and Techniques) for more information.

1 The Foundation Row - Prepare the needle with 1.5m of single thread and tie a keeper bead 15cm from the end.

2 Thread on eight repeats of 1C and 2A. Pass the needle through the same hole in the first C bead to make a ring (fig 1).

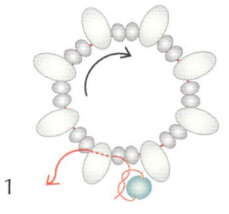

fig 1

Place the ring over the neck of the bauble - it needs to fit snugly so you may need to adjust the bead count.

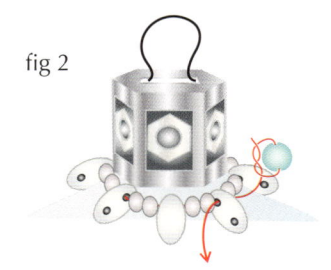

fig 2

If you need to make an adjustment, add or subtract A beads equally from all eight sections to keep the C beads evenly spaced around the ring (fig 2).

3 Remove the ring from the bauble and pass the needle through the same holes in all the beads again to make the ring firm.

Pass the needle through the outer hole of the first C bead to be on the outer edge of the ring (fig 3).

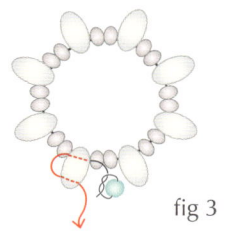

fig 3

4 The Netting - The first row of netting hangs from the outer row of Twin bead holes around the ring.

Thread on 3A, 1B, 2A, 1B and 3C. Pass through the last 1B and 3C again to make a ring (fig 4).

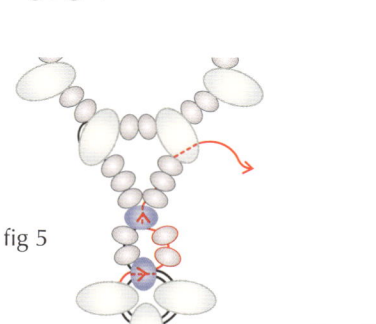

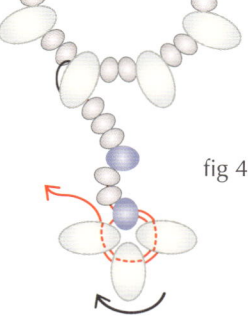

fig 4

fig 5

Pass through the same B bead again and thread on 2A.

Pass up through the previous B bead and thread on 3A. Pass through the outer hole of the next C bead around the ring (fig 5).

Repeat Step 4 seven more times to complete the first row of netting containing eight snowdrop motifs.

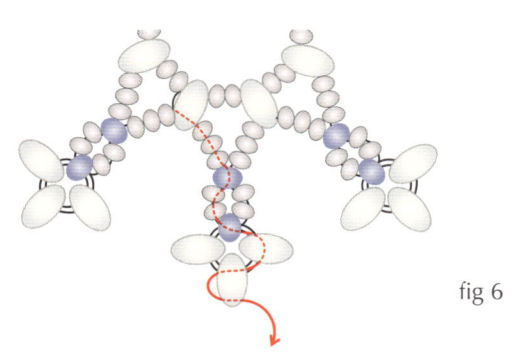

fig 6

5 Referring to fig 6, pass down through the first netted motif to emerge from the outer hole of the central C bead (fig 6).

The needle is now in the correct position to start the second row of netting.

6 The second row of netting hangs from the outer hole of the middle C bead on each motif. It is made using the same technique as the first row although the 3A count is increased to 6A to allow for the increasing width of the bauble.

Referring to fig 7 throughout, thread on 6A, 1B, 2A, 1B and 3C.

Pass the needle through the last 1B and 3C again to make a ring (as fig 4).

fig 7

Pass the needle through the same B bead again and thread on 2A.

Pass the needle up through the previous B bead and thread on 6A. Pass the needle through the outer hole of the next C bead around the ring (fig 7).

Repeat seven more times to complete the row.

Reposition the needle for the start of the third row to emerge from the outer hole of the central C bead on the first motif of the second row (fig 8).

fig 8

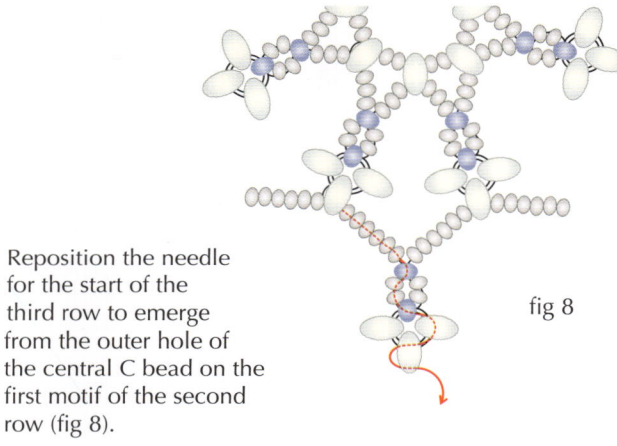

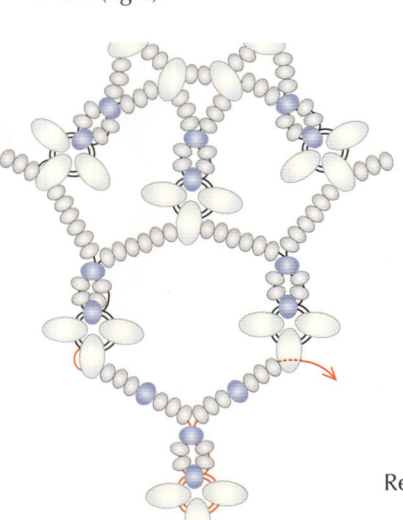

7 Following the same technique thread on 3A, 1B, 3A, 1B, 2A, 1B and 3C.

Make the ring, thread on 2A and pass up through the previous 1B (as figs 4 and 5).

Thread on 3A, 1B and 3A and pass through the next C bead around the decoration (fig 9).

Repeat seven more times to complete the row.

fig 9

Reposition the needle to emerge from the outer hole of the middle C bead of the first motif (as fig 8) ready to start the first fringe strand.

8 The Fringe Strands – There are sixteen fringe strands.

One strand hangs from each of the eight snowdrop motifs and one strand bridges across each gap (dangling from the extra B beads added in the previous row).

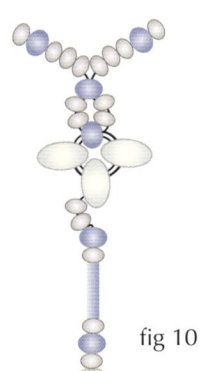

Thread on 2A, 1B, 1A, 1D, 1A, 1B, 1A, 1E, 1B, 2A, 1B and 3C.

Pass through the last 1B and 3C to make a ring as before.

Pass through the B bead, the inner holes of the next 2C and the outer hole of the middle C (fig 10).

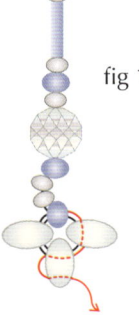

fig 10

fig 11

9 Referring to fig 11 thread on 2A, 1B, 1A, 1F, 1B and 3A.

Pass the needle back up the last 1B, 1F, 1A and 1B to pull the 3A into an anchor.

Thread on 2A and pass through the C bead of the adjacent snowdrop motif (fig 11).

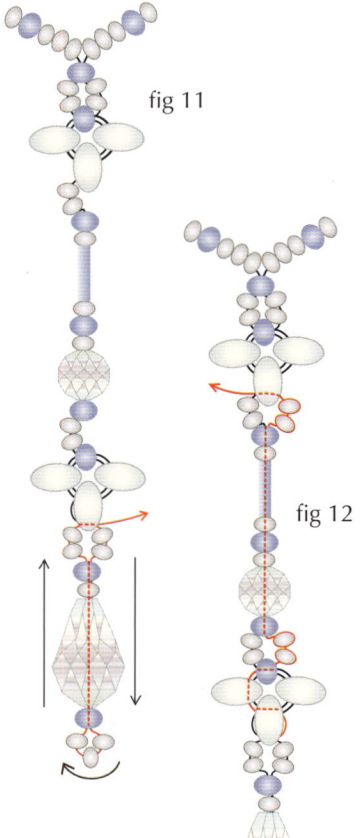

fig 12

10 Referring to fig 12 pass the needle through the inner hole of the same C bead, the inner hole of the following 1C and the next 1B.

Thread on 2A. Pass the needle up through the previous B on the main strand and the following seven beads.

Thread on 2A and pass through the middle C bead of the snowdrop motif (fig 12).

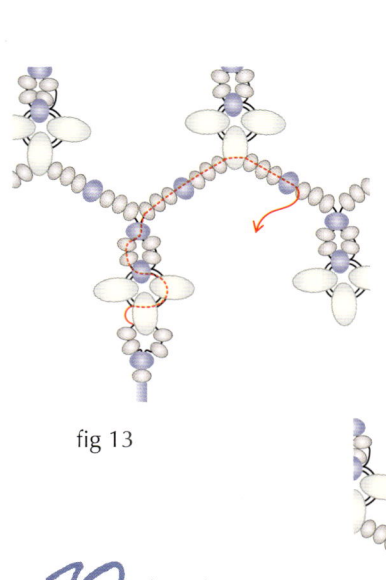

fig 13

11 Pass up through the beads of the motif and the third row of netting to emerge from the first B bead of the next repeat (fig 13).

12 Thread on 7A, 1B, 1E, 1B, 8A, 1D, 1A, 1B, 1A, 2D, 1A, 1B, 1A, 1E, 1B, 2A, 1B and 3C.

Pass the needle through the last 1B and 3C as before to make a ring.

Referring to fig 14 pass through the B bead again, the inner holes of the next 2C and the outer hole of the middle C.

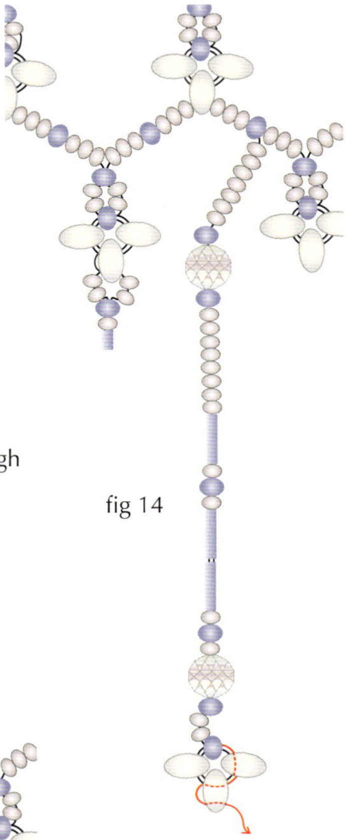

fig 14

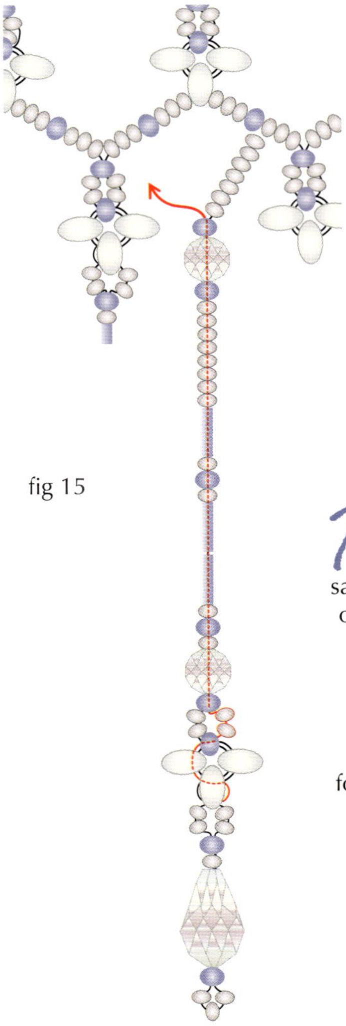

fig 15

Repeat Step 9 to add an F bead to the bottom of the strand.

13 Pass through the inner hole of the same C bead, the inner hole of the following 1C and the next 1B.

Thread on 2A. Pass up through the previous B on the main strand and the following twenty-one beads to emerge from the first B bead of this fringe strand (fig 15).

14 Thread on 7A. Referring to fig 16 pass the needle through the preceding B bead along the last row of netting and the following 3A, 1C, 3A and 1B.

This completes the fringe strand.

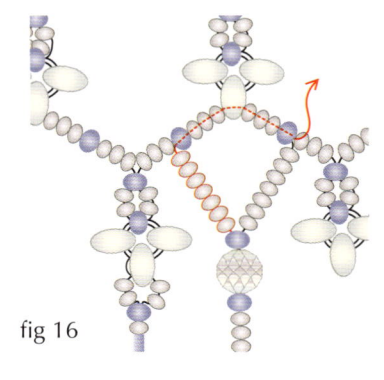

fig 16

Reposition the needle to emerge from the outer hole of the middle C bead on the next snowdrop motif around the netting ready to make the next fringe strand.

Repeat from Step 8 seven times. Finish off the thread ends neatly and securely and place the decoration over the bauble.

15 The Hanging Loop – Prepare the needle with 1m of double thread and tie a keeper bead 15cm from the ends.

Thread on 1E and 1B. Pass back through the E bead to pull the B into an anchor (fig 17).

Thread on 1B and 50A. Pass back through the B bead just added, the E and the B bead anchor (fig 18).

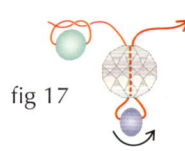

fig 17

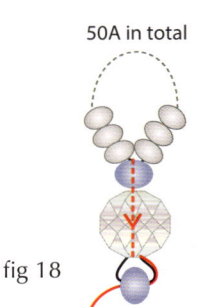

50A in total

fig 18

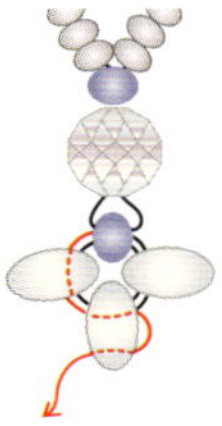

fig 19

fig 20

16 Thread on 3C.

Pass through the previous B bead as before to make a ring/snowdrop motif.

Pass through these four beads again to make the motif firm and reposition the needle to emerge from the outer hole of the central C bead (fig 19).

Thread on 2A, 1B, 1G and 1B.

Pass through the metal loop at the top of the bauble and back up through the 1B, 1G and 1B just added.

Thread on 2A and pass through the central C bead of the motif (fig 20).

Pass through the beads of the connection to the bauble again and finish off the all remaining thread ends neatly and securely.

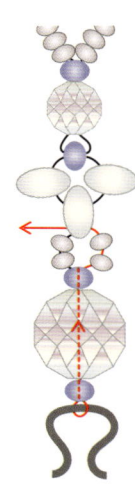

Robin Bauble

You Will Need

Materials

One 40mm frosted brown glass bauble
6g of size 10 silver lined brown seed beads A
3g of size 10 silver lined grey seed beads B
3g of size 10 silver lined red seed beads C
3g of size 10 chalk white seed beads D
3g of size 10 chalk red seed beads E
Two 4mm black fire polished glass beads F
3g of size 8 silver lined brown seed beads G
Eight 4mm red fire polished glass beads H
One 6mm white pearl round bead J
One 12x6mm copper capri twisted dagger bead K
One 12mm copper capri fire polished faceted bead L
Ash and white size D beading thread

Tools

A size 10 beading needle
A pair of scissors to trim the threads

When the red, red robin comes bob, bob, bobbin' along, you know Christmas is not so far away ...especially if he is wearing a Santa hat.

The Decoration is Made in Five Stages

The face, including the beak, is made first.

A foundation row of beads is made to fit the neck of the bauble.

A beaded net, to support the face and cover the bauble, is made next.

The hat is made to cover the metal bauble cap.

The hanging loop is added to the top of the bauble.

1 **The Face** - Each eye, with its surrounding rings, is made separately. An extra, midline row stitches the two eyes together and supports the beak.

Prepare the needle with 1.5m of single ash colour thread and tie a keeper bead 15cm from the end.

2 Thread on 1F and 4B.

Pass the needle through the F bead again to make a strap of 4B on the side (fig 1). Repeat to make a second strap on the other side of the F bead.

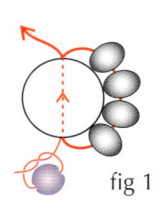

fig 1

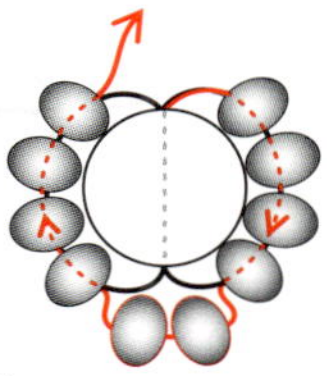

Pass through the first strap of 4B and thread on 2B. Pass through the second strap to pull the new 2B across the hole at the end of the F bead (fig 2).

Thread on 2B and pass through the following 4B beads to emerge at the end of the first strap (fig 3).

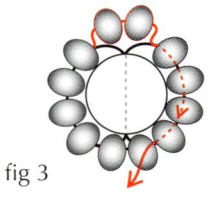

This completes the first ring around the eye (12B in total).

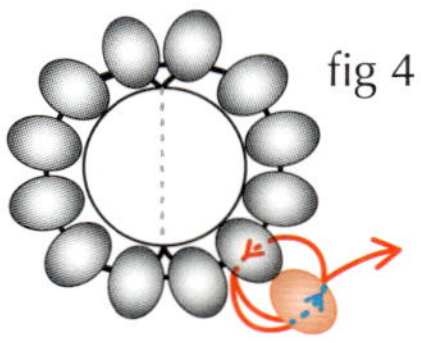

fig 2

fig 3

fig 4

3 Thread on 1C. Pass through the B bead on the previous ring and back through the new 1C (fig 4).

Thread on 2C. Pass through the next 1B along the previous row and back through the new 2C (fig 5).

Thread on 2C. Pass through the next 1B along the previous row and back through the new 2C (as fig 5).

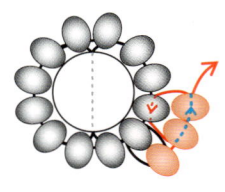

fig 5

This is Square stitch - adding one bead (as in fig 4) is standard Square stitch, adding two or more beads to a single bead on the previous row (as fig 5) is an increase stitch in Square stitch.

4 Repeat the 1C, 2C and 2C Square stitches three times. Pass the needle through the first 1C of the row to complete the ring (20C in total) (fig 6).

Pass through all the C beads just added to neaten the row. Finish with the needle emerging from the first 1C of the row (as fig 6).

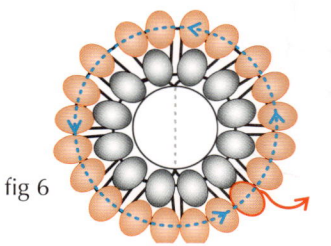

fig 6

5 Thread on 2C. Pass through the 1C of the previous row and back through the new 2C (fig 7) - note the needle is pointing in the opposite direction to the previous row.

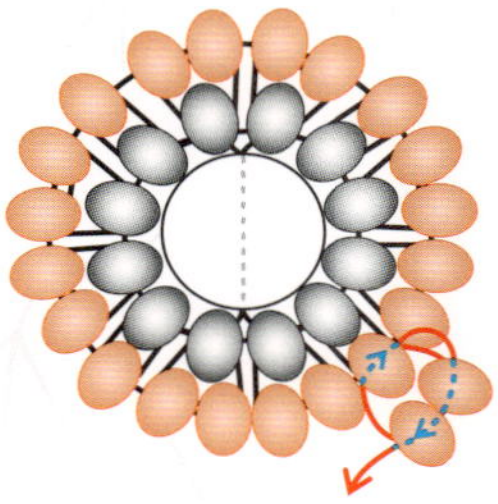

fig 7

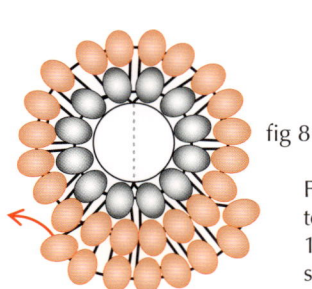

fig 8

Following the same Square stitch technique as in Step 3, add one 1C stitch, one 2C stitch, one 1C stitch and one 2C stitch (fig 8).

Remove the needle and let the thread end hang loose. Repeat from Step 1 to make a second eye.

6 Arrange the two eye motifs as fig 9 - note the long thread ends point downwards with the holes in the F beads at 45° to the centre line.

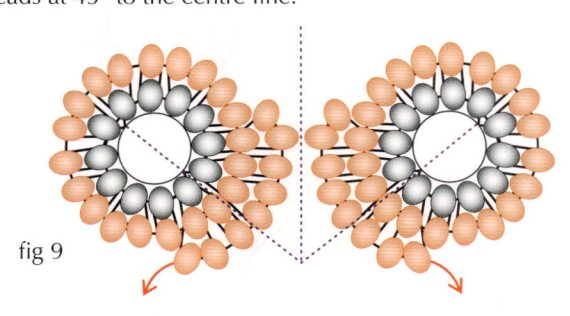

fig 9

Finish off both thread ends on the right eye neatly and securely without blocking the holes in the C beads.

Finish off the keeper bead thread on the left eye similarly. Attach the needle to the remaining thread end on the left eye.

Referring to fig 10, pass the needle through the 5C beads of the second ring that support the last row worked and the following 4C of the last row on this eye.

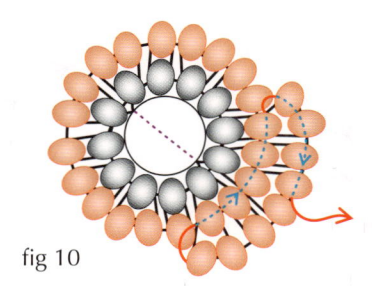

fig 10

7 The Midline Row - Thread on 1C. Pass through the previous 1C on the motif and back through the new 1C to start a new row of Square stitch (fig 11).

Repeat to add a 1C Square stitch.

fig 11

Thread on 2C. Pass through the next 1C of the previous row and back through the first 1C only of the new stitch (fig 12).

This short row forms the midline of the face and is now Square-stitched to the side of the other eye.

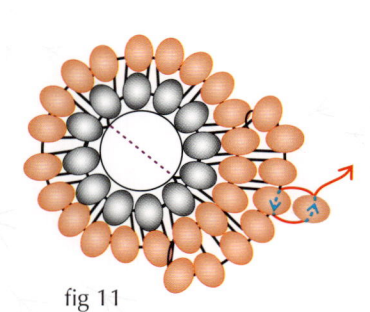

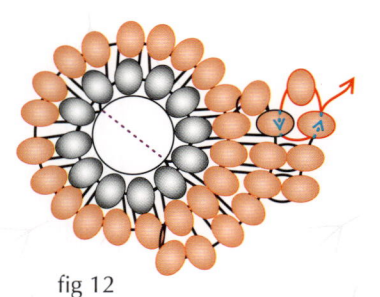

fig 12

8 Bring the other eye alongside the needle position. Align the motifs as in fig 9 so the F bead holes are at the correct angle and the two short rows (made in Step 5) are mirrored across the centre line.

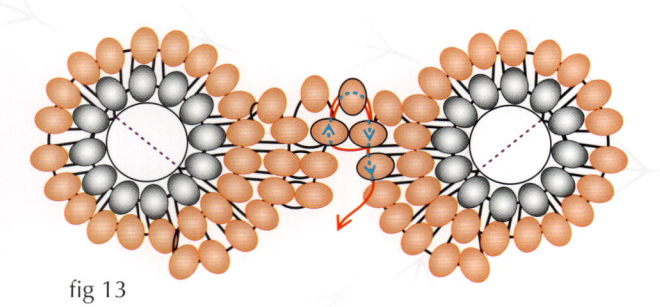

fig 13

Thread on 1C. Referring to fig 13, pass the needle down the second C bead of the end 2C stitch on the right eye. Pass back up the original 1C on the midline row, through the added 1C and down the 1C on the right eye. Pass through the following 1C (fig 13).

Square stitch this 1C and the following 1C to the adjacent C beads on the midline row (see fig 14).

Pass through the following 2C to emerge at the edge of the right eye (fig 14).

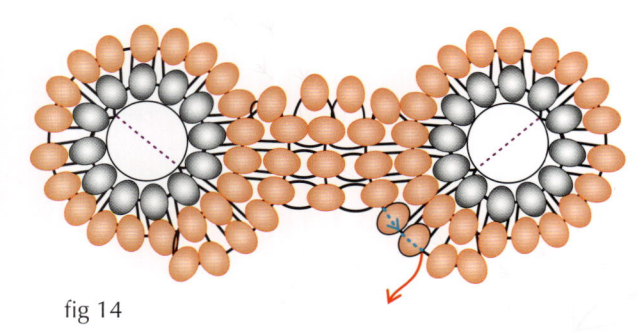

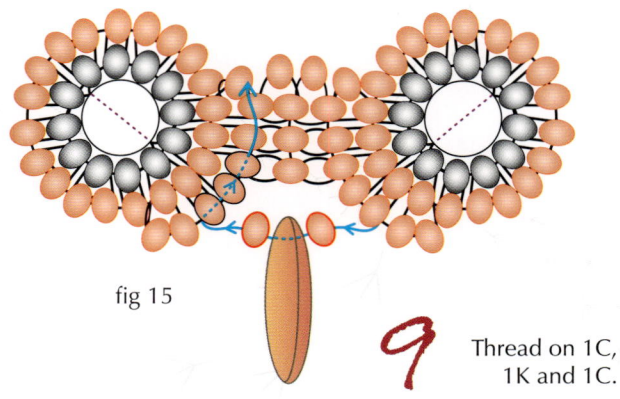

fig 14

fig 15

9 Thread on 1C, 1K and 1C. Pass through the third, fourth and fifth C beads up the side of the left eye (fig 15).

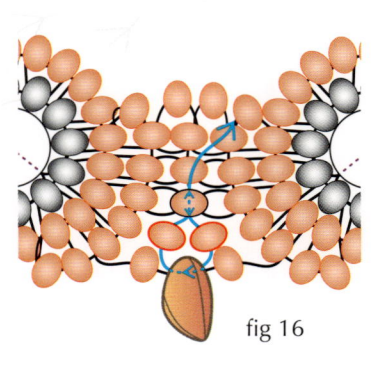

Pass down the adjacent 1C (bottom C bead) of the midline row and thread on 1C.

Pass through the K bead and thread on 1C.

Pass up the bottom 1C of the midline row (fig 16).

fig 16

10 Referring to fig 17 pass down the adjacent 1C on the right eye and the following 1C. Pass through the K bead and down the third 1C from the bottom of the left eye. Pass through the 1C on this side of the K bead, through the K and the following 1C (fig 17).

Square stitch 1C to this C bead (fig 18).

Thread on 4C. If necessary tip the K bead outward to be in the correct attitude for the beak.

Square stitch the last 1C added to the 1C on the left-hand side of the K bead so the hole end of the K bead is encircled with C beads (fig 19).

Pass the needle through the 1C, 1K and 1C just above the last row worked and back through the 5C just added to make the beak firm.

Finish off the thread end without blocking any holes around the edge of the beadwork.

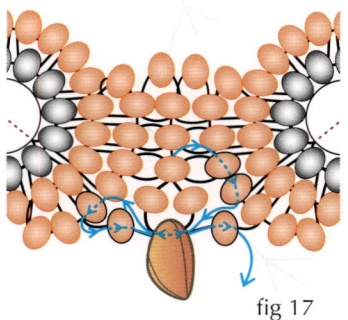

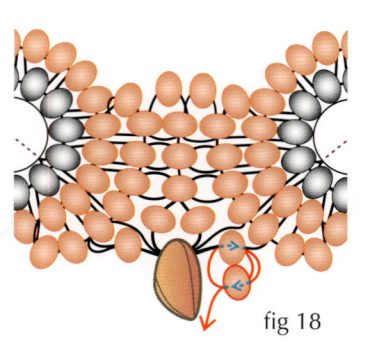

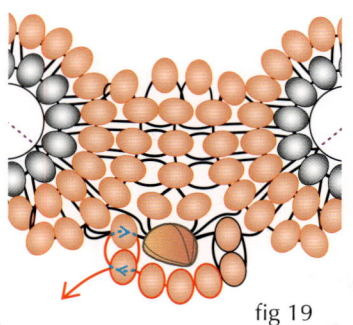

fig 17

fig 18

fig 19

11   **The Foundation Row** - Prepare the needle with 1.5m of single ash colour thread and tie a keeper bead 15cm from the end.

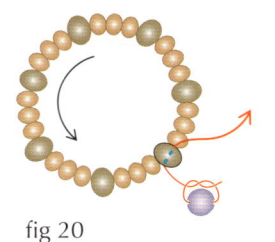

Thread on seven repeats of 1G and 3A. Pass through the first G bead to make a ring (fig 20).

Place the ring over the neck of the bauble.

fig 20

The ring needs to fit snugly. If you need to make an adjustment, add or subtract A beads equally from all seven sections to keep the G beads evenly spaced around the ring.

Pass the needle through the beads again to make the ring firm and remove the ring from the bauble.

12   **The Netting** - Row One - Thread on 3A, 1G and 3A. Pass back up the G bead to pull the 3A into a picot to anchor the strand.

Thread on 3A. Pass through the next G bead around the ring (fig 21). Repeat four times.

Thread on 4A.

fig 21

Referring to fig 22, pass through the third C bead along the top edge of the left eye and thread on 4A.
Pass through the next 1G around the ring (fig 22).

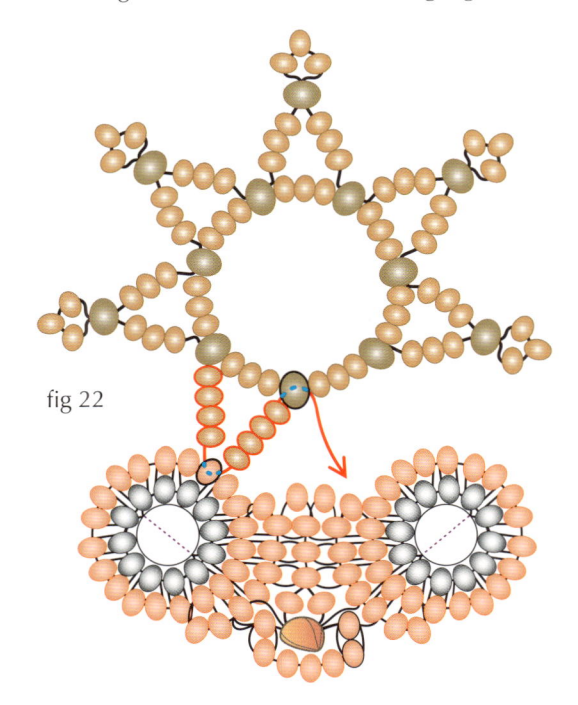

fig 22

13   Thread on 5A. Referring to fig 23, pass through the top 2C between the eyes and thread on 1A.

Pass up the fourth A just added and thread on 2A.

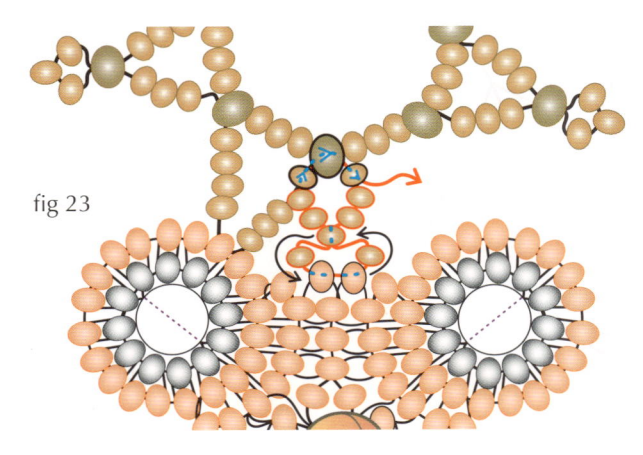

fig 23

Pass through the last 1A of the previous connection, the G on the ring and the first 1A just added (fig 23).

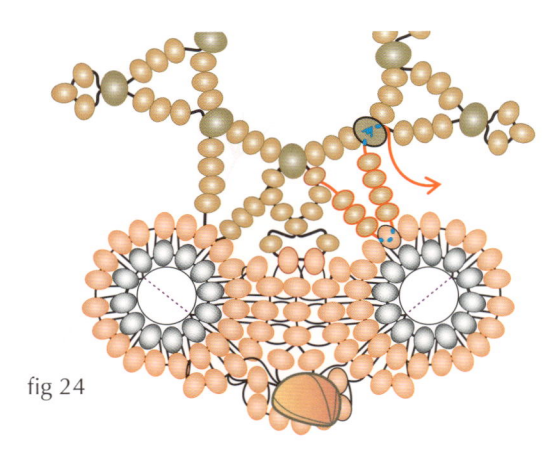

fig 24

Thread on 3A and pass through the third 1C along the top edge of the right eye. Thread on 4A and pass through the following G bead of the ring (fig 24).

This completes the row.

14 Pass the needle down the first 3A, 1G and 2A added on the first row to emerge from the middle A bead of the first picot (fig 25). This is the correct position to begin Row Two.

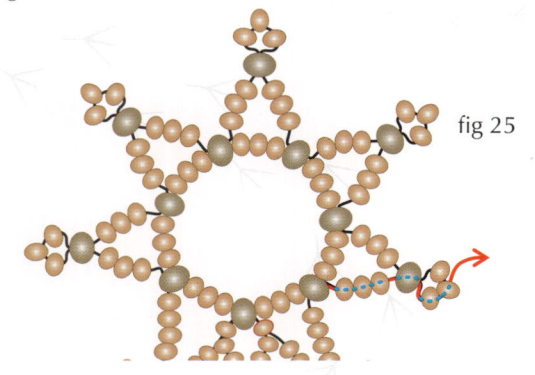

fig 25

Row Two - Thread on 6A, 1G and 3A. Pass the needle back up the G bead to make a 3A picot.

Thread on 6A and pass through the middle 1A of the the next Row One picot around the bauble (fig 26).

Repeat three times.

fig 26

15 Thread on 4B. Count 5C around the left eye from the first row connection. Pass through this C bead and the following (sixth) C bead (see fig 27).

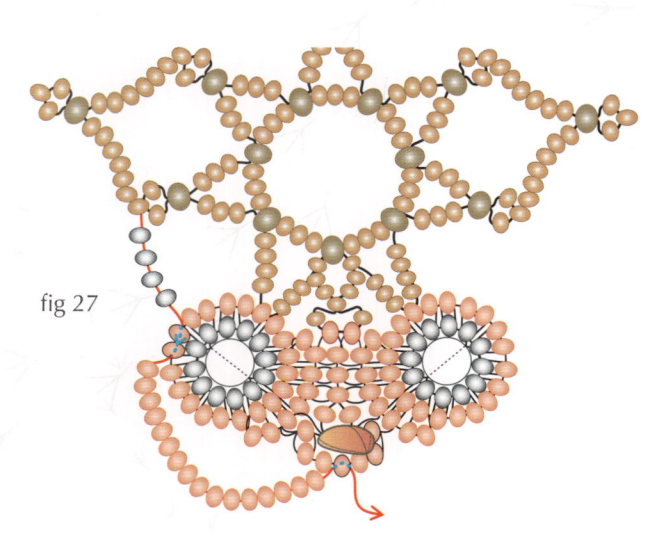

fig 27

Thread on 17C and pass the needle through the centre 1C below the K (beak) bead (fig 27).

Thread on 4C. Pass through the last 1C of the swag just made, the centre C bead underneath the K bead and the first 1C just added to make a ring of 6C beneath the beak (fig 28).

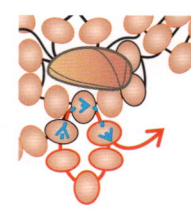

fig 28

16 Thread on 16C and pass through the sixth and fifth C beads along the top edge of the right eye (fig 29).

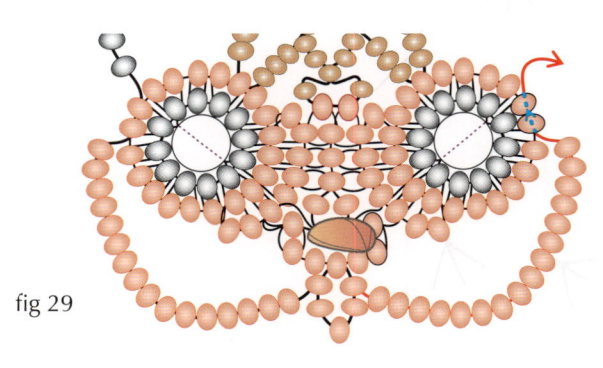

fig 29

Thread on 4B and pass through the middle 1A of the following first row picot to match the other side of the work and complete the row.

Pass the needle through the following 6A, 1G and 2A to emerge from the middle A of the first Row Two picot (as fig 25) - this is the correct position to begin Row Three.

17 Row Three - Thread on 7A, 1G and 3A. Pass back up the G bead to make a 3A picot.

Thread on 7A and pass through the middle 1A of the next Row Two picot around the bauble (as fig 26). Repeat twice.

Thread on 7A, 1G and 3A.

Pass the needle back up the G bead to make a 3A picot.

Thread on 7B. Pass through the third and fourth C beads of the adjacent 17C swag (fig 30).

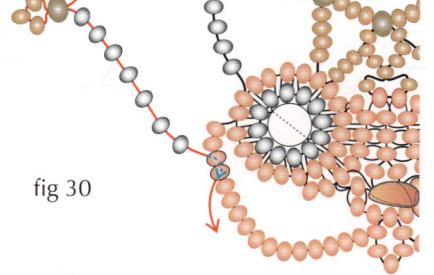

fig 30

24

18
Thread on 18C. Pass through the 1C at the bottom of the 6C ring made in fig 28.

Thread on 4C. Pass through the last 1C of the new swag, the 1C on the 6C ring and the first 1C just added to make a new 6C ring (fig 31).

fig 32

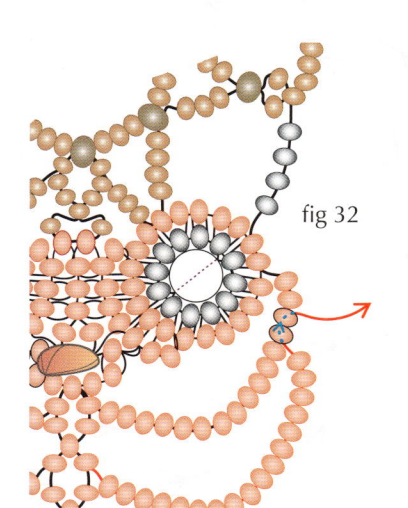

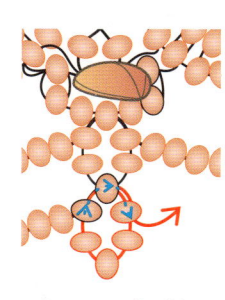

fig 31

Thread on 17C and pass through the fourth and third C beads before the end of the swag hanging below the right eye (fig 32).

To complete the row thread on 6B, 1G and 3A. Pass back up the G bead to make a picot and thread on 7A. Pass through the middle 1A of the following Row Two picot.

19
Reposition the needle for the fourth row by passing through the first 7A, 1G and 2A of Row Three to emerge from the middle A bead of the picot (as fig 25).

Row Four - Thread on 7A, 1H and 3A. Pass back up the H bead to make a 3A picot. Thread on 7A and pass through the middle 1A of the next Row Three picot around the bauble (as fig 26).

Repeat twice.

20
Thread on 7B, 1H and 3B. Pass back up the H bead to make a 3B picot. Thread on 7B.

Referring to fig 33, pass the through the sixth C bead of the following swag (count carefully - this is 8C down from the attachment of the B bead swag on the previous row - see fig 33).

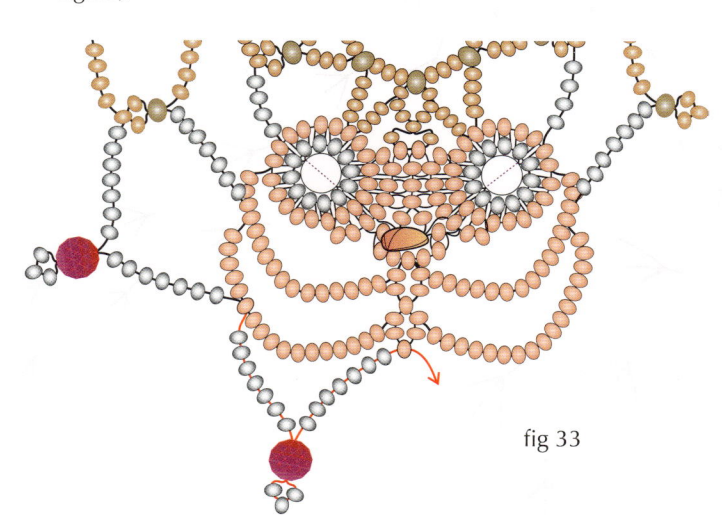

fig 33

Thread on 7B, 1H and 3B. Pass back up the H bead to make the picot. Thread on 7B and pass through the bottom 1C of the 6C ring made in fig 31 (fig 33). This is the centre front.

Working a mirror image of the previous three stitches, complete the row with two pointed picot swags in B beads and a final pointed picot swag in A beads.

Finish off the thread ends neatly and securely without blocking the holes in the beads of the Foundation Row. Place the net over the bauble.

21
The Hat - This is made in four stages - a tight band of Ladder-stitched beads around the bauble cap, the red funnel of the hat, the bobble and a final band of Ladder-stitched beads to form the fur trim around the base.

The Tight Band - Prepare the needle with 1.2m of single white thread and tie a keeper bead 25cm from the end.

Thread on 2D, 4E and 2D. Pass up through the first four beads and down the second to make two columns (fig 34).

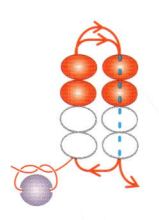

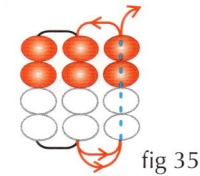

fig 34

Thread on 2D and 2E. Pass down the previous column and up the new four beads (fig 35).

fig 35

Thread on 2E and 2D. Pass up the previous column and down the new four beads (fig 36).
This is Ladder stitch.

Repeat the last two stitches until you have 16 columns.

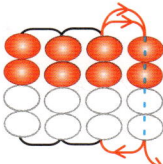

fig 36

22 Wrap the strip around the metal bauble cap to check the sizing - it needs to fit snugly. If required, add two or four more columns (the total number of columns must be an even number).

The following instructions are based on 16 columns - notes are given to expand the beading if you have more than 16 columns on your band.

Number the columns 1-16 (18 or 20) starting with column 1 where the needle is currently positioned.

23 **The Red Funnel** - Vertical rows of E beads are now added to the top edge of the column strip. The rows increase and then decrease in length to make the funnel bend over into the classic Santa Hat profile.

The needle should be emerging at the D bead end of column 1. Pass up column 2.

fig 37

Thread on 7E. Thread on 3E and Ladder stitch to the top 3E of the 7E (fig 37).

Thread on 6E and pass down column 4 on the main band (see fig 38).

Total row length added is 9E.

Pass up the 2D of the column 5 and the 2E of column 6 (fig 38).

fig 38

Thread on 11E. Ladder stitch the last 3E added to the top 3E of the previous stitch (fig 39).

Total row length added is 11E.

fig 39

Ladder stitch 3E to the top 3E of the 11E and thread on 10E. Pass down column 7 (fig 40).

Total row length added is 13E.

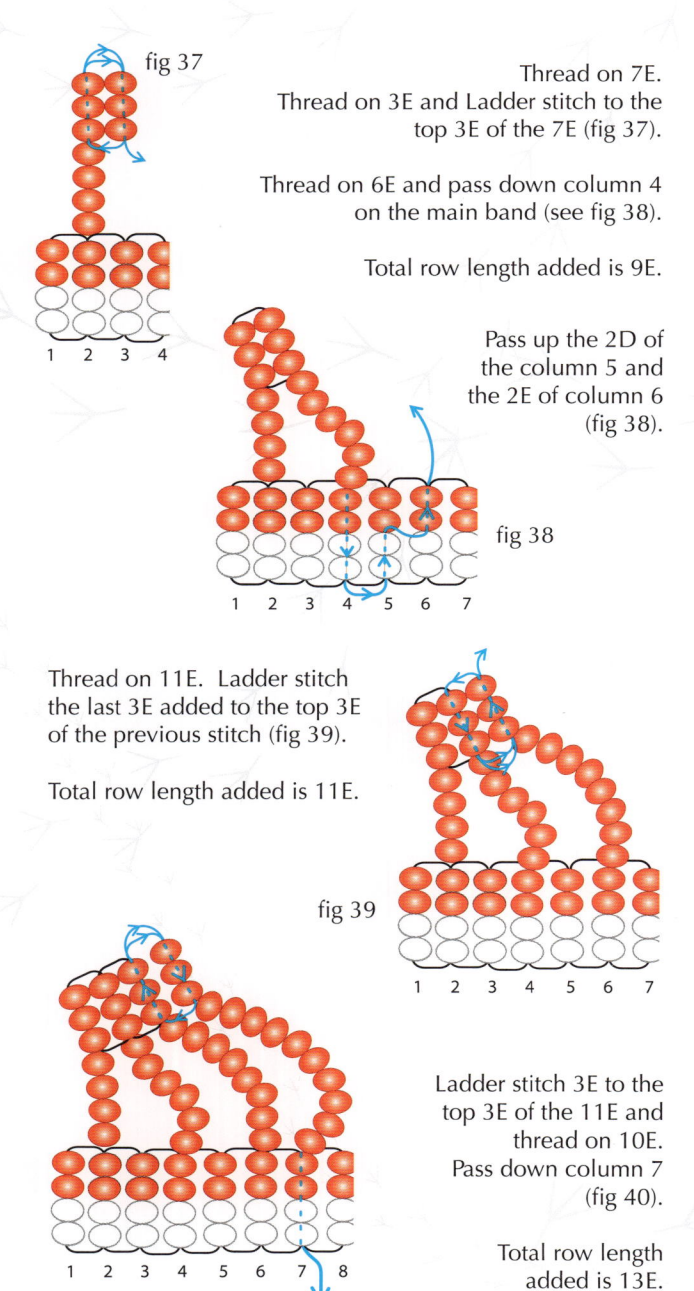

fig 40

24 Pass up column 8 and thread on 15E. Ladder stitch the top 3E to the top 3E of the previous row (as fig 39).
Total row length added is 15E.

Ladder stitch 3E to the top 3E of the 15E (as fig 40) and thread on 14E. Pass down column 9.
Total row length added is 17E (see fig 41).

The last two rows repeated the technique of the previous two rows - the procedure swaps back and forth dependant on whether the next row is started at the bottom (at the column strip) or the top (where the top 3C beads are Ladder-stitched to the adjacent row).

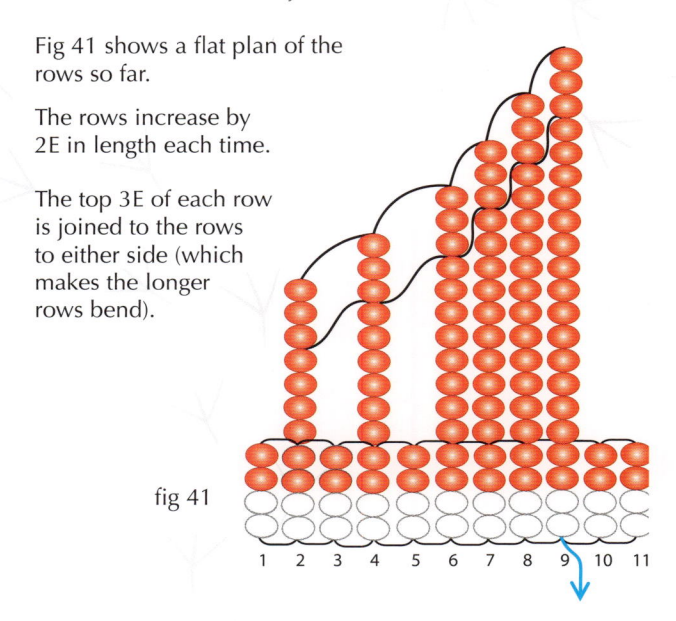

Fig 41 shows a flat plan of the rows so far.

The rows increase by 2E in length each time.

The top 3E of each row is joined to the rows to either side (which makes the longer rows bend).

fig 41

If you had 16 columns at the end of Step 22 you now start to decrease the row length. Go to Step 25.

If you had 18 columns at the end of Step 22 you need to add two more rows - 19E to column 10 and 17E to column 11. Add these two rows. Go to Step 25.

If you had 20 columns at the end of Step 22 you need to add 4 more rows - 19E to column 10; 21E to column 11; 19E to column 12 and 17E to column 13. Add these four rows. Go to Step 25.

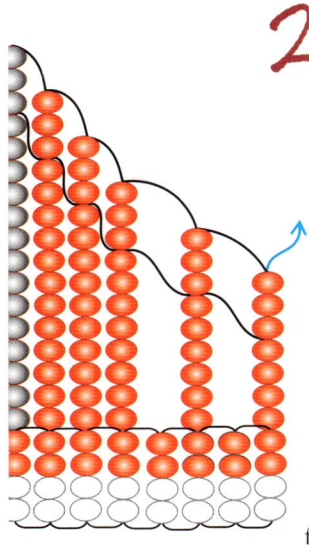

25 Fig 42 shows the required decrease rows in red. The previous 17E row is shown in grey.

Note these row lengths (15E, 13E, 11E, 9E and 7E) mirror the rows added to columns 8, 7, 6, 4 and 2.

Add these five rows using the same technique as shown in Step 23.

fig 42

26 The needle will emerge from the top of the last row added as shown in fig 42.

Ladder stitch the top 3C of this row to the top 3C of the first 7C row (column 2) to close up the top of the funnel. The bottom seam will be stitched in Step 28.

Pinch and fold the top of the funnel so the top 3C of each row gathers together (see top view in fig 43).

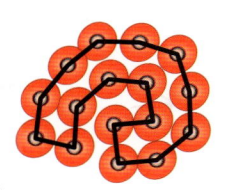

Make a few stitches across the end of the rows to hold the bundle tight.

Finish with the needle emerging at the centre of the top surface ready to add the bobble.

fig 43

27 The Bobble - Thread on 1D, 1J and 6D. Pass the needle through the J bead again to make the 6D into a strap on the side (fig 44).

Thread on 6D and make a second strap.

Repeat six times to add eight 6D straps in total.

Thread on 1D. Pass back down the J bead and through the first 1D just above the C beads (fig 45).

Pass down the top 3E of the nearest E bead row to strengthen the connection to the top of the hat.

Finish off the thread end neatly and securely.

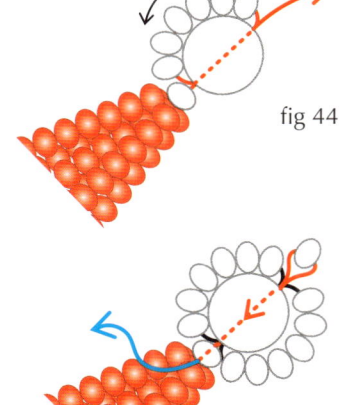

fig 44

fig 45

28 Remove the keeper bead from Step 21 and attach the needle to this thread end.

Make a Ladder stitch to link the first column of 2D and 2E to the last column of 2D and 2E to complete the bottom band.

Finish off this thread end neatly and securely. Push the completed band over the metal cap.

29 The Fur Trim - This is made from a second Ladder-stitched band.

Referring to Step 21 start a new four-bead high Ladder stitch band using white thread and D beads only.

Extend the band until it is long enough to wrap around the outside of the previous band now in situ around the metal bauble cap (20 - 24 columns).

Link the first 4D column to the last 4D column with a Ladder stitch.

Remove the first band from the metal cap. Slip the new, larger band over the top of the first band so the bottom rows are flush. Slip stitch the underside of the two bands together. Place the completed hat over the metal cap.

Position the hat so it bends to the side of the robin's face and the metal loop at the top of the bauble can be accessed between two of the longer E bead rows.

Make two or three stitches to connect the completed hat to the Foundation Row of the netting. Finish off the thread ends neatly and securely.

30 The Hanging Loop - Prepare the needle with 1m of single ash colour thread and tie a keeper bead 15cm from the end.

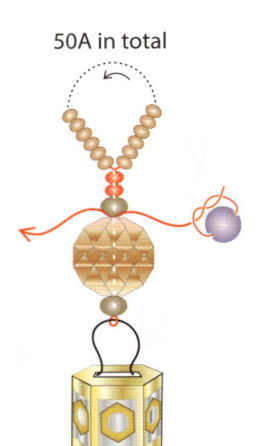

50A in total

Thread on 1L and 1G. Pass the needle through the metal loop at the top of the bauble and back up the G and L beads.

Thread on 1G, 2C and 50A.

Pass the needle back down the 2C and 1G beads to draw up the loop (fig 46).

Pass the needle through all the beads and the metal loop twice more to strengthen the loop.

fig 46

Finish off the thread ends neatly and securely.

Finlandia Tree

You Will Need

Materials

to Make a Silver Tree

4g of size 10 silver lined crystal seed beads A
3g of size 10 chalk white seed beads B
2g of size 2 silver lined bugle beads C
Two 6mm crystal fire polished faceted glass beads D
Three 4mm crystal fire polished faceted glass beads E
One 8mm crystal fire polished faceted glass bead F
One 7mm silver star bead G
One 50mm silver plated headpin
White size D beading thread

to Make a Gold Tree

4g of size 10 silver lined gold seed beads A
3g of size 10 ivory ceylon seed beads B
2g of size 2 silver lined gold bugle beads C
Two 6mm crystal fire polished faceted glass beads D
Three 4mm crystal fire polished faceted glass beads E
One 8mm crystal fire polished faceted glass bead F
One 7mm gold star bead G
One 50mm gold plated headpin
Gold size D beading thread

Tools

A size 10 beading needle
A pair of scissors to trim the threads

a completed Finlandia Tree measures approximately
10 x 3.5cm including the hanging loop

These snow-fringed miniature fir trees will delight everyone. Lightweight, they will dangle from the finest of twigs and look fabulous against dark green foliage.

The Decoration is Made in Three Stages

Three rings of pointed branches are made first. The bugle bead trunk is made as a separate unit. The tree is assembled from the prepared sections and the hanging loop is added to the top of the decoration.

1 The Branches
The three layers of branches are all made using a similar technique - the smallest (top) layer is constructed first.

The Small Branch Ring - This ring will support seven interlinked branches. Prepare the needle with 1.2m of single thread and tie a keeper bead 15cm from the end.

Thread on 7A. Pass the needle through the first A bead to bring the beads into a ring (fig 1).

Pass through the beads again to make the ring more firm. Make sure the needle is emerging from the first A bead as shown in fig 1.

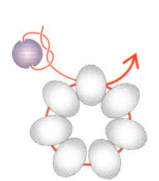

fig 1

2
Thread on 1A, 1C, 1B, 2A and 3B. Leaving aside the last 3B to anchor the strand, pass the needle back through the last 2A threaded and the following 1B and 1C (fig 2).

Thread on 1A and pass through the A bead on the ring and the following 1A (fig 3).

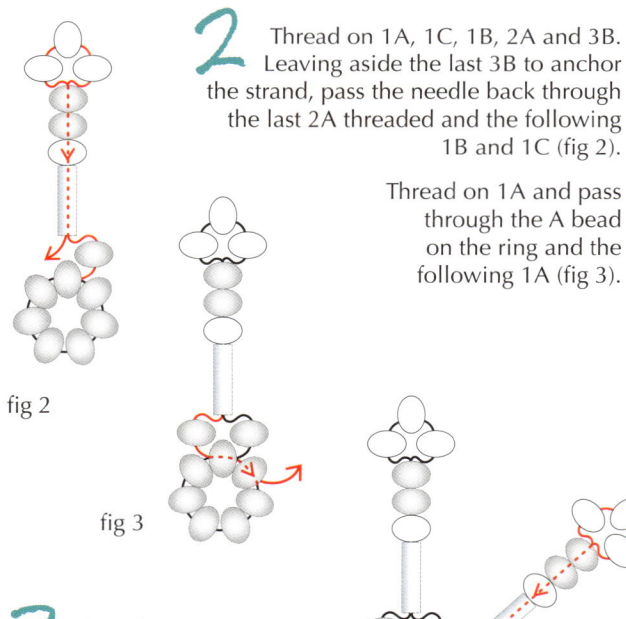

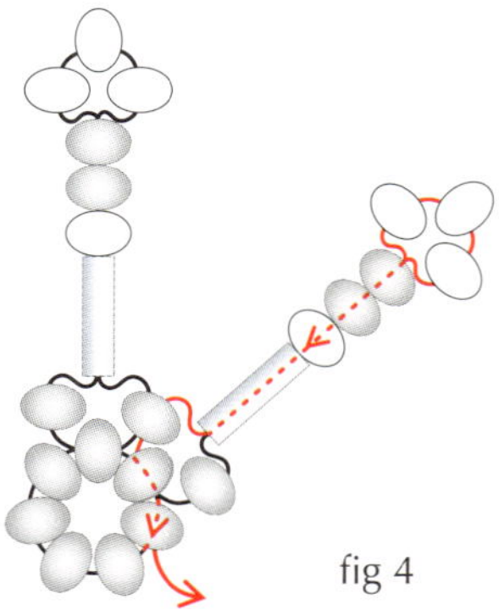

fig 2

fig 3

3
Thread on 1A, 1C, 1B, 2A and 3B. Leaving aside the last 3B to anchor the strand, pass back through the last 2A threaded and the following 1B and 1C (as fig 2).

Pass through the adjacent 1A at the base of the previous branch, the A bead on the ring at the base of the current branch and the following 1A of the ring (fig 4).

fig 4

Repeat Step 3 four more times (six branches).

4
The seventh branch needs to link to both the first and the sixth branches.

The needle should be emerging from the last blank A bead of the ring. Pass it up through the adjacent 1A at the base of the first branch (fig 5).

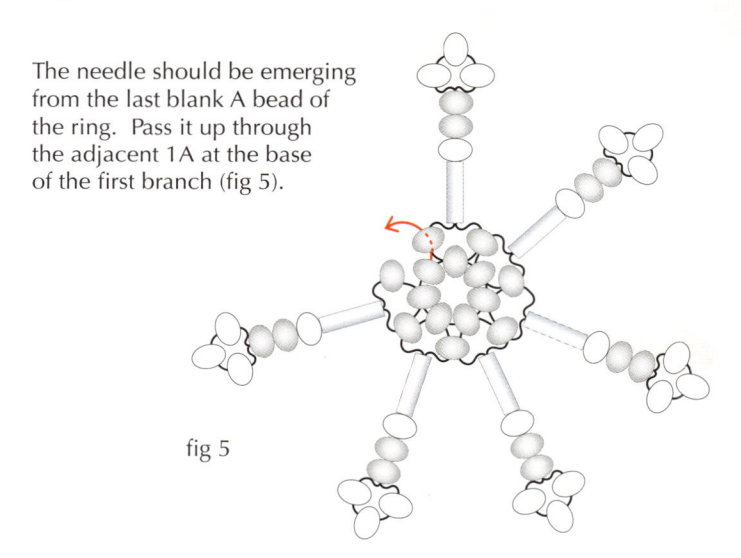

fig 5

Thread on 1C, 1B, 2A and 3B. Complete the remainder of the branch as before.

Referring to fig 6, reposition the needle to emerge from the end of the first C bead.

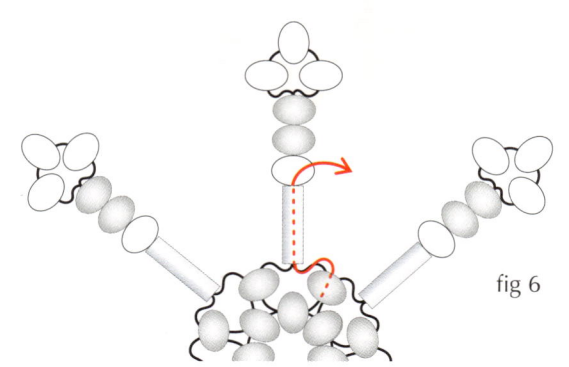

fig 6

29

5 The branches are linked together at the end of each C bead.

fig 7

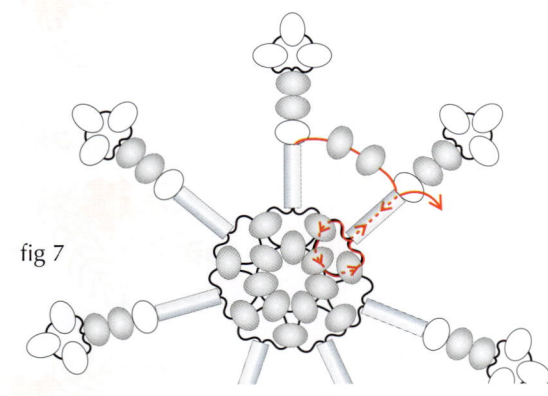

Thread on 2A.
Referring to fig 7, pass up the C bead on the next branch, through the 3A at the top of this C bead (the A beads at the start and end of the point sequence and the A bead on the ring) and back down the same C bead (fig 7).

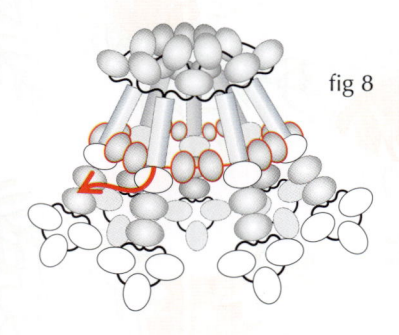

fig 8

Repeat six times to link all seven branches together to create a cone (fig 8).

Finish with the needle emerging from the bottom of the first C bead (as in fig 8).

Pass the needle through the 2A of the first link made in Step 5 to emerge on the inside of the cone.

6 Thread on 1A. Push this A bead to the inside of the cone and up against the second A bead of the link just passed through.

fig 9

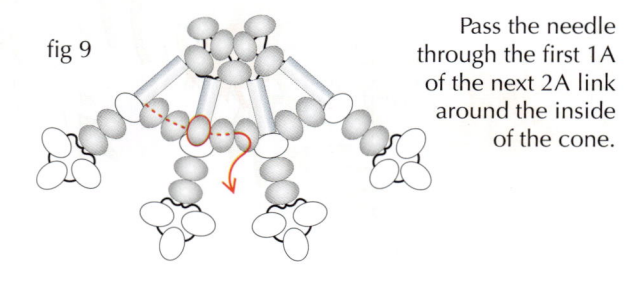

Pass the needle through the first 1A of the next 2A link around the inside of the cone.

The new A bead should slot into place between the two 2A links on the inside of the cone and behind the first B bead of the branch (fig 9 showing the inside of the cone).

The following steps are all worked on the inside of the cone.

7 Thread on 2B. Pass through the 3B beads at the tip of the previous branch (fig 10).

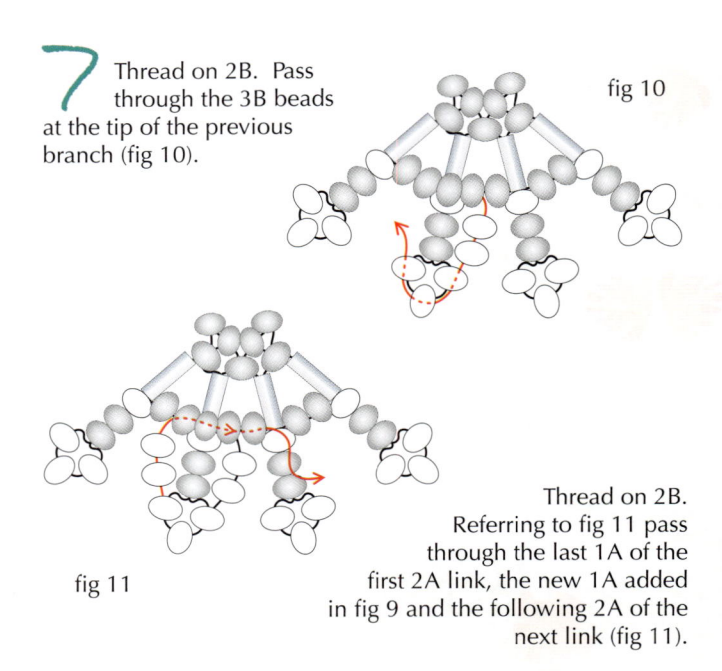

fig 10

fig 11

Thread on 2B. Referring to fig 11 pass through the last 1A of the first 2A link, the new 1A added in fig 9 and the following 2A of the next link (fig 11).

Repeat Step 6 to add 1A to the inside of the cone between this 2A link and the next.

8 Thread on 2B. Pass through the 3B beads at the tip of the previous branch (as fig 10).

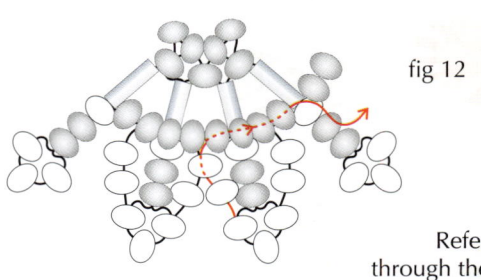

fig 12

Thread on 1B. Referring to fig 12 pass through the first 1B along the side of the of the previous branch, through the following 1A of this 2A link, the 1A just added and the following 2A of the next link (fig 12).

Repeat Step 6 and Step 8 four times.
Repeat Step 6 once.

9 The needle should be emerging from the first A bead of the first 2A link. To complete the seventh branch you need to make links to the B bead edging of both the sixth and the first branches.

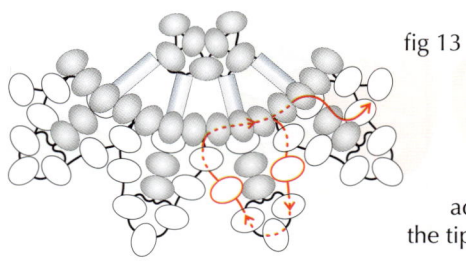

fig 13

Pass down the adjacent 1B towards the tip of the first branch and thread on 1B. Pass through the 3B at the tip of the seventh branch.

Thread on 1B and complete the link as before (fig 13). Finish off both thread ends neatly and securely.

10 **The Middle Branch Ring** - This ring will support eight branches. Prepare the needle with 1.2m of single thread and tie a keeper bead 15cm from the end.

Thread on 8A and make a ring as in Step 1.

For the first branch thread on 3A, 1C, 1B, 2A and 3B.

Pass back through the 2A and the following 1B, 1C and 2A (fig 14).

Thread on 1A and finish the branch as before (fig 15). This is the same method as shown in figs 2 and 3).

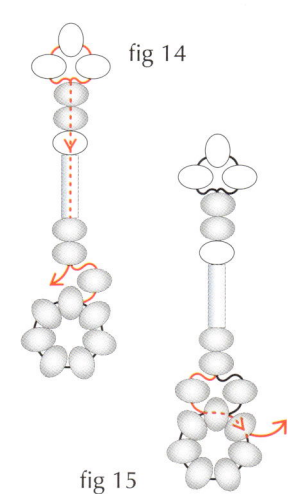

fig 14

fig 15

11 For the second branch thread on 3A, 1C, 1B, 2A and 3B. Pass back through the 2A and the following 1B, 1C and 2A.

Pass the needle through the adjacent 1A at the base of the previous branch, the A bead on the ring at the base of the current branch and the following 1A of the ring (as fig 4). Repeat five times (seven branches).

As on the Small Branch Ring, the eighth (last) branch needs to link to both the seventh and the first branches through the A beads at the base. Referring to fig 5 pass the needle up through the first 1A of the first branch. Thread on 2A, 1C, 1B, 2A and 3B. Complete the branch as before.

Reposition the needle to emerge from the end of the C bead on the first branch (as fig 6) ready to add the links between the branches.

12 The links are 3A beads long.

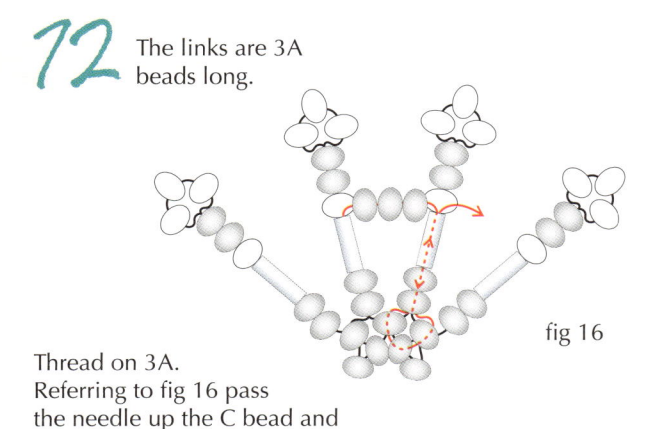

fig 16

Thread on 3A. Referring to fig 16 pass the needle up the C bead and the following 2A of the next branch.

Pass the needle through the 3A at the base of the branch and back down the same branch to emerge at the base of the same C bead as before (fig 16).

Repeat to link all eight branches together and make a cone. Finish with the needle emerging from the bottom of the first C bead (as fig 8).

Pass the needle through the 3A of the first link to emerge on the inside of the cone.

13 Thread on 1A. Pass through the first 2A of the following 3A link to slot the new 1A into the gap between the two 3A links on the inside of the cone (as Step 6).

14 Thread on 3B. Pass through the 3B beads at the tip of the previous branch and thread on 3B.

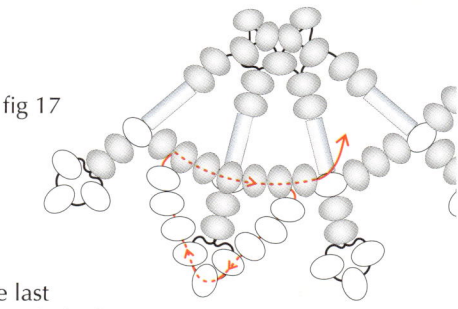

fig 17

Pass through the last 2A of the previous link, the new 1A and the following 3A of the next link (fig 17).

Repeat Step 13.

15 Thread on 3B. Pass through the 3B beads at the tip of the previous branch and thread on 2B.

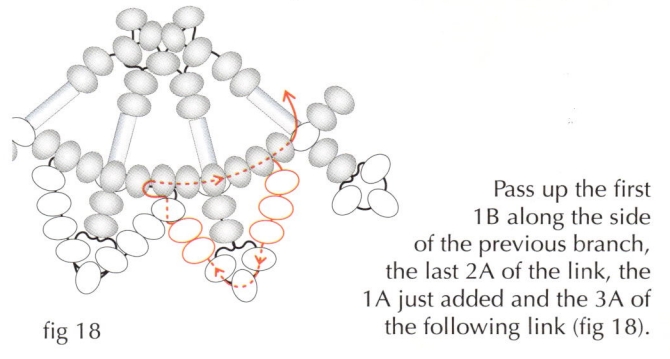

fig 18

Pass up the first 1B along the side of the previous branch, the last 2A of the link, the 1A just added and the 3A of the following link (fig 18).

Repeat Step 13 and Step 15 five times. Repeat Step 13 once.

31

16 The eighth branch needs to link to both the first and the seventh branches.

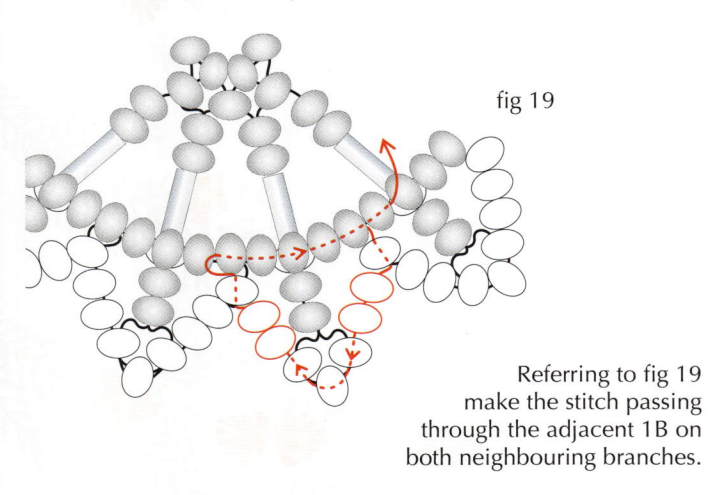

fig 19

Referring to fig 19 make the stitch passing through the adjacent 1B on both neighbouring branches.

Finish off both thread ends neatly and securely.

17 **The Large Branch Ring** - This ring will support ten branches and is made using the same method.

Prepare the needle with 1.2m of single thread and tie a keeper bead 15cm from the end.

Thread on 10A and make a ring as in Step 1.

Thread on 5A, 1C, 1B, 2A and 3B for the first branch and make as before (fig 20). Complete the remaining nine branches to match as before.

Add ten 3A links as in Step 12.

Complete the branches as in Steps 13 to 16 and finish off the thread ends neatly and securely.

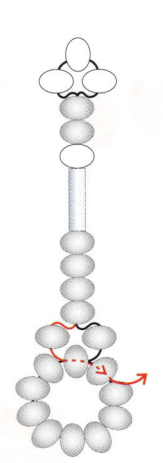

fig 20

18 **The Tree Trunk** - This is made in Square stitch.

Prepare the needle with 1m of single thread and tie a keeper bead 15cm from the end.

Thread on 3C for the first row.

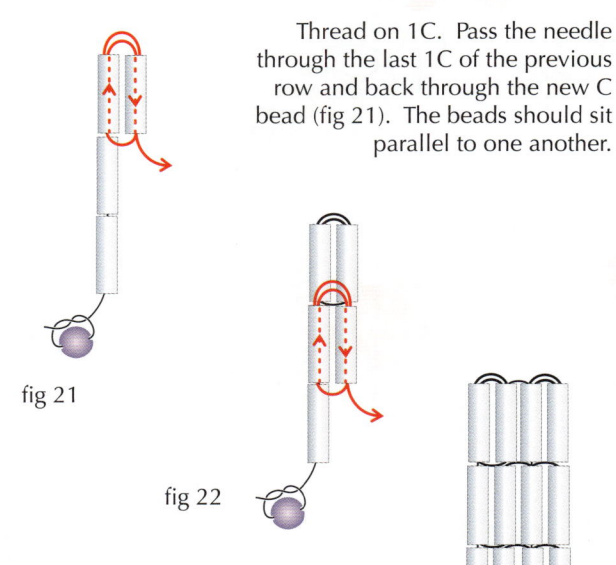

Thread on 1C. Pass the needle through the last 1C of the previous row and back through the new C bead (fig 21). The beads should sit parallel to one another.

fig 21

fig 22

Thread on 1C and repeat (fig 22). Repeat once more to complete the row.

Add two more rows of 3C (fig 23).

fig 23

Roll the four rows into a slim tube so Row One meets Row Four. Using the same Square stitch technique, link these two rows together to secure the tube.

Finish off both thread ends neatly and securely.

19 Assembling the Tree - Prepare the needle with 1m of double thread and tie a keeper bead 15cm from the ends. The tree is assembled from the top, threading down towards the base of the trunk.

Thread on 1D and pass the needle down through the centre of the 7A ring at the top of the Small Branch Ring.

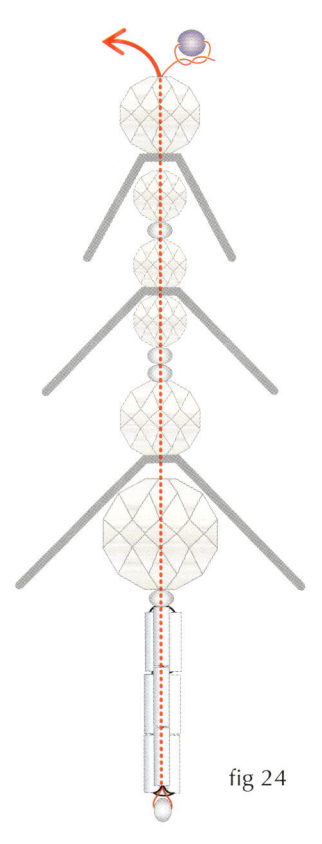

Thread on 1E, 1A and 1E. Pass down through the centre of the Middle Branch Ring.

Thread on 1E, 2A and 1D. Pass down through the centre of the Large Branch Ring.

Thread on 1F and 1A. Pass down the centre of the trunk tube and thread on 1A.

Leaving aside the last 1A to anchor the work, pass the needle back up the centre of the trunk and all the following beads and branch rings to emerge at the keeper bead (fig 24).

Carefully adjust the tension in the thread so everything sits snugly together.

fig 24

20 Thread on 2B, 1G, 1B and 40A. Pass back down the 1B, 1G and 2B to pull the 40A into a large loop (fig 25).

Finish the thread ends neatly and securely.

Carefully thread a straight headpin up through the centre of the trunk and the following beads just added until the head is flush with the base of the trunk. If the pin will not pass all the way up the tree, trim 1cm from the top of the pin and try again.

The headpin helps to hold the core of the tree straight. If you wish, a dab of craft glue will ensure it cannot be dislodged.

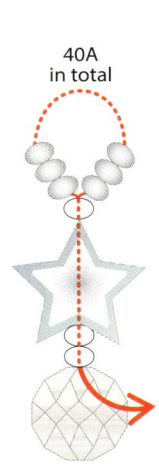

40A in total

fig 25

Heavenly Bauble

You Will Need

Materials

One 40mm frosted blue glass bauble
10g of size 10 frost crystal seed beads A
10g of size 10 silver lined crystal seed beads B
4g of size 8 silver lined crystal seed beads C
Seventeen 4mm crystal AB fire polished beads D
Eight 6mm crystal AB fire polished faceted beads E
Nine 4mm round white pearl beads F
Four 15x5mm white frost glass wing beads G
Twenty-one 5mm silver filigree bead caps H
Twelve 8mm silver filigree bead caps J
Twelve 10mm silver filigree bead caps K
White size D beading thread

Tools

A size 10 beading needle
A pair of scissors to trim the threads

Delicate lace-winged angels dance around this dainty bauble design. The halos and layered skirts are made from filigree bead cups. If you want even more twinkle: intersperse the filigree skirt layers with graduated cup sequins.

The Decoration is Made in Four Stages

A foundation row is fitted around the neck of the bauble.

The shorter hanging strands, which incorporate the beaded angel wings, are made.

The longer hanging strands are added in between the shorter strands.

The hanging loop is added to the top of the bauble.

Extra Info....

The filigree bead cups; H, J, and K, are threaded into the bead sequences to form the halos and skirts of the angels. It is important to thread the cups in the correct direction so the cup finishes 'upwards' or 'downwards' as required (see diagrams below).

Upwards - sits with the open cup uppermost (like a crown)

Downwards - sits with the dome uppermost (like a skirt)

The instructions state '1H up' or '1H down' (or 1J or 1K, up or down, dependent on the size of cup required).

1. The Foundation Row

Prepare the needle with 1.2m of single thread and tie a keeper bead 15cm from the end.

Thread on eight repeats of 1C and 2A. Pass the needle through the first C bead to make a ring (fig 1).

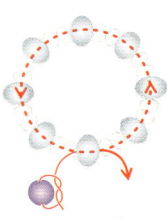

fig 1

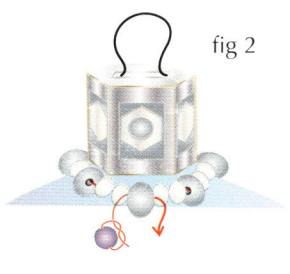

fig 2

Place the ring over the neck of the bauble - it needs to fit snugly so you may need to adjust the bead count.

If you need to make an adjustment, add or subtract A beads equally from all eight sections to keep the C beads evenly spaced around the ring (fig 2).

When you have the best fit possible, remove the ring from the bauble and pass the needle through the beads again to make the ring firm. Finish with the needle emerging from a C bead (as fig 2).

2. The Short Strands

These strands each support one large angel with seed bead wings.

Thread on 24A, 1H up, 1F, 1B, 1D, 1B, 1H down, 2B, 1J down, 2B, 1K down, 3B, 1K down, 1D, 15A, 1C, 1A, 1H down, 1E, 1H up, 1A and 3B.

Pass back up the 1A, 1H, 1E and 1H to pull the last 3B into an anchor (fig 3).

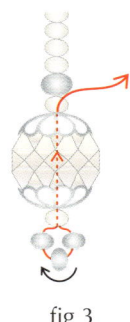

fig 3

Pass up the following 31 beads and cups to emerge from the top D bead (fig 4). This D bead supports the wings.

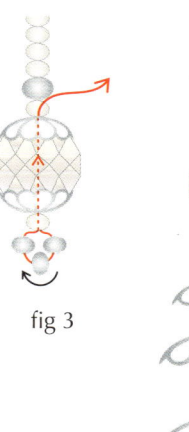

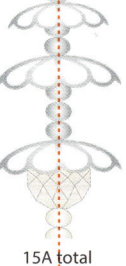

15A total

fig 4

35

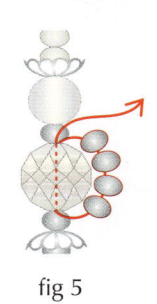

3 **The Wings** - Thread on 4B. Pass back up the D bead to make a strap on the side of the D bead (fig 5).

Pass the needle through the first 3B just added (fig 6).

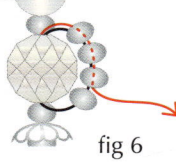

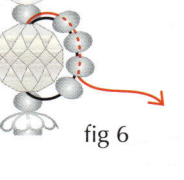

fig 5

fig 6

fig 7

Thread on 5B. Pass down through the middle 2B on the 4B strap and the following 4B of the new loop (fig 7).

Thread on 5B. Pass up the third and fourth B of the previous loop and the following 3B of the new loop (fig 8).

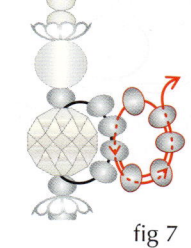

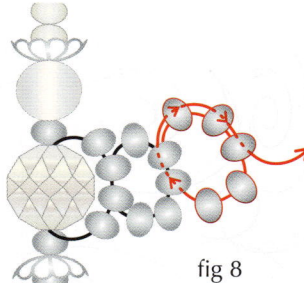

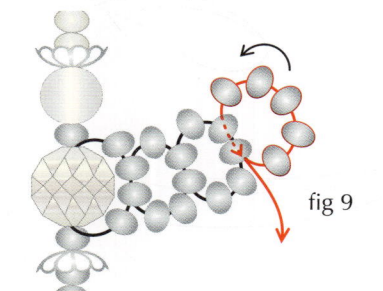

fig 8

Thread on 5B. Pass down the second and third B of the previous loop (fig 9).

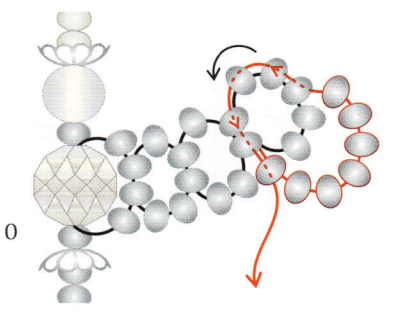

fig 9

fig 10

4 Thread on 7B.

Referring to fig 10, pass through the third, fourth and fifth B of the previous loop, down the 2B between the previous two loops and the first 1B just added (fig 10).

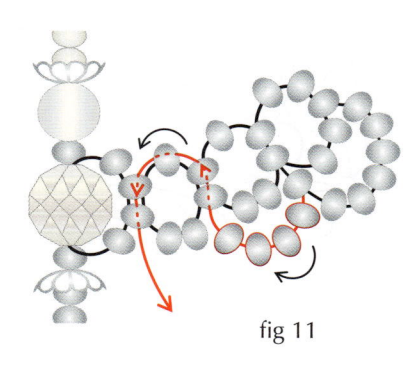

fig 11

Thread on 4B. Referring to fig 11, pass up the 2B between the first and second loops, the following 1B along the top of the wing and down the middle 2B of the first 4B strap (fig 11).

5 Thread on 4B. Referring to fig 12 pass up through the last 1B of the previous 4B added and the following 2B between the first two loops.

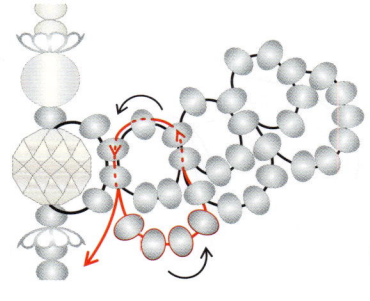

Continue through the following 1B along the top of the wing and down the middle 2B of the first 4B strap (fig 12).

fig 12

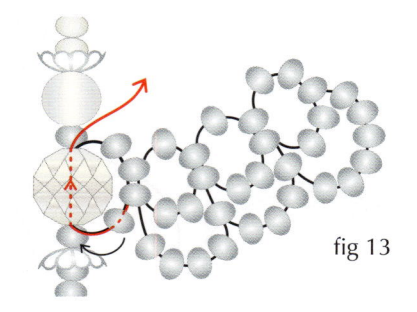

fig 13

Pass through the following 1B and up through the D bead (fig 13). The top edge of the wing now needs to be reinforced.

36

6 Pass through the first 2B along the top edge and thread on 1B. Pass through the next 1B along the top edge and thread on 1B. Pass through the following 1B along the top edge (fig 14).

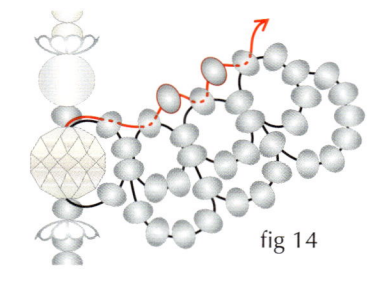

fig 14

Referring to fig 15, pass through the following 11B to emerge on the top edge of the wing once more. Pass through the following 3B along the top edge and the last 3B of the first 4B strap (fig 15).

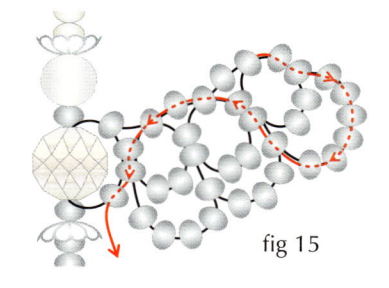

fig 15

Pass up through the D bead (fig 16). The wing on this side of the D bead is complete.

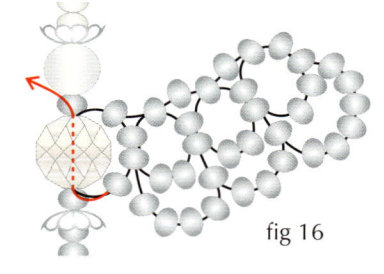

fig 16

Repeat from Step 3 to complete a second wing on the opposite side of the D bead (see fig 17).

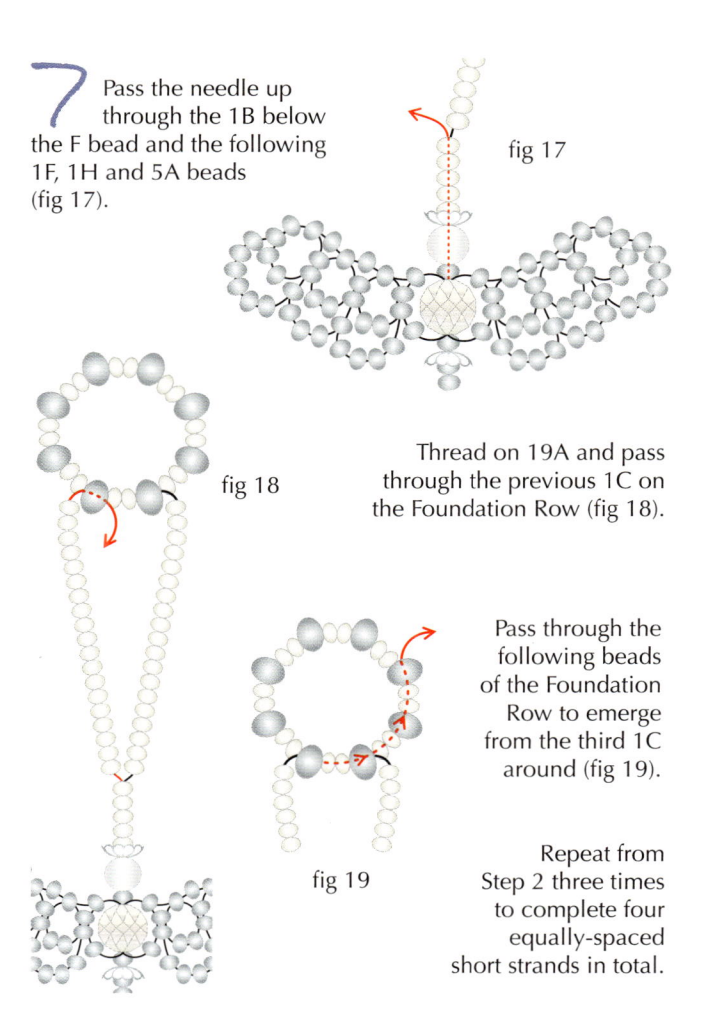

Extra Info....
In the following steps a medium size (J) filigree cup will be used to form small flower motifs.

To make these flowers the filigree bead cup is threaded through the petal-shaped holes rather than through the central hole.

The diagram shows a plan of the holes in a bead cup with the holes numbered 1 to 8 clockwise.

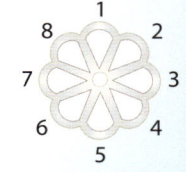

The needle will pass downwards through holes 8 and 5 and upwards through holes 5 and 2.

7 Pass the needle up through the 1B below the F bead and the following 1F, 1H and 5A beads (fig 17).

fig 17

fig 18

Thread on 19A and pass through the previous 1C on the Foundation Row (fig 18).

Pass through the following beads of the Foundation Row to emerge from the third 1C around (fig 19).

fig 19

Repeat from Step 2 three times to complete four equally-spaced short strands in total.

8 The Long Strands - These are decorated with smaller angels. These angels have G bead wings.

The needle should be emerging from the first C bead of the Foundation Row (above the first 19A of the first short strand). Pass the needle down the following 6A of this Short Strand (fig 20).

Thread on 4A.

Pass through hole 8 on a J filigree to emerge on the inside of the cup.

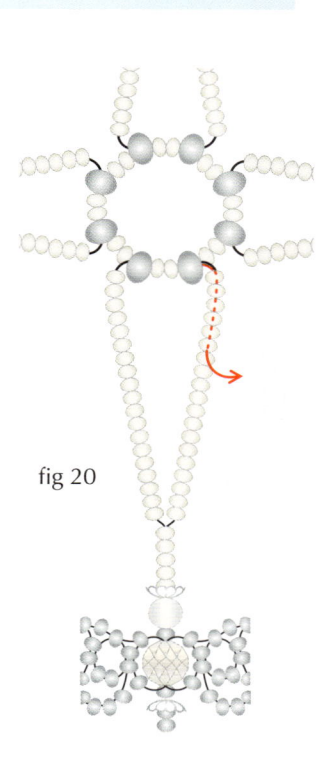

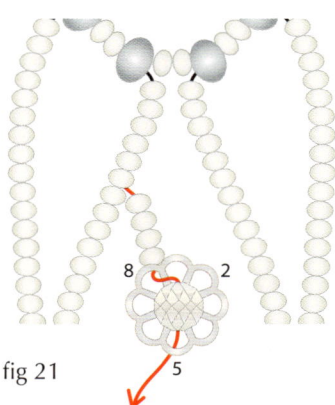

fig 20

fig 21

Thread on 1D and pass through hole 5 to emerge on the outside of the cup (fig 21).

The D bead should sit inside the cup in the middle of the space.

37

9 Thread on 35A, 1H up, 1F, 1G (curving upwards), 1C, 1J down, 2C, 1K down, 2C, 6A, 1C, 1A, 1E, 1A, 1D, 1A and 3B.

Pass the needle back up the last 1A, 1D, 1A, 1E, 1A and 1C to pull the bottom 3B into an anchor (as fig 3).

Pass up through the following beads to emerge immediately below the J bead filigree cup added in fig 21.

Pass up through hole 5 (outside to inside of the cup) and up through the D bead.

Pass up through hole 2 in the J filigree to emerge on the outside of the cup (fig 22).

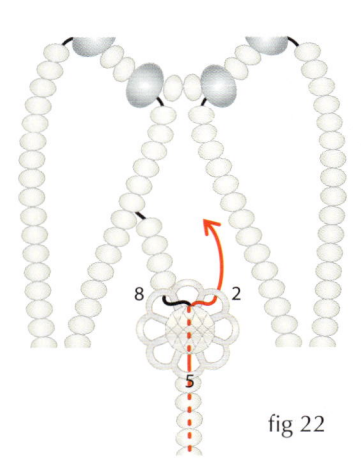

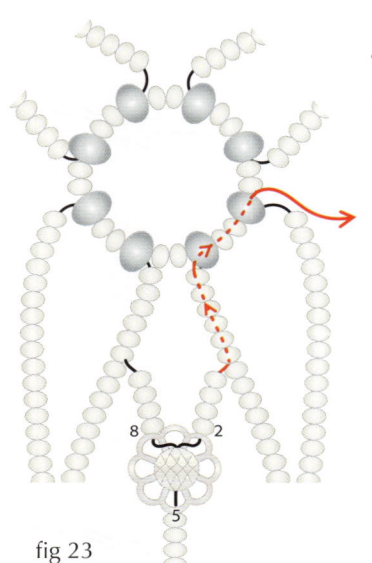

fig 22

10 Thread on 4A.

Locate the nearside of the next short strand around the bauble. Pass up the top 6A beads on this side of the short strand to centre the new long strand between the two short strands.

Pass through the following 1C, 2A and 1C around the Foundation Row to emerge from the next C bead around (fig 23).

fig 23

Repeat Steps 8, 9 and 10 three more times to complete four long strands in total.

Place the net over the bauble.

11 Before you finish off any thread ends, hold up the net-draped bauble and observe how the B bead angel wings are sitting. With just one pass of thread through the seed beads the tips of the wings can curl forward, causing them to close together, rather than remaining flat on either side of the supporting D bead.

If the wings on your angels need more support you can add more thread through the wing B beads. This extra thread fills the bead holes, stiffening and strengthening the wings.

First, make sure no existing thread ends need to be finished off between the B beads of the wings or next to the D beads at the centre of the wings. If there are any such thread ends, attach the needle to each end in turn and pass through the beadwork until they are clear of the wings. Now finish off these thread ends neatly and securely.

Prepare the needle with a new 80cm length of thread and tie a keeper bead 15cm from the end. Pass the needle up through the D bead supporting the wings.

Referring to fig 24 pass down through the first 3B beads of the strap around the D bead, under and up the first loop, down the other side of the second loop and around the end of the third loop (fig 24).

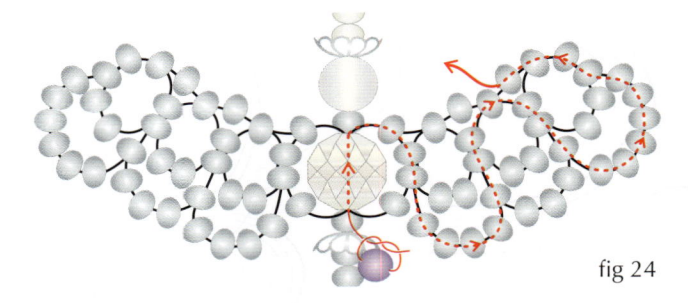

fig 24

Referring to fig 25, pass along the top row of the wing, down through the last 3B of the 4B bead strap around the D bead and up the D bead.

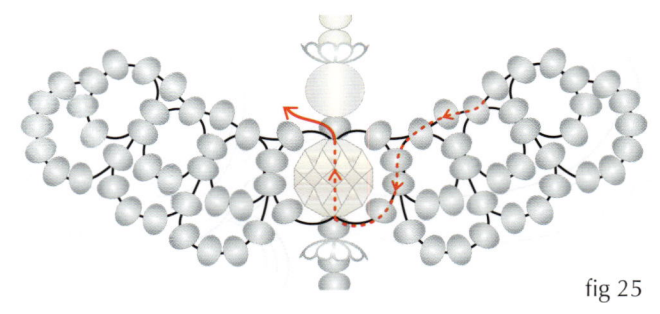

fig 25

Repeat the thread path shown in figs 24 and 25 on the other wing.

The wings should be much stiffer. Repeat the thread path again if the needle will pass through the beads.

The bead holes of the wings and the D bead will be very full of thread making a concealed knot impossible. Fortunately no knots are necessary as this thread is not securing any beads in the design: it just adds additional stiffness. The two ends of this stiffening thread can be trimmed tight against the beadwork.

Repeat on any remaining wing sets as necessary.

Heavenly Inspirations

Twinkle Angel Earrings

A simple adaptation of the smaller angel motif from the Heavenly Bauble design makes a pair of delicately sparkling earrings.

Materials
Two 15x5mm white frost glass wing beads G
Two 5mm silver filigree bead caps H
Two 8mm silver filigree bead caps J
Two 10mm silver filigree bead caps K
Two 4mm opal white faceted crystal beads L
Four 4mm clear AB faceted crystal beads M
Four size 10 ceylon white seed beads N
Two headpins and a pair of earfittings

Thread onto a headpin 1N, 1M, 1K down, 1M, 1J down, 1N, 1G, 1L and 1H up.

Trim to 8mm and turn a loop using round-nosed pliers. Attach the earfitting and repeat for the second earring.

Twinkle Tree Earrings

A stack of filigree bead caps makes a delightful little tree.

Thread four size 8 brown seed beads onto a headpin.

Add two 10mm, two 8mm and two 5mm filigree bead caps using one size 8 silver lined crystal seed bead between each bead cap layer.

Thread on one 4mm crystal AB fire polished bead.

Trim to 8mm and turn a loop using round-nosed pliers. Attach the earfitting and repeat for the second earring.

---

12 The Hanging Loop - Prepare the needle with 1.2m of single thread and tie a keeper bead 15cm from the end.

Thread on 1D. This D bead supports the two wings on the hanging loop.

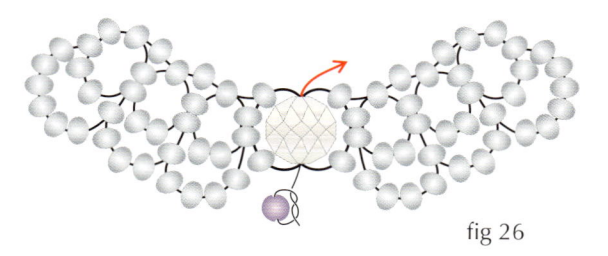

fig 26

Repeat Steps 3 to 6 to add a B bead wing on each side of the D bead. The needle will finish at the 'top' of the D bead (fig 26).

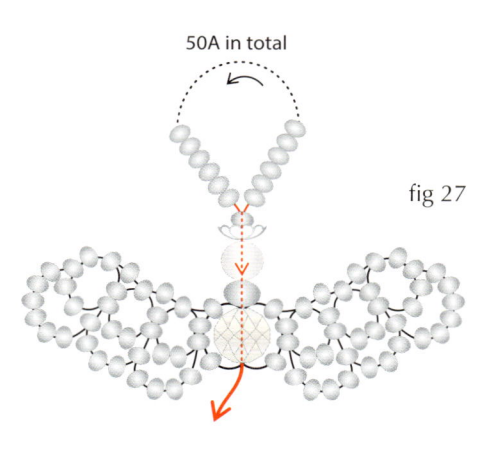

50A in total

fig 27

Thread on 1C, 1F, 1H up and 51A.
Pass the needle back down the first 1A of the 51A and the following 1H, 1F, 1C and 1D to draw up a loop of 50A (fig 27).

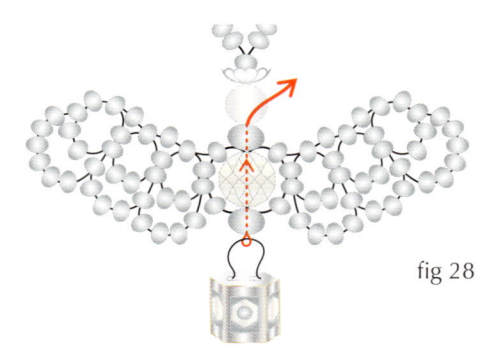

fig 28

Thread on 1C and pass the needle through the metal loop at the top of the bauble. Pass back up the 1C just added and the following 1D and 1C (fig 28).

Pass twice through all the remaining beads of the angel motif, the loop and the connection to the bauble to reinforce.

If necessary, stiffen the wings using an extra thread length as in Step 11.

Finish off the thread ends neatly and securely.

39

Comet Bauble

You Will Need

Materials

One 60mm frosted dark blue glass bauble
10g of size 10 silver lined crystal seed beads A
4g of size 8 frost silver lined crystal seed beads B
6g of size 6 frost silver lined crystal seed beads C
15g of size 3 silver lined crystal bugle beads D
Twelve 6mm crystal AB fire polished beads E
Seven 8mm crystal AB fire polished beads F
Twelve 8x6mm clear AB faceted oval crystal beads G
White size D beading thread

Tools

A size 10 beading needle
A pair of scissors to trim the threads

A multitude of bugle beads and a constellation of stars adorn this decoration. Straight-sided bugle beads scatter light less than rounded seed beads which makes the fringing shimmer and glisten like hundreds of tiny mirrors.

The Decoration is Made in Seven Stages

The zig-zag band of bugle beads is made first.

The six eight-point stars for the fringe strands are made as separate motifs.

A foundation row to fit the neck of the bauble is made next.

The foundation row is connected to the bugle band.

The fringing is completed.

The large stars are made and attached to the foundation row.

The hanging loop is made and attached to complete the design.

Extra Info....

Bugle beads are cut lengths of fine glass tube. Although the tubes are made to exacting standards and the bugle beads cut with precision, some breakage and slightly uneven bead lengths do occur.

A large number of bugle beads are used in this design and it is important that matching bugles are used for each section. Discard any beads with obvious breaks and any that are noticeably short or too long.

1 **The Bugle Band** - The bugle band is made in Ladder stitch using 96D beads. Referring to the Extra Info box above, sort out 96D that match well together.

Prepare the needle with 1.8m of single thread and tie a keeper bead 15cm from the end.

Thread on 2D. Pass up the first D and back down the second D (fig 1). Repeat the stitch to reinforce the connection.

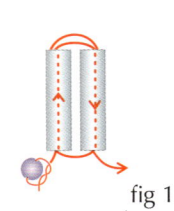

fig 1

2 Thread on 1D. Pass down the previous 1D and back up the new 1D (fig 2). Repeat the stitch to reinforce the connection.

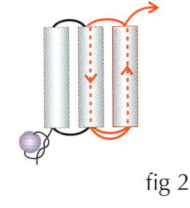

fig 2

Thread on 1D. Pass up the previous 1D and back down the new 1D (fig 3). Repeat the stitch to reinforce the connection. This is Ladder stitch.

Repeat Step 2 until you have made a strip of 14D.

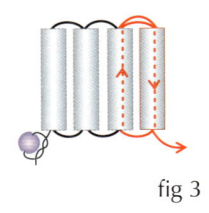

fig 3

3 Thread on 1A, 1B, 1G, 1B, 1A, 1D, 1A, 1B and 1A. Pass down the last D bead of the Ladder stitch section and up the first five beads just added (fig 4).

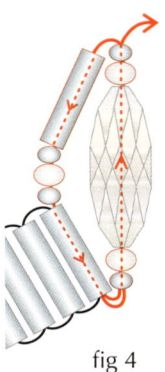

fig 4

Thread on 1D, 1A, 1B, 1A and 1D.

Pass up the first five beads of the previous stitch and down the 1D, 1A, 1B, 1A and 1D beads just added to complete a diamond frame (fig 5).

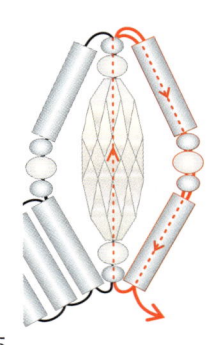

fig 5

The diamond frame needs to be reinforced. Following the same thread paths, pass through the beads of the motif again finishing with the needle emerging as fig 5.

4 Thread on 1D and Ladder stitch to the current 1D (fig 6). Reinforce the stitch as before.

Repeat the Ladder stitch technique until this section is 14D long.

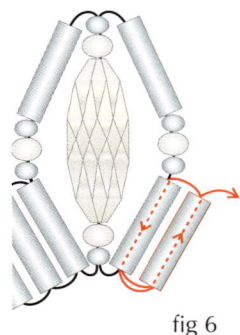

Repeat Step 3 to make a diamond frame facing in the opposite direction (fig 7).

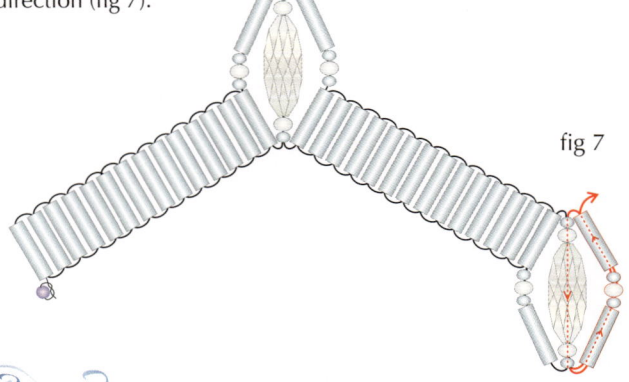

fig 6

fig 7

41

5 Repeat Step 4. The diamond frame made at the end of this repeat will match the orientation of the first frame (fig 8). A zig-zag pattern is starting to appear.

fig 8

Repeat Step 4 twice to make two more 14D sections and two more diamond frames.

fig 9

Add one 14D section only (fig 9).

A sixth diamond is required to link the two ends of the band together.

fig 10

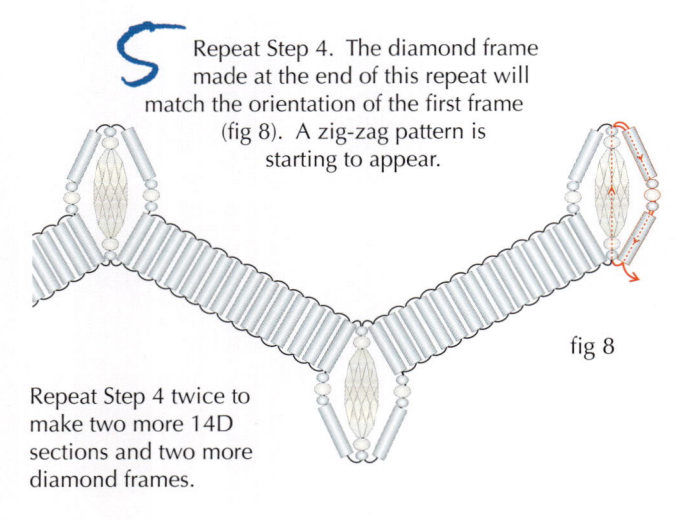

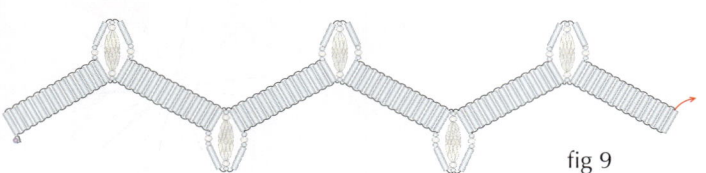

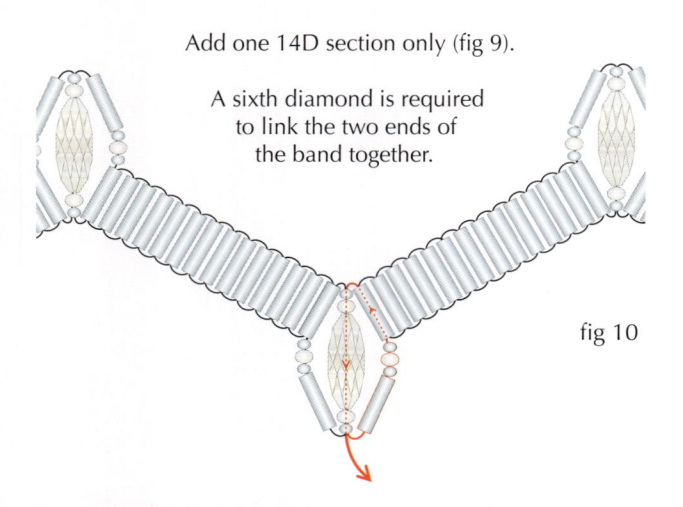

Thread on 1A, 1B, 1G, 1B, 1A, 1D, 1A, 1B and 1A. Pass up the last D bead of the previous Ladder stitch section and down the first five beads just added as before.

Thread on 1D, 1A, 1B and 1A. Making sure the band is not twisted pass up through the first 1D from Step 1 and down the 1A, 1B, 1G, 1B and 1A at the centre of the new diamond frame (fig 10).

Reinforce the frame as before.
Remove the needle leaving the thread end loose and set the band aside.

6 The Eight-Point Stars - These are made as separate motifs to ease the assembly of the fringe stranding.

Prepare the needle with 1m of doubled thread and tie a keeper bead 15cm from the ends.

Thread on 1F, 1A, 1B, 1A, 1B, 1A, 1B and 1A. Pass through the F bead to make a strap on the side.

Thread on 1A, 1B, 1A, 1B, 1A, 1B and 1A. Pass through the F bead again to make a second strap (fig 11).

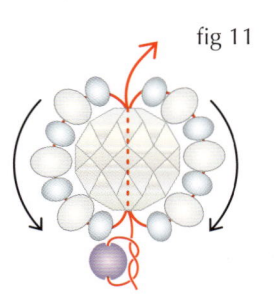

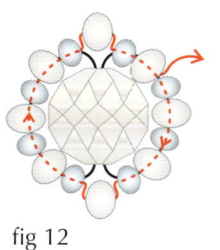

fig 11

Pass the needle through the seven beads of the first strap and thread on 1B. Pass through the seven beads of the second strap and thread on 1B. Pass through the first 1A and 1B of the first strap again (fig 12).

fig 12

The two new B beads sit above the holes in the F bead completing an alternating frame of seed beads.

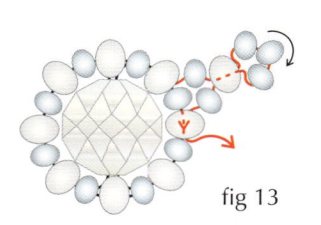

7 Thread on 1A, 1B and 3A. Pass the needle back through the B bead to pull the 3A into a neat picot.

fig 13

Thread on 1A and pass through the next 1B around the frame (fig 13).

Repeat seven times to add eight picot points in total (fig 14).

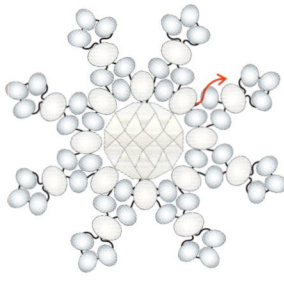

fig 14

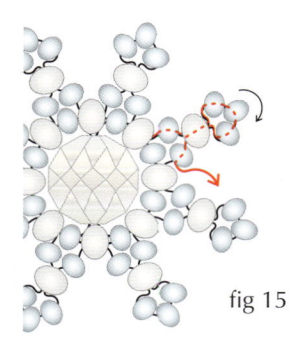

8 Pass the needle through the beads of the following picot point to emerge from the last 1A (fig 15).

fig 15

Skipping past the next B bead of the frame, pass through the beads of the next picot point around (fig 16).

Repeat seven more times to link all eight points together and reinforce the star.

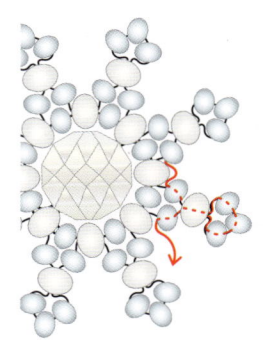

fig 16

9 Reposition the needle to emerge from the B bead above the hole at one end of the central F bead (fig 17).

fig 17

Thread on 1A, 1D, 1A, 1G, 1A, 1B and 3A.

Pass back up the last B bead and the following beads to emerge at the B on the frame.

fig 18

Pass through this B bead in the same direction to centralise the strand just made (fig 18).

Carefully adjust the thread tension so the strand falls vertically and softly from the edge of the frame.

Finish off both thread ends neatly and securely without blocking the hole in the B bead at the opposite end of the F bead.

Repeat from Step 6 to make five more identical motifs.

10 The Foundation Row - Prepare the needle with 1.5m of single thread and tie a keeper bead 15cm from the end.

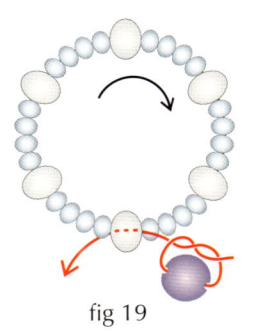

Thread on six repeats of 1C and 4A.

Pass the needle through the first C bead to make a ring (fig 19).

Place the ring over the neck of the bauble - it needs to fit snugly so you may need to adjust the bead count.

fig 19

If you need to make an adjustment, add or subtract A beads equally from all six sections to keep the C beads evenly spaced around the ring.

When the ring is a good fit, pass through all the beads again to emerge as fig 19. Remove the ring from the bauble.

11 Connecting to the Bugle Band - The foundation row is now linked to the bugle band.

Looking around the bugle band there are three upward pointing diamond frames and three pointing downwards. The three upward pointing frames connect to the foundation row.

Thread on 2A, 1B, 8A, 1D, 1A, 1B and 2A.

Locate an upward pointing diamond frame on the bugle band. Pass through the 1D, 1A, 1B, 1A and 1D down one side of the frame (fig 20).

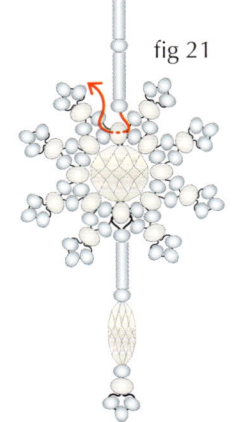

fig 20

fig 21

Thread on 1A, 1B, 25A, 1D, 1A, 1D, 1A, 1D, 1A, 1D, 1A, 1C, 1A, 1D, 1A, 1D and 1A. Pick up a prepared eight-point star motif and pass the needle through the B bead sitting above the F bead hole (fig 21).

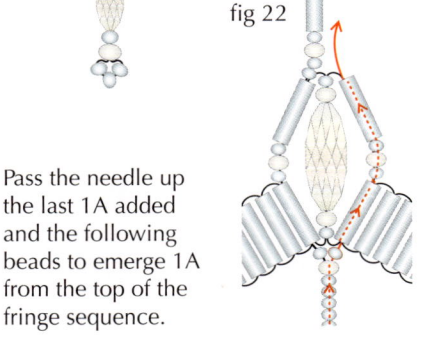

fig 22

Pass the needle up the last 1A added and the following beads to emerge 1A from the top of the fringe sequence.

fig 23

Thread on 1A and pass up the 1D, 1A, 1B, 1A and 1D along the other side of the diamond frame (fig 22).

Carefully tension the thread so the new long strand falls straight and softly from the bottom point of the diamond frame.

12 Referring to fig 23 thread on 1A. Pass up the second 1A towards the foundation row and the following 1B, 1A, 1D, 8A and 1B. Thread on 2A and pass through the C bead on the foundation ring to centralise the strand below this C bead.
Pass through the following beads of the ring to emerge from the second C bead around (fig 23).

Repeat Steps 11 and 12 twice more to make the connections to the remaining two upward pointing diamond frames. Leave the thread end attached and remove the needle.

13 Completing the Fringing
Prepare the needle with 1.5m of single thread and tie a keeper bead 15cm from the end.

Pass the needle down the seventh D of the bugle band preceding the long strand just made to emerge from the lower edge of the band (fig 24).

fig 24

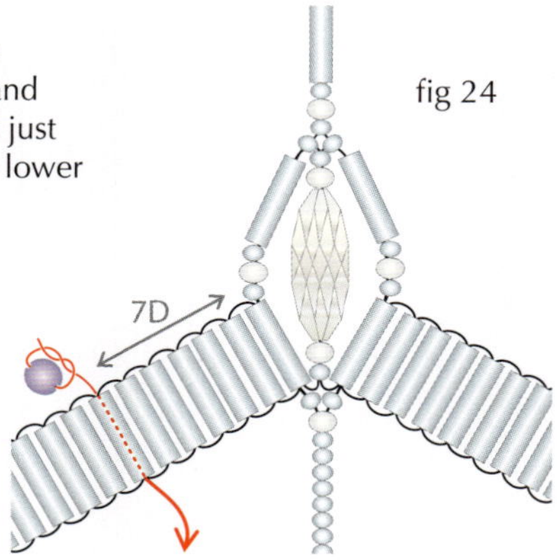

fig 25

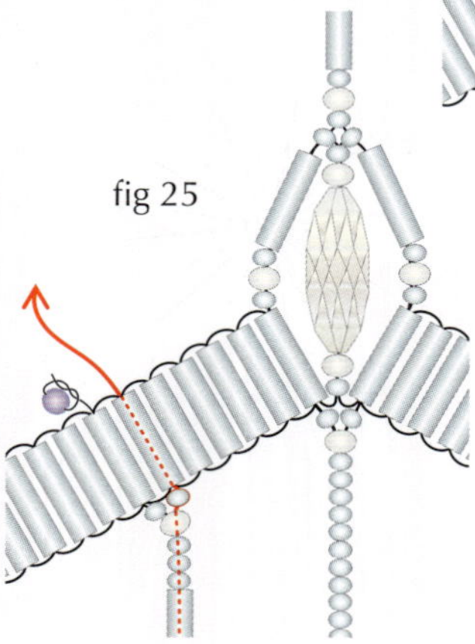

* Thread on 1A, 1B, 3A, 1D, 1A, 1D, 1A, 1C, 1A, 1D, 1A, 1E, 1A, 1B and 3A.

Pass back up the last 1B and the following beads to emerge 1A before the start of the sequence. Thread on 1A and pass up through the next D bead closer to the diamond frame along the bugle band (fig 25).

Carefully tension the thread so the strand falls softly from the edge of the band as before.

Pass down, up and down the next 3D towards the same diamond frame to emerge from the lower edge of the band once more.

14
Thread on 1A, 1B, 10A, 1D, 1A, 1D, 1A, 1D, 1A, 1D, 1A, 1C, 1A, 1D, 1A, 1E, 1A, 1B and 3A.

Pass back up the last 1B and the following beads to emerge 1A before the start of the sequence. Thread on 1A and pass up through the previous D bead along the bugle band (fig 26). Tension the thread as on previous strands.

fig 26

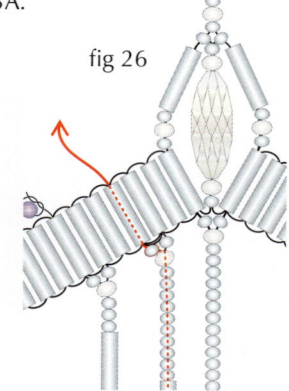

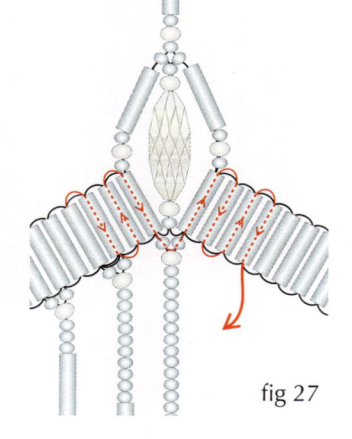

Weave up and down the D beads of the band and the beads around the lower edge of the diamond frame to emerge from the bottom of the fourth D bead of the following section of bugle band (fig 27).

fig 27

15
Add a fringe strand to match Step 14 passing the needle up the previous D bead of the bugle band to mirror the previous fringe strand made.

Working towards the next diamond frame, pass down, up and down the next 3D to emerge from the lower edge of the band once more.

Add a fringe strand as in Step 13 passing the needle up the next D bead of the band to mirror the first two strands (see fig 28).

16
Reposition the needle to emerge from the bottom of the next diamond frame along the bugle band (fig 28).

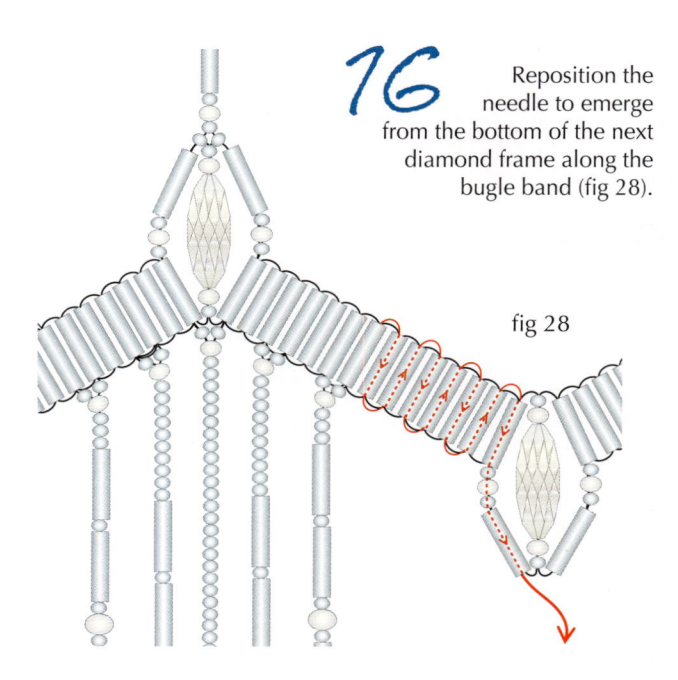

fig 28

Thread on 1A, 1B, 3A, 1D, 1A, 1D, 1A, 1C, 1A, 1D, 1A, 1D and 1A. Attach a prepared eight-point star motif to the bottom of this strand as shown in fig 21. Pass back up the strand beads to emerge 1A from the top of the sequence. Thread on 1A and pass up the 1D, 1A, 1B, 1A and 1D on the other side of the diamond motif (as fig 22).

Weave the needle up and down the next bugle band section to emerge from the lower edge of the eighth D bead (7D from the next frame as fig 24).

Working towards the next diamond frame repeat twice from * in Step 13 to complete the fringe stranding.

fig 29

17 **The Large Stars -** Prepare the needle with 1.5m of single thread and tie a keeper bead 25cm from the end.

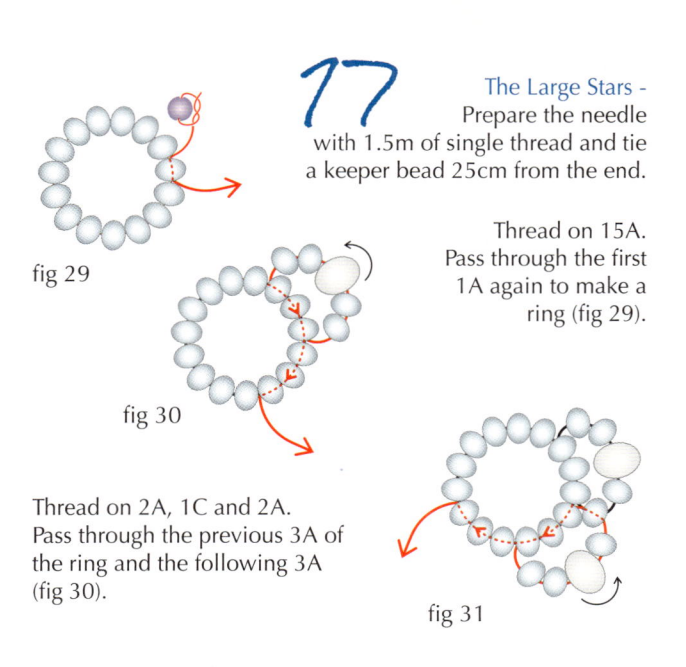

Thread on 15A. Pass through the first 1A again to make a ring (fig 29).

fig 30

Thread on 2A, 1C and 2A. Pass through the previous 3A of the ring and the following 3A (fig 30).

fig 31

18 Thread on 2A, 1C and 1A. Pass through the first 1A of the previous stitch, the 3A just passed through on the ring and the following 3A (fig 31). Repeat twice.

To make the last stitch of the row pass through the last 1A of the first stitch and thread on 1A, 1C and 1A.

Pass through the first 1A of the fourth stitch and the 3A of the ring (fig 32).

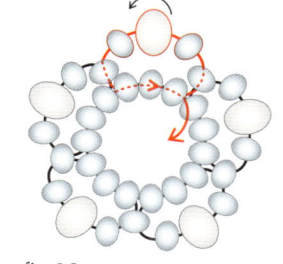

fig 32

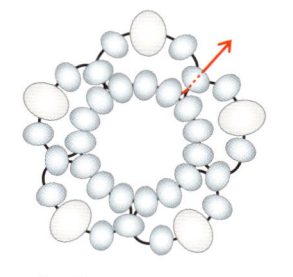

Pass through the 1A between the first and last stitches to reposition the needle for the next row (fig 33).

fig 33

fig 34

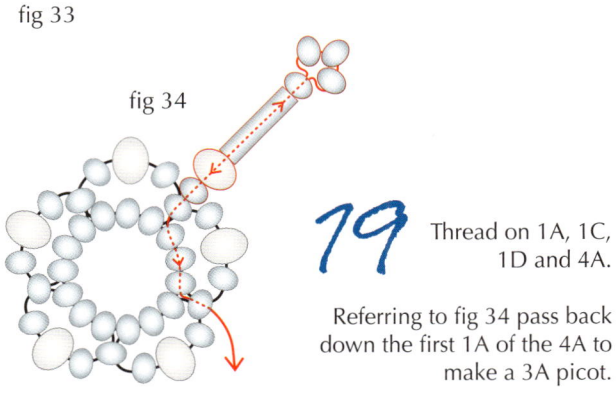

19 Thread on 1A, 1C, 1D and 4A.

Referring to fig 34 pass back down the first 1A of the 4A to make a 3A picot.

Pass down the following 1D, 1C and 1A just added, the 1A of the previous row, through 3A of the ring and the next 1A of the previous row (fig 34).

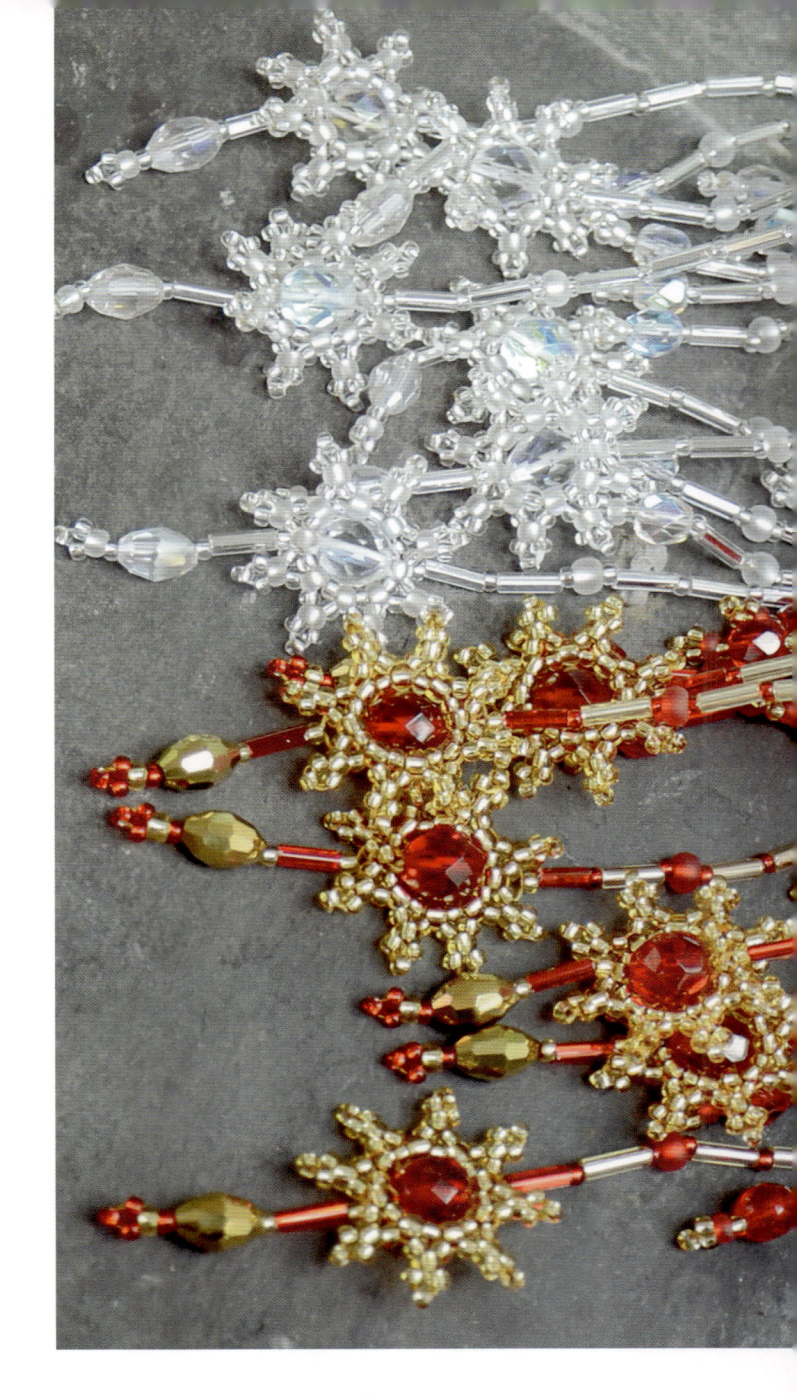

20 Repeat Step 19 four times to add five spikes in total (fig 35).

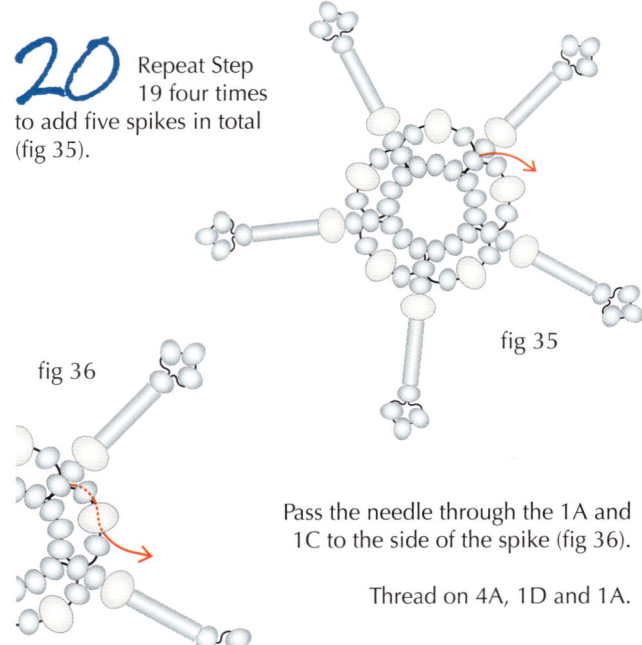

fig 35

fig 36

Pass the needle through the 1A and 1C to the side of the spike (fig 36).

Thread on 4A, 1D and 1A.

45

fig 37

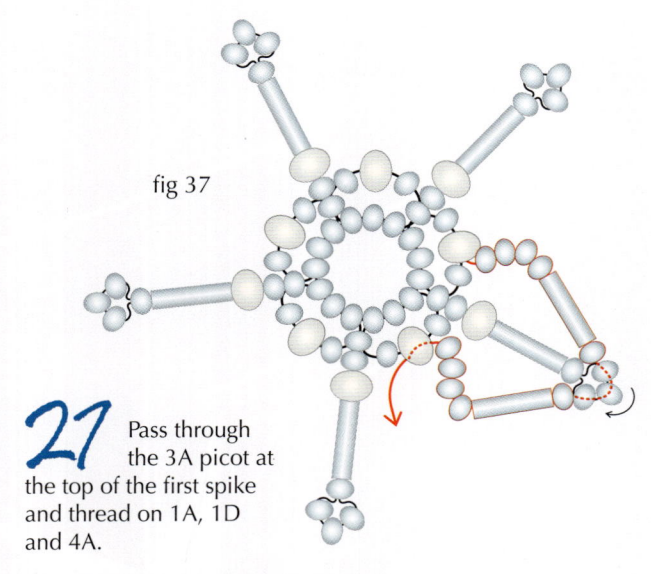

21 Pass through the 3A picot at the top of the first spike and thread on 1A, 1D and 4A.

Pass through the next C bead (fig 37).

22 Referring to fig 38, thread on 2A. Pass in the opposite direction through the second A of the 4A just added. Thread on 1A, 1D and 1A and pass through the 3A picot of the next spike *. Thread on 1A, 1D and 4A and pass through the next C bead (fig 38).

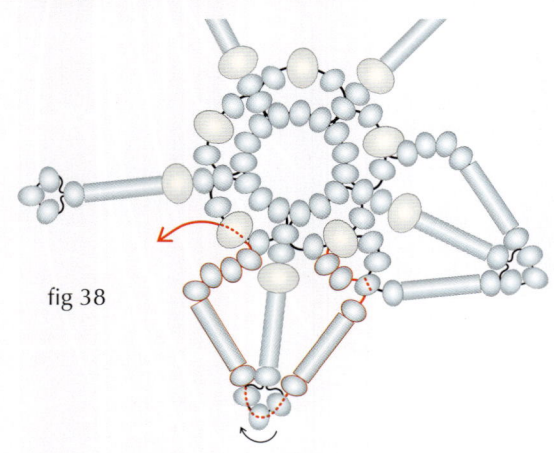

fig 38

Repeat Step 22 three more times.

Repeat Step 22 to *.
To complete the row thread on 1A, 1D and 1A. Pass through the third A added in Step 21. Thread on 2A and pass through the C bead between the points (fig 39).

fig 39

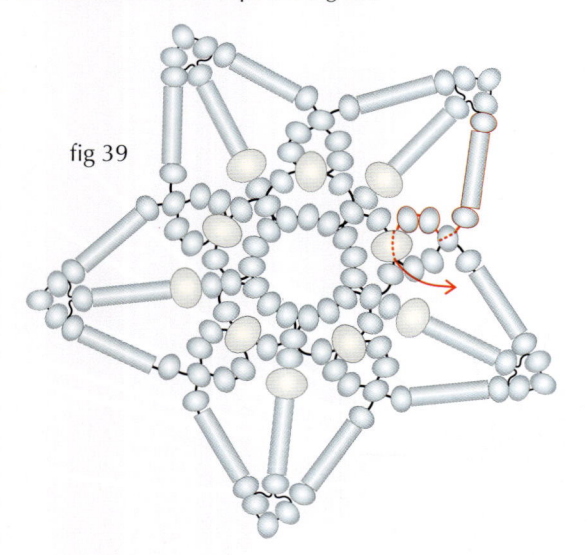

fig 40

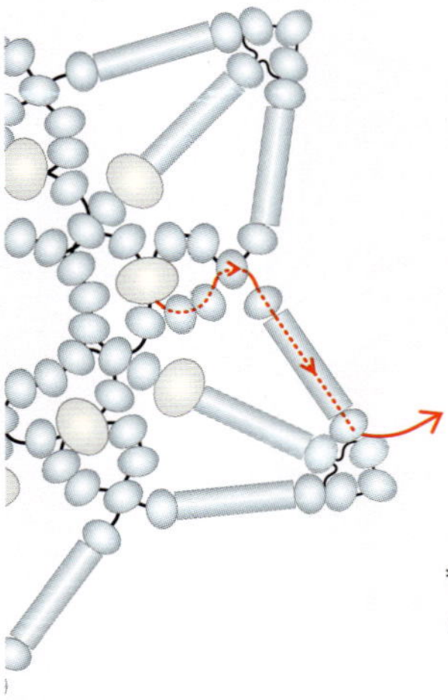

23 The star needs to be reinforced.

Pass the needle through the following 4A, 1D and 1A added in Step 21 (fig 40).

*Referring to fig 41 pass the needle down the adjacent 1A under the picot and up the original A bead to make a Square stitch (fig 41).

fig 41

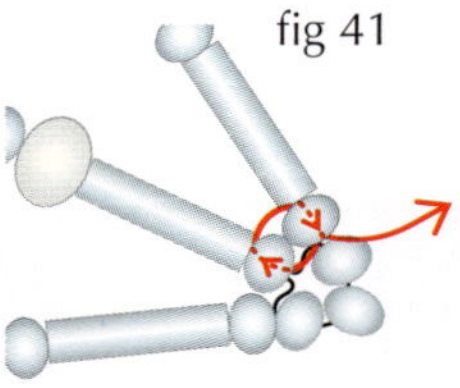

Pass through the 3A of the picot and the following 1A. Square stitch this 1A to the same 1A under the picot (fig 42).

fig 42

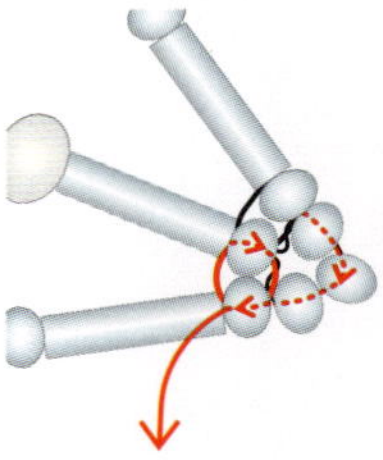

Pass through the following 1D and 1A. Skipping across the top of the next 1A, pass up the 1A and 1D along the side of the next star point (fig 43).

fig 43

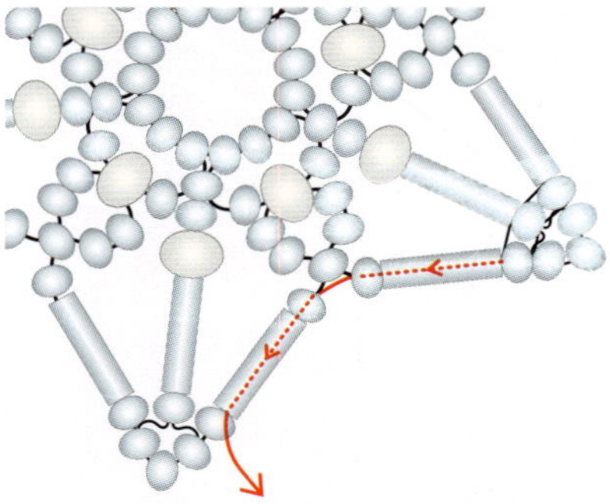

Repeat from * four times. Note - the star will become slightly convex which helps it to sit against the curve of the bauble.

Finish off this thread end neatly and securely.

Remove the keeper bead. Attach the needle to this thread end and reinforce the centre 15A ring. Finish off the thread end neatly and securely.

Repeat from Step 17 twice to make two more large stars.

24 Attaching the Large Stars -
Re-attach the needle to the long thread end on the foundation row.

fig 44

Thread on 7A and 1B. Pass the needle through the 1A at the tip of a picot on the first large star.

Pass back up through the beads just added and the following beads around the foundation row to emerge immediately before the second C bead along (fig 44).

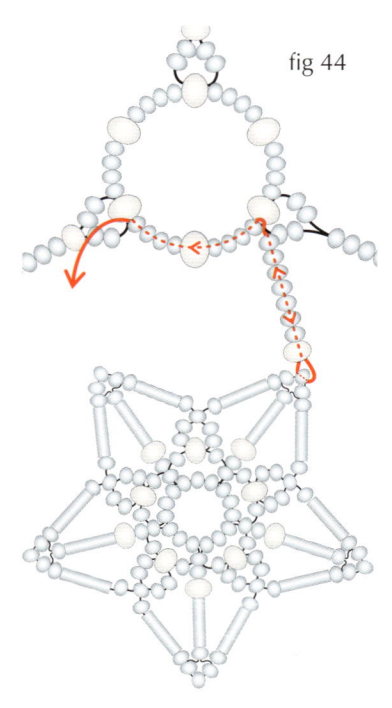

Thread on 7A and 1B. Pass through the 1A at the tip of the next picot star point around the same motif. Pass back up the beads just added and the following 1C on the foundation row.

Repeat twice more to attach the remaining two large stars.

Finish off all remaining thread ends and place the beading over the bauble.

25 The Hanging Loop - Using a 1.5m length of doubled thread repeat Step 6 to fig 17 in Step 9 to make an eight-point star.

The needle should be emerging from a B bead adjacent to the F bead hole.

50 A in total

Thread on 4A, 1B, 2A, 1C and 50A.

fig 45

Pass back down the C and the following 2A, 1B and 4A to draw up the loop. Pass through the B bead on the star in the same direction (fig 45).

Pass through the F bead at the centre of the star and the B bead adjacent to this end of the F bead hole.

Thread on 4A, 1B, 1A and 1C.

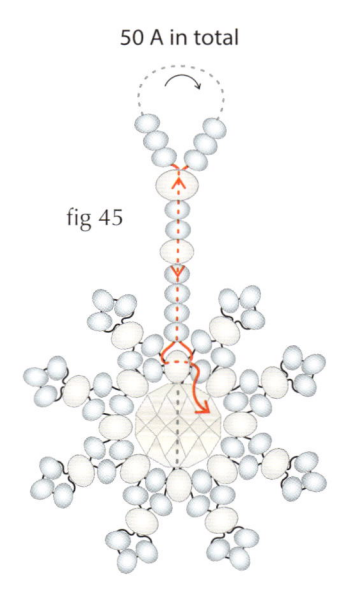

Pass the needle through the metal loop at the top of the bauble and back up the beads just added. Pass through the same B bead on the star to centralise the connection.

Reinforce this connection to the bauble loop and finish off all remaining thread ends neatly and securely.

Candle Decoration

You Will Need

Materials

to Make a Gold Candle Clip

4g of size 10 silver lined gold seed beads A
4g of size 10 ceylon cream seed beads B
2g of size 10 silver lined orange seed beads C
7g of size 3 ceylon cream bugle beads D
2.5g of size 3 silver lined gold bugle beads E
One 9x7mm topaz AB fire polished drop bead F
One 5mm gilt filigree bead cup G
One gilt tree clip with a single spring attachment
6cm of 8mm external diameter clear plastic tubing
12cm of 0.6mm gold plated half-hard wire
Gold size D beading thread

to Make a Silver Candle Clip

4g of size 10 silver lined crystal seed beads A
4g of size 10 ceylon white seed beads B
2g of size 10 silver lined pale blue seed beads C
7g of size 3 ceylon white bugle beads D
2.5g of size 3 silver lined crystal bugle beads E
One 9x7mm crystal AB fire polished drop bead F
One 5mm silver filigree bead cup G
One silver tree clip with a single spring attachment
6cm of 8mm external diameter clear plastic tubing
12cm of 0.6mm silver plated half-hard wire
White size D beading thread

Tools

A size 10 beading needle
A pair of scissors to trim the threads
Wire cutters and round-nosed pliers

finished candle measures approximately 85x15mm

Candles bring a warm light on dark winter evenings. In two styles, the first design sits on top of the tree bough in a glittering cup of bugle beads; the second, on page 55, hangs from the bough.

The Decoration is Made in Six Stages

The candle cylinder is made first.

The candle holder is made next and attached to the base of the candle cylinder.

The top of the candle cylinder is added.

The 'waxy drips' are stitched to the side of the candle.

The flame is made as a separate unit.

The candle is assembled on the clip.

Extra Info....

The bugle bead body of the candle is worked in Peyote stitch using a double thickness of thread.

Passing through bugle beads can cause a drag on the thread. Occasionally one side of a double thread is dragged more than the other, causing little loops to form between the beads. Watch out for these little loops - it is important to make sure that both sides of the double thread pull through completely to maintain an even tension.

1 The Candle Cylinder - Prepare the needle with 1.5m of double thread. Bring the two cut ends together and tie a keeper bead 15cm from these ends.

2 Row 1 - Thread on 8D.

Row 2 - Thread on 1D. Pass back through the seventh bead of the previous row (fig 1).

fig 1

Thread on 1D and pass back through the fifth D of the previous row (fig 2). Repeat to the end of the row to add two more D beads above alternate D beads (fig 3).

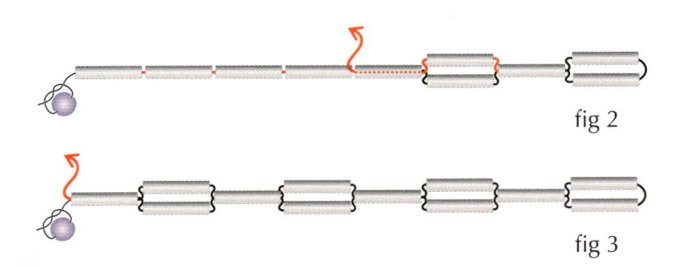

fig 2

fig 3

You have created a row with a key and keyhole appearance. On the next row the new beads will sit in the keyholes and, in turn, make a new set of keys.

3 Row 3 - Thread on 1D. Pass the needle back through the last D added on the previous row (a key bead) to pull the new bead into the keyhole at the end of the row (fig 4).

fig 4

Thread on 1D and pass through the next key bead along. Repeat to the end of the row.
This is Peyote stitch.

Row 4 - Add the first 1D of the row as before (fig 5). Work to the end of the row to add 1D in each keyhole.

fig 5

Repeat the same technique until there are 15D beads up each edge (30 rows worked). You will need to add in more thread to complete the 30 rows. Do not tie any knots - add the new thread on a keeper bead leaving the old thread ends hanging loose.

4 Stitching the Seam - Roll the beadwork to bring Row 1 up against Row 30 and interlock the edges.

Pass the needle back and forth, to zip the seam together (fig 6).

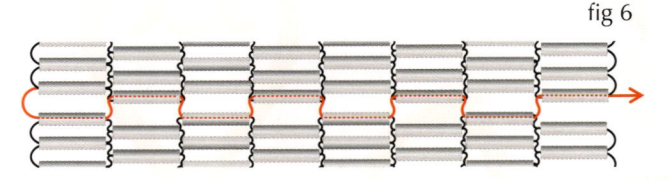

fig 6

Remove any keeper beads and finish off the thread ends neatly and securely between the beads at one end of the cylinder only - leave the other half of the cylinder knot-free. The knot-free end will be the top end of the candle. Mark the top end with a temporary tag of thread.

5 The Candle Holder - A wide fan of A and E beads is made first. The edges of the fan are then connected to produce a shallow filigree cone.

Prepare the needle with 1.5m of single thread and tie a keeper bead 15cm from the end.

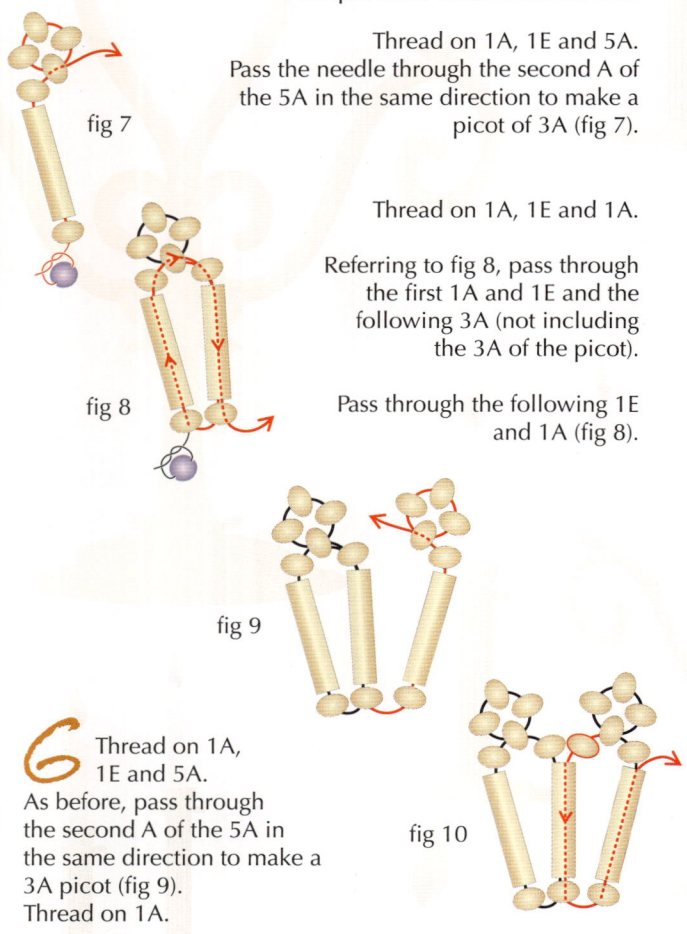

Thread on 1A, 1E and 5A. Pass the needle through the second A of the 5A in the same direction to make a picot of 3A (fig 7).

fig 7

Thread on 1A, 1E and 1A.

Referring to fig 8, pass through the first 1A and 1E and the following 3A (not including the 3A of the picot).

Pass through the following 1E and 1A (fig 8).

fig 8

fig 9

6 Thread on 1A, 1E and 5A. As before, pass through the second A of the 5A in the same direction to make a 3A picot (fig 9). Thread on 1A.

fig 10

Referring to fig 10 pass down the previous 1E and the 1A beneath it. Pass up the first 1A and the following 1E of this step (fig 10).

Thread on 5A. Pass in the same direction through the second A of the new 5A to make the picot as before.

Thread on 1A, 1E and 1A.

Referring to fig 11 pass up the 1A at the base of the previous E bead, the following 1E and 3A (not including the 3A of the picot).

Pass through the following 1E and 1A (fig 11).

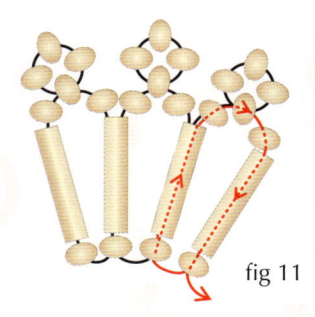

fig 11

The E beads are starting to form the desired 'fan-shape'. Make sure the single A beads at the bottom of the E beads are sitting snugly together to emphasize the effect.

Repeat Step 6 until you have used 15E beads. The needle should finish at the top of the 15th E bead (as fig 10).

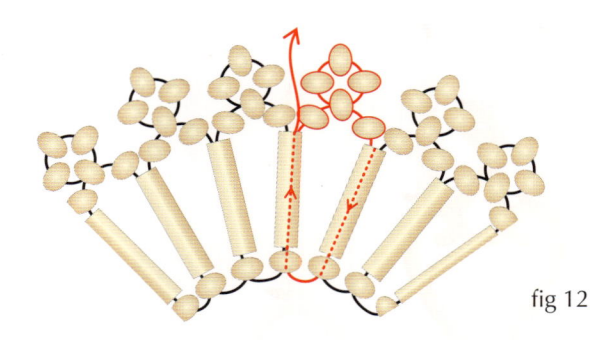

fig 12

7 Thread on 5A. Referring to fig 12 make the picot as before and thread on 1A.

Pass down the first E bead of the fan and the 1A beneath it. Pass back up the 1A and 1E on the other end of the fan to complete the join and create a shallow cone.

The top (wide) edge of the cone is now decorated with a row of loops and reinforced with several passes of thread.

8 Referring to fig 13, pass the needle through the following 1A of the previous stitch.

*Pass through the adjacent 1A of the picot. Thread on 3A and pass down the last 1A of the first picot (fig 13). This creates a 3A bridge between the picots.

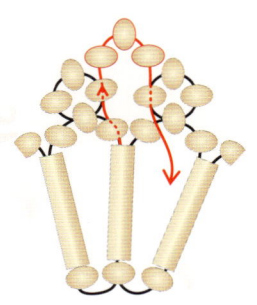

fig 13

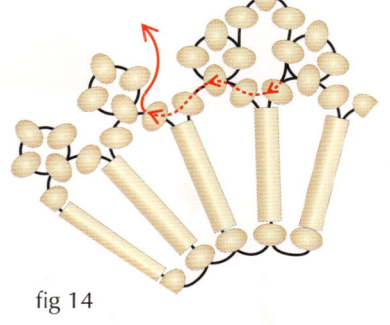

fig 14

Referring to fig 14, pass through both single A beads on each side of the E bead and the following 3A along the inner row.

Note - make sure you pass through each inner row bead in the correct direction - the row should pull into a neat zig-zag line (also see fig 15).

Repeat from * to add a 3A bridge in each gap.

To reinforce the beadwork pass the needle through the innner A bead ring above the E beads (45A beads) (fig 15). If the needle will fit through the holes again, repeat the pass once more.

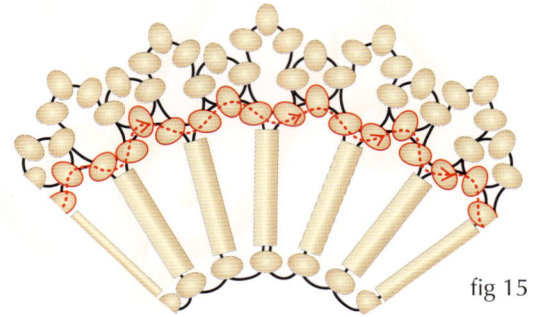

fig 15

50

9 Pass down the adjacent 1E and 1A beads to emerge at the narrow end of the cone. The A beads along this lower edge are now Square-stitched together to make the base of the cone firm.

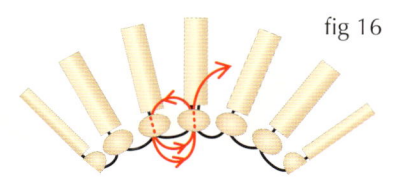

fig 16

Pass up the next 1A along, down the previous 1A and back up the new 1A (fig 16).

Pass down the next 1A, up the previous 1A and down the new 1A (fig 17).

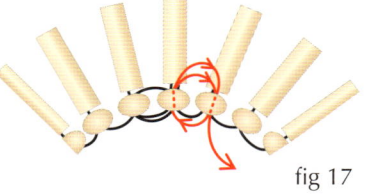

fig 17

Repeat the stitches shown in figs 16 and 17 until all 15A around the narrow end of the cone are linked together. Finish with the needle pointing upwards from an A bead (as fig 16) and on the outside of the cone.

Extra Info....
When the cone is attached to the candle cylinder the stitches pass between the D bead bugles of the cylinder (not through the D bead holes) so it does not matter if there are knots blocking the D bead holes.
Make sure the next few steps are worked around the bottom end of the cylinder keeping the knot-free top for adding the 'waxy drips' in Steps 12-15.

10 Linking the Candle Holder to the Candle Cylinder - Slide the clear plastic tubing into the candle cylinder so the cut end of the plastic is just proud of the bottom end of the beadwork.
Tip - If the tube is a very tight fit - a little talc or the tiniest bit of cornflour will make it slide in easier.

Slide the narrow end of the cone over the protruding plastic tube and up against the bottom of the candle cylinder so the cone cups around the base of the candle (fig 18).

fig 18

This will stretch out the bottom 15A row of the cone to match up with the fifteen gaps between the D beads at the base of the cylinder.

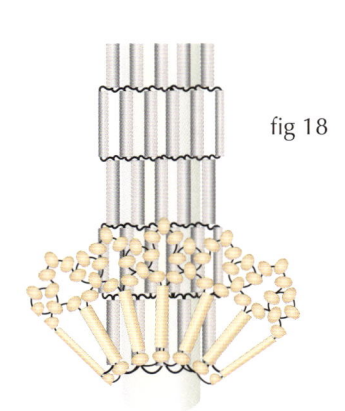

To make the connecting stitches the needle must emerge on the inside of the candle cylinder - at present the plastic tube is in the way. You will need to slide the tube back into the candle cylinder to make the stitch and slide it down again to line up the next stitch.

11 Hold the beadwork upside-down so you can see the bottom of the candle cylinder and the holes in the A beads at the bottom of the cone. The needle is emerging from one of these A beads pointing towards the adjacent E bead and on the outside of the cone.

fig 19

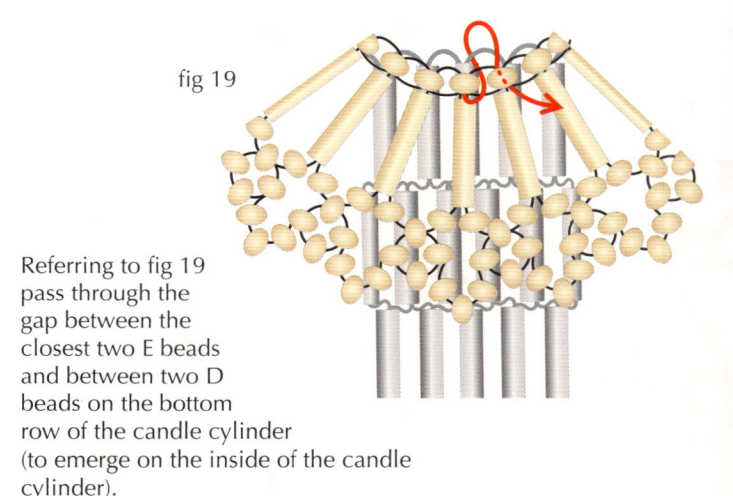

Referring to fig 19 pass through the gap between the closest two E beads and between two D beads on the bottom row of the candle cylinder (to emerge on the inside of the candle cylinder).

Pass down the next 1A bead around the base of the cone (fig 19). The stitch should pull tight against the thread loop between the D beads on the candle cylinder.

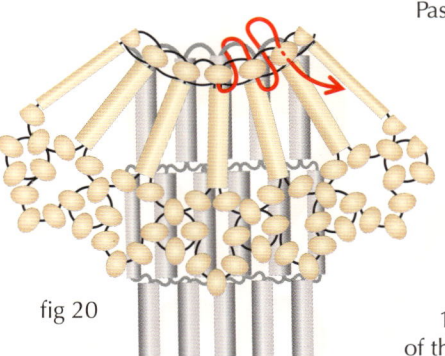

Pass the needle through the next gap between two E beads around the cone and between the next two D beads on the bottom row of the candle cylinder (to emerge on the inside of the candle cylinder).

fig 20

Pass down the following 1A bead around the base of the candle holder (fig 20).

Repeat thirteen times to complete the seam. Finish off the thread end neatly and securely.

51

12 The Candle Top
Prepare the needle with 1.5m of single thread and tie a keeper bead 15cm from the end. Pass through 1D on the top of the candle cylinder to emerge at the top edge.

Thread on 1B. Pass down the next 1D and up the first 1D. Pass through the new B bead (fig 21).

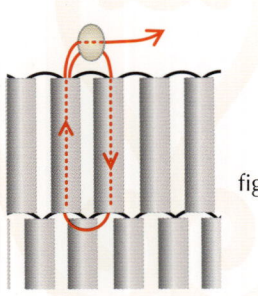

fig 21

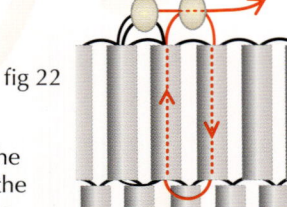

fig 22

Thread on 1B. Pass down the second 1D along, back up the previous 1D and through the new B bead (fig 22).

Repeat the stitch shown in fig 22 thirteen times to add 15B in total. Pass through the first 1B of the row to close up the ring.

13
*Thread on 1B. Pass through the previous 2B on the ring and back through the new 1B (fig 23).

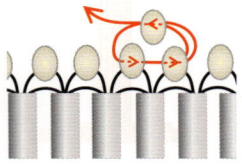

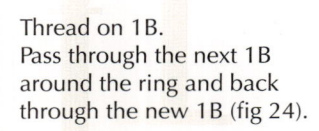

fig 23

Thread on 1B. Pass through the next 1B around the ring and back through the new 1B (fig 24).

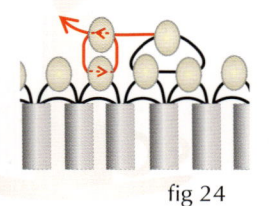

fig 24

Repeat from * four times to add 10B in total.

Pass the needle through the 10B beads twice to pull them into a neat, tight ring. Pass the needle through the closest B bead on the 15B (outer) ring to be in the correct position to start the 'waxy drips' down the outside of the candle cylinder.

14 The 'Waxy Drips'
These attach to the 15B beads of the outer ring and to the threads between the D beads of the candle cylinder.

Extra Info....
Each D bead is approximately 5B beads in length. With this is mind, you can make drips 5B, 10B or 15B beads in length quite easily however this makes a very regular repeat pattern which is uncharacteristic of real drips. The following technique will show you how to add extra B beads to vary the drip lengths more imaginatively.

15
Thread on 5B. Use the tip of the needle to pick up a thread between the first and second band of D beads directly below the B bead on the top ring.

Pass back up the 5B beads and the B bead on the ring (fig 25).

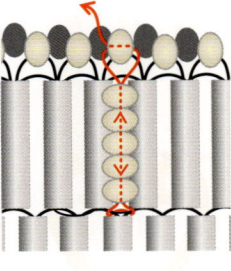

fig 25

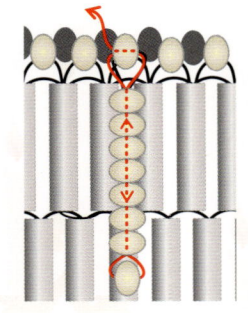

Pass back down the new 5B and thread on 3B. Leaving aside the last 1B to anchor the strand, pass back up the previous 2B, the 5B of the first stitch and the 1B of the ring (fig 26).

Pass through the next 1B of the ring.

fig 26

Thread on 10B. Use the tip of the needle to pick up a thread between the second and third band of D beads directly below the B bead on the ring.

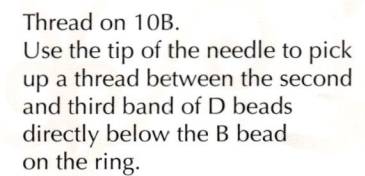

Pass back up the 10B and through the same 1B on the ring (fig 27).

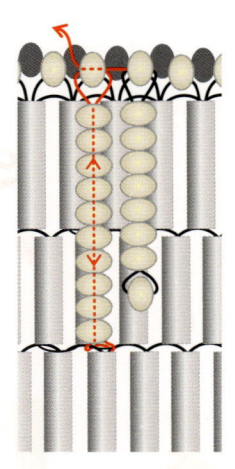

fig 27

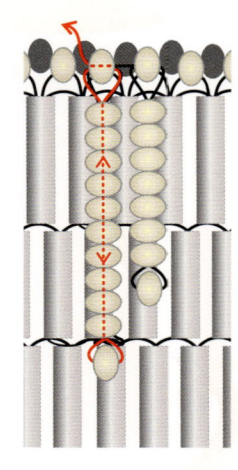

Pass back down the 10B and thread on 1B. Leaving aside the 1B to anchor the thread, pass back up the 10B and the 1B of the ring (fig 28).

Pass through the next 1B of the ring.

You have added a drip of 8B and a drip of 11B.

fig 28

Repeating the same technique add one drip per B bead of the 15B outer ring. A suggested pattern is given below but any variation between 5B and 18B (requiring 15B for the first stitch) will work well.

Suggested pattern for the thirteen remaining 'drips' - 6B, 5B, 8B, 11B, 16B, 9B, 13B, 6B, 10B, 8B, 6B, 18B, and 14B.

When the 'drips' are complete finish off the thread end neatly and securely.

16 The Candle Flame

Prepare the needle with 1.2m of single thread and tie a keeper bead 15cm from the end.

Extra Info....
If you are making the silver version of the candle, swap the A and C beads in Steps 16 to 18 to give better colour definition around the F bead at the centre.

Thread on 1F (wide end to narrow end) and 10A. Pass through the F bead again to bring the A beads into a strap on the side (fig 29). Thread on 10A and repeat to make a second strap.

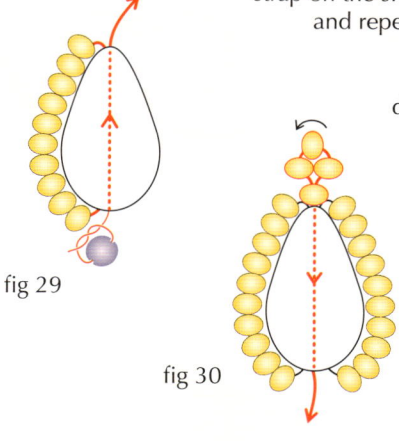

Thread on 4A. Pass back down the first 1A of the 4A and the F bead to make a tight picot at the top of the work (fig 30).

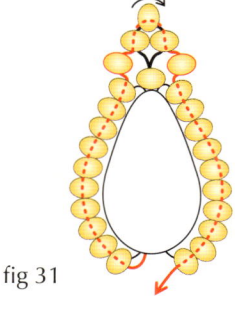

fig 29

fig 30

Pass through the first 10A and thread on 1A.

Pass through the 3A of the picot and thread on 1A.

fig 31

Pass through the second 10A beads to complete a frame around the F bead (fig 31).

17

Thread on 1C. Pass through the previous 1A and back through the new 1C to make a Square stitch (fig 32).

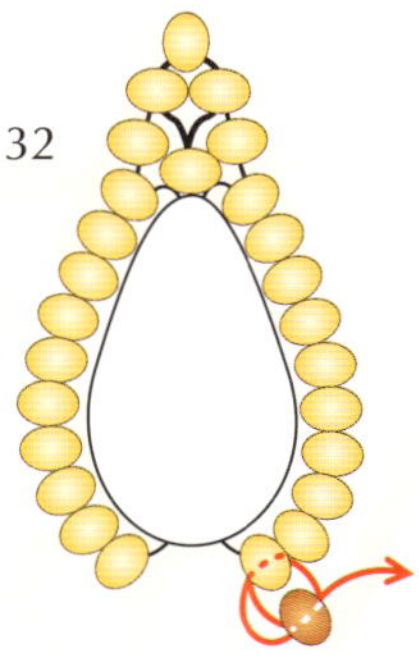

Thread on 2C. Pass through the next 1A and back through the new 2C to make an increase Square stitch (fig 33).

Repeat these two stitches once.

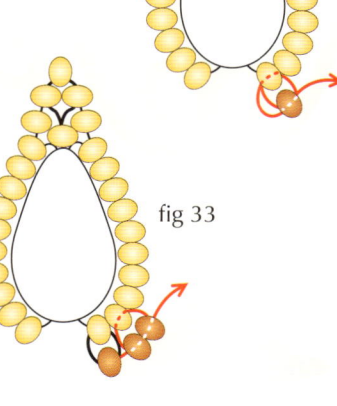

fig 32

fig 33

Repeat the single bead stitch shown in fig 32 eight times - the last stitch links to the side of the picot (see fig 34).

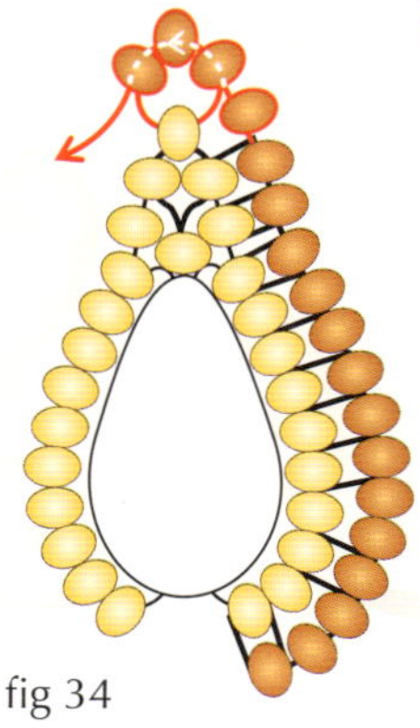

fig 34

Thread on 4C. Pass through the 1A at the top of the picot and through the last 3C again to form a triangle at the top of the flame (fig 34). Thread on 1C.

18 Thread on 1C and Square stitch to the A bead on this side of the picot as before (fig 35).

Add seven single Square stitches, one increase stitch, a single stitch, one increase stitch and one single stitch to complete this side of the flame (fig 36).

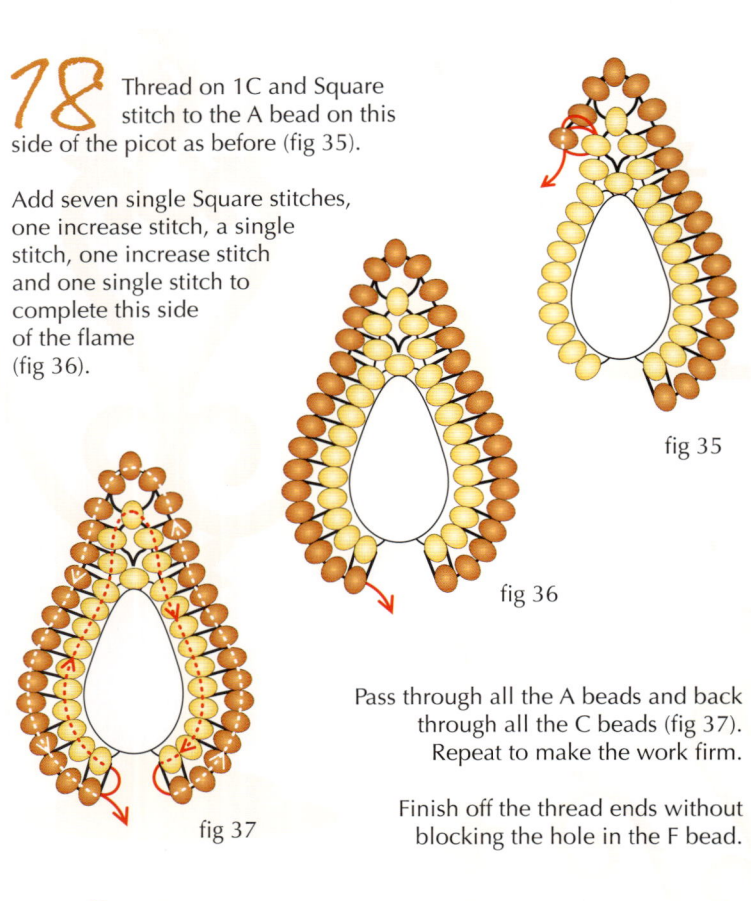

fig 35

fig 36

fig 37

Pass through all the A beads and back through all the C beads (fig 37). Repeat to make the work firm.

Finish off the thread ends without blocking the hole in the F bead.

19 Assembling the Candle - Remove and trim the plastic tube carefully so it matches the length of the candle cylinder. Push it inside the candle cylinder.

Make a 4mm hook at the end of the wire (fig 38).

Gently squeeze open the tree clip so you can access the bottom of the vertical spring.

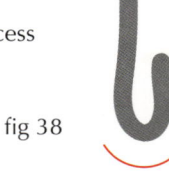

fig 38

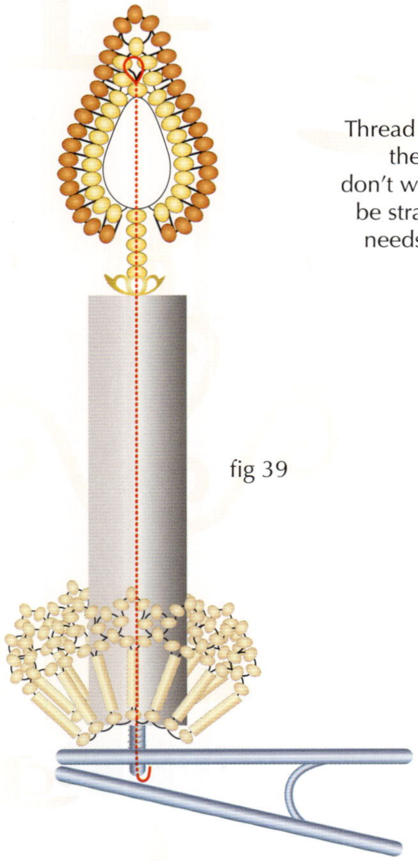

Thread the plain wire end up through the spring. It's a bit awkward but don't worry if the wire bends as it can be straightened out again. The hook needs to catch on the bottom of the spring (see fig 39).

Thread the cylinder onto the wire so the cut end sticks out of the 10B hole at the top.

Thread 1G (cupped side uppermost) and 5A onto the wire. Pass the wire up through the F bead of the flame and the 1A above it.

Push everything down the wire and firmly onto the top of the clip.

Trim the excess wire to 8mm and make a neat loop (fig 39).

fig 39

54

Hanging Candle Decoration

The simpler hanging candle is made using the same basic method. Final assembly is a little different and uses a large bead filigree bead cup to keep the work neat.

20 Follow Steps 1 to 4 to make the candle cylinder.

Slide the plastic tube into the cylinder.

Follow Steps 12 to 18 to add the 'waxy drips' and to make the flame.

21 **Assembling the Hanging Candle** - Attach a new 60cm thread to emerge at the bottom of the candle cylinder.

Remove and trim the plastic tube so it is 4mm shorter than the length of the candle cylinder. Push it inside the candle cylinder so it fits snugly against the inside of the top B bead disc.

fig 40

Make a 4mm loop at the end of the wire.

Referring to fig 40 thread on 1H (cupped side down) and the cylinder so the cut wire end sticks out of the 10B hole at the top. The H cup should pull inside the bottom of the bead cylinder.

Thread 1G (cupped side uppermost) and 5A onto the wire. Pass the wire up through the F bead of the flame and the 1A above it.

Trim the excess wire to 8mm and make a neat loop adjacent to the A bead.

Looking around the bottom edge of the beaded cylinder you can see the thread loops from the ends of the Peyote stitch rows.

Slip stitch these thread loops to the outer edge of the H cup to secure it inside the bottom of the tube.
Finish off the thread end neatly and securely.

Pass the length of transparent monofilament thread through the top wire loop to suspend the completed decoration.

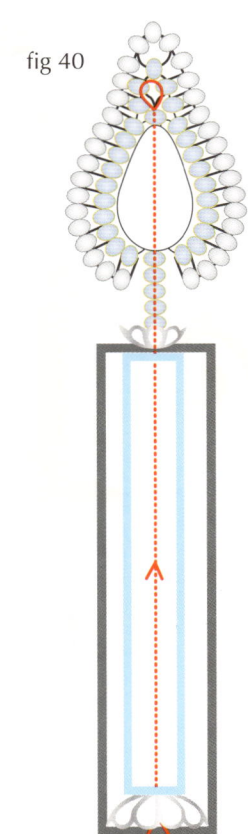

You Will Need

Materials
to Make a Silver Hanging Candle

2g of size 10 silver lined crystal seed beads A
5g of size 10 ceylon white seed beads B
2g of size 10 silver lined pale blue seed beads C
7g of size 3 ceylon white bugle beads D
One 9x7mm crystal AB fire polished drop bead F
One 5mm silver plated filigree bead cup G
One 10mm silver plated filigree bead cup H
6cm of 8mm external diameter clear plastic tubing
12cm of 0.6mm silver plated half-hard wire
20cm of fine transparent monofilament thread
White size D beading thread

55

Lotus Bauble

You Will Need

Materials

One 60mm frosted teal glass bauble
11g of frost metallic gold Twin beads A
5g of frost opaque turquoise Twin beads B
6g of frost opaque teal Twin beads C
14g of size 10 frost metallic gold seed beads D
5g of size 10 frost opaque turquoise seed beads E
3g of size 10 frost opaque teal seed beads F
1g of size 10 frost opaque blue AB seed beads G
3g of size 8 frost metallic gold seed beads H
Thirty-one 4mm sapphire fire polished glass beads K
Ten 6mm teal fire polished glass beads L
Six 6x5mm frost gold Nib-Bit two-hole beads N
Gold size D beading thread

Tools

A size 10 beading needle
A pair of scissors to trim the threads

Turquoise and lapis fan-like lotus flowers bloom amongst the hieroglyphs and courtly wall paintings in ancient Egyptian art. Combined with golden feather motifs they fashion a luxury decoration fit for a Pharoah.

The Decoration is Made in Five Stages

The five large fan motifs with dangling strands are made first.

A foundation row around the neck of the bauble is made next.

A row of feather motifs and loops (to support the fans) is added to the ring.

The fans are connected to the loops created in the previous stage.

The hanging loop is made and attached to the top of the bauble.

This design uses two-hole Twin beads. If you have not used Twin beads before see page 9 (Tips and Techniques) for more information.

Extra Info....
Nib-Bit beads have two parallel holes - one across the wide end and one across the narrow end.

The instructions will indicate which hole to use when necessary.

1 The Large Fan Motif - Prepare the needle with 1.5m of single thread and tie a keeper bead 15cm from the end.

The fan is worked up from the hole in the wide end of the Nib-Bit. Only use this hole until instructed to change.

Thread on 1N and 3A.
Pass the needle through same holes on the four beads again (fig 1).

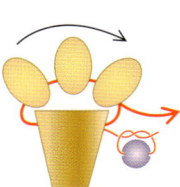

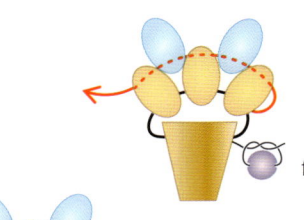

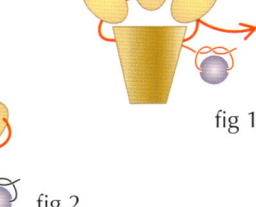

fig 1

fig 2

fig 3

2 Row 2 - Pass through the outer hole in the current A bead and thread on 1B. Pass through the outer hole of the next A bead along and thread on 1B. Pass through the outer hole of the last A bead (fig 2).

The row needs to be reinforced. Pass the needle through the lower holes of the A beads and back through the row just made (fig 3).

3 Row 3 - Thread on 1B and pass through the outer hole of the last B on Row 2.
Thread on 2B and pass through the next B bead along. Thread on 1B (fig 4).

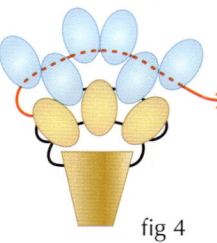

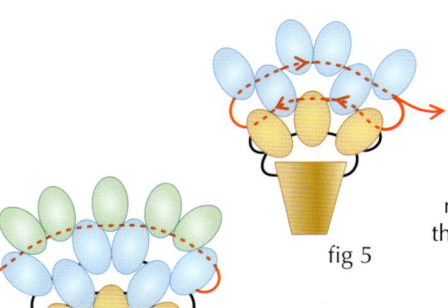

fig 4

Reinforce the row by passing through the previous row of holes and the row just made (fig 5).

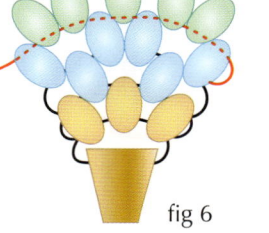

fig 5

fig 6

4 Row 4 - Pass through the outer hole of the current B bead and thread on 2C.

Pass through the outer hole of the next B bead along and thread on 1C. Pass through the next B and thread on 2C. Pass through the last B of the previous row (fig 6).
Reinforce the new row as before (see figs 3 and 5).

Row 5 - Thread on 1C. Pass through the outer hole of the last C added on Row 4.

Thread on 1C and pass through the next C along. Repeat three times.

Thread on 1C (fig 7).

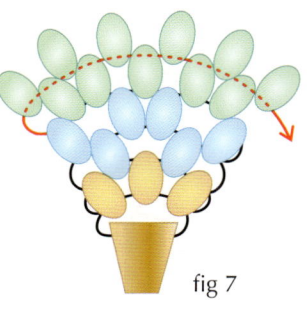

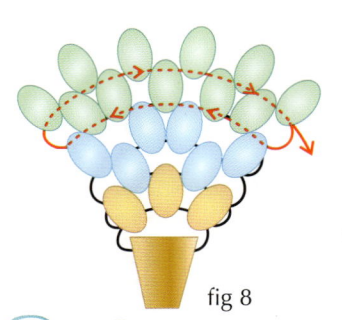

fig 7

fig 8

Pass the needle through the holes of Row 4 and back through Row 5 (fig 8).

57

5 Row 6 - Referring to fig 9 pass through the outer hole of the current C bead and thread on 1D and 1H. Pass through the outer hole of the next C bead along Row 5.

fig 9

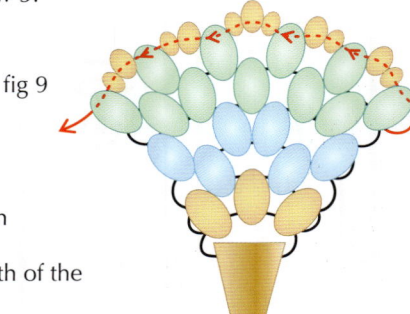

Add 1D and 1H in the next gap.
Add 1D, 1H and 1D in the following gap.
Add 1H and 1D in both of the last two gaps (fig 9).

Pass the needle back through the holes of Row 5 only to emerge from the lower hole of the end C bead.

6 The needle is in the correct position to start the first fringe strand.

Thread on 21D, 1E, 1H, 3E, 1H, 1K and 2A.

Pass back up the K bead to pull the 2A into an anchor. Pass through the following H bead in the same direction so it sits across the top of the K bead (fig 10).

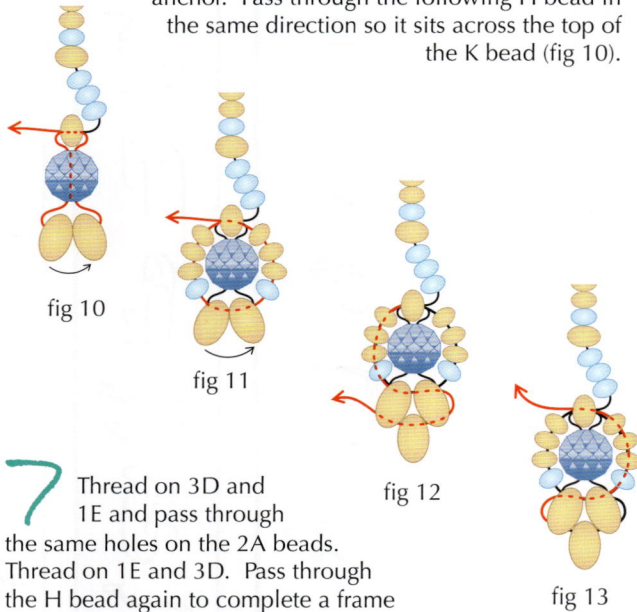

fig 10

fig 11

7 Thread on 3D and 1E and pass through the same holes on the 2A beads. Thread on 1E and 3D. Pass through the H bead again to complete a frame around the K bead (fig 11).

fig 12

fig 13

Pass the needle through the first 3D, 1E and 2A of the frame. Pass the needle through the outer hole of this A bead and thread on 1A. Pass the needle through the outer hole of the following A bead (fig 12).

Pass the needle through the inner holes of the 2A and the following 1E, 3D and 1H beads (fig 13).

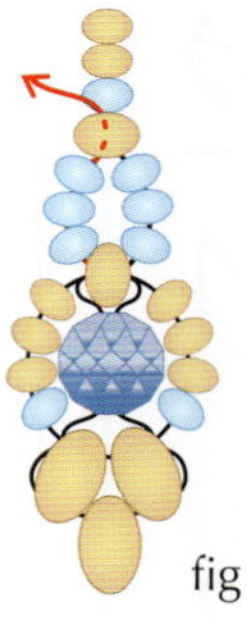

Thread on 3E. Pass the needle back up the H bead on the main strand to centre the frame below it (fig 14).

Pass back up through the remaining beads of the fringe strand to emerge at the edge of the fan.

fig 14

8 The needle must be repositioned for the next fringe strand.

Referring to fig 15 throughout, pass through the same hole in the C bead at the edge of the fan and through the following C bead hole of Row 4.

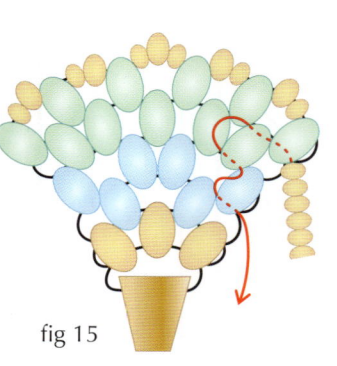

Pass back through the lower hole of the same C bead and the lower hole of the next B bead to emerge at the edge of the fan (fig 15).

fig 15

Thread on 28D, 1F, 1H, 3F, 1H, 1K and 2A.

Pass the needle back up the K bead to pull the 2A into an anchor. Pass through the following H bead, in the same direction, so it sits across the top of the K bead (as fig 10).

Swapping the E beads for F beads, repeat Step 7 to complete the frame around the K bead.

58

9 The needle must be repositioned for the third fringe strand.

Referring to fig 16 throughout, pass through the same hole in the B bead at the edge of the fan and the following B bead hole of Row 2.

Pass back through the lower hole of the same B bead and the lower hole of the next A bead to emerge at the edge of the fan (fig 16).

Thread on 10E, 1A, 1F, 1H, 1F, 24D, 1F, 1H, 3G, 1H, 1L and 1A.

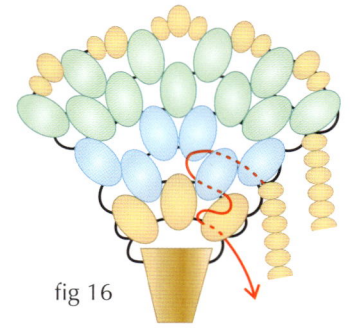

fig 16

Pass the needle back up the L bead to pull the A bead up into an anchor.

Pass through the following H bead, in the same direction so it sits across the top of the L bead (as fig 10). This fringe strand supports a feather motif.

10 Thread on 3D, 1E, 1D, 1G and 1A.

fig 17

Pass through the same hole in the A bead anchor and thread on 1A, 1G, 1D, 1E and 3D.

Pass through the H bead at the top of the L bead to complete the frame (fig 17).

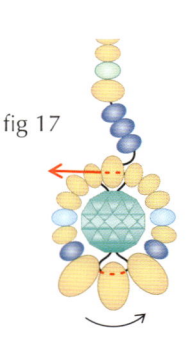

Pass the needle through the following nine beads of the frame to emerge from the same hole on the third A bead of the frame.

11 Pass through the outer hole of the current A bead. Thread on 1A and pass through the outer hole of the middle A bead. Thread on 1A and pass through the following 1A (fig 18).

Pass back through the inner holes of the first 3A and the first four holes of the row just worked.

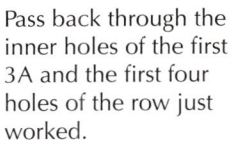

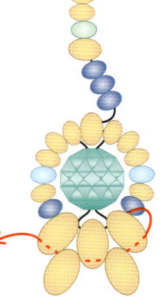

fig 18

Pass through the outer hole of the last A bead added (fig 19).

Thread on 2A and pass through the outer hole of the following 1A to pull the 2A into the central gap (see fig 20).

fig 19

Pass the needle back through the holes of the previous row and the first three holes of the row just completed (fig 20).

fig 20

12 Pass through the outer hole of this A bead and thread on 1A. Pass through the outer hole of the following A bead (fig 21).

Pass the needle back through the feather rows and the beads of the frame to emerge from the H bead at the far side of the L bead (fig 22).

fig 21

fig 22

fig 23

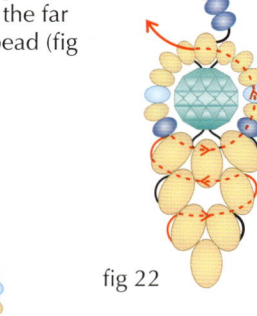

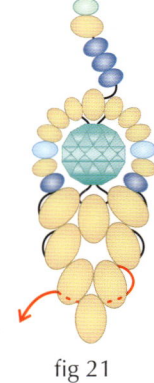

Thread on 3G and pass up through the closest H bead of the fringe strand to centralise the L bead and feather motif below this bead (fig 23).

59

13 Pass up through the following 1F, 24D, 1F and 1H beads. Thread on 1F and pass up through the vacant hole of the following 1A (see fig 24).

Thread on 10E. Pass through the 3A beads just above the N bead (fig 24).

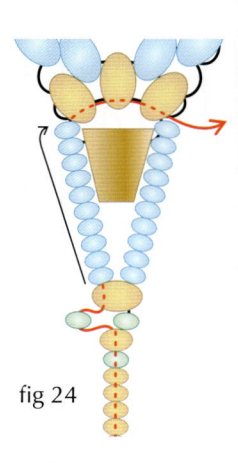

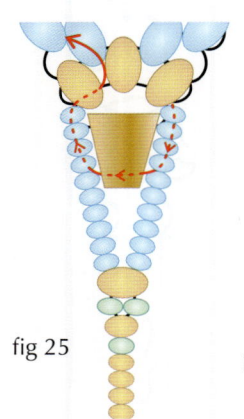

fig 25

fig 24

Pass down through the following 4E and pass through the hole across the narrow end of the N bead.

Pass up through the top 4E of the 10E just added and the first 1A following that (fig 25).

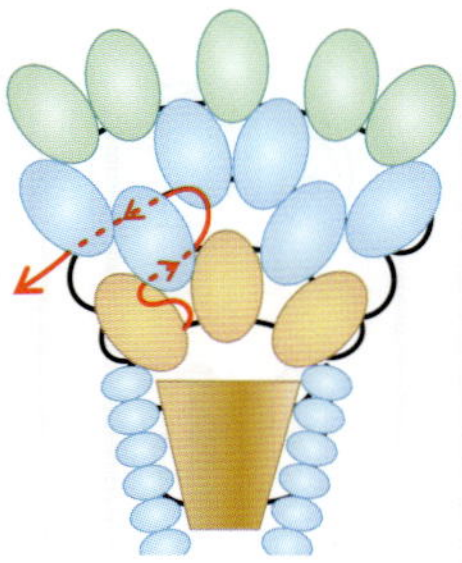

fig 26

14 Refer to fig 26 to reposition the needle for the fourth fringe strand.

Make one strand to match the second fringe strand (as in Step 8).

Reposition the needle for the fifth fringe strand by mirroring the thread path shown in fig 15.
Make the fifth strand to match the first fringe strand (as in Steps 6 and 7).

Finish off the thread end neatly and securely without blocking the holes in the top row of the fan. Remove the keeper bead and finish off this thread end similarly.

Repeat from Step 1 four more times to make five fans in total.

Set all the fans aside for the moment.

15 The Foundation Row - Prepare the needle with 1.5m of single thread and tie a keeper bead 15cm from the end.

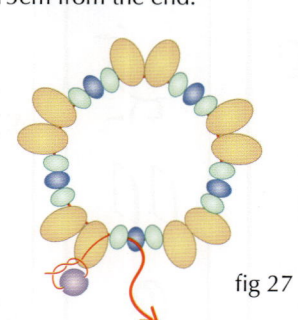

Thread on five repeats of 1F, 1G, 1F and 2A.

Pass the needle through the first F bead to make a ring of beads (fig 27).

fig 27

16 Place the ring over the neck of the bauble - it needs to fit snugly without the thread showing between the beads.

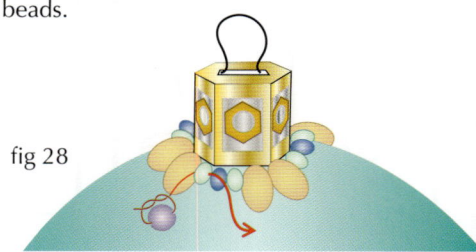

fig 28

If you need to make an adjustment, remove the ring and re-thread with five repeats of 1F, 2G, 1F and 2A (or, for a larger ring try 2F, 1G, 2F and 2A). The five pairs of A beads need to be equally spaced around the bauble neck (fig 28).

Remove the ring from the bauble and pass the needle through all the beads again to make the work firm.

17 Making the Connecting Loops - Pass through the foundation row to emerge from the second A bead along.

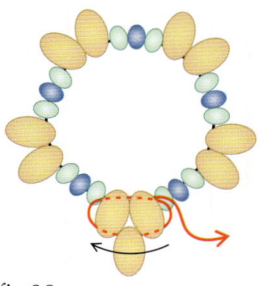

Pass the needle through the outer hole of this A bead and thread on 1A.

Pass through the outer hole of the following 1A and back through the inner holes of the 2A of the foundation row to make a trio of A beads (fig 29).

fig 29

Repeat four more times to add 1A to each 2A pair (see fig 30).

Pass the needle through the holes of the first trio to emerge from the outer hole of the middle A bead (fig 30).

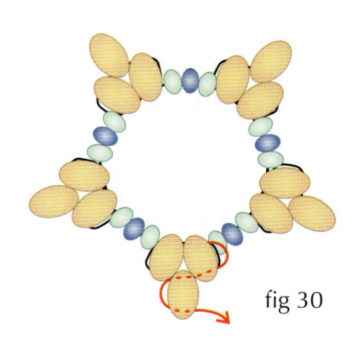

fig 30

60

18

Thread on 1F, 4G, 1H and 4G.

Pass back up the F bead and through the hole in the A bead (fig 31).

Make sure the new loop is hanging centrally from the tip of the A bead.

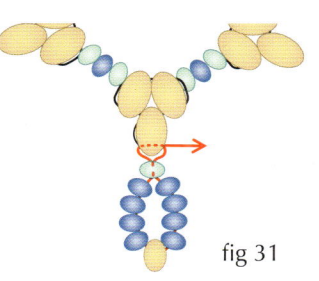

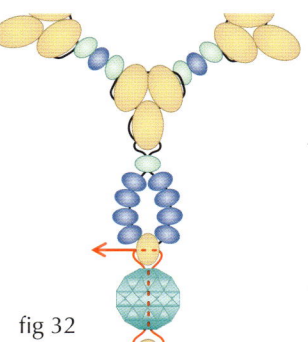

fig 31

Pass the needle back down the 1F, 4G and through the H bead.

Thread on 1L and 1A. Pass back up the L bead to pull the A bead into an anchor and pass through the H bead so this bead sits across the top of the new L bead (fig 32).

fig 32

19

A frame is now added around the new L bead. Thread on 3D, 1F, 1D, 1G and 1A.

Pass through the same hole in the A bead anchor and thread on 1A, 1G, 1D, 1F and 3D. Pass through the H bead at the top of the L bead to complete the frame (as fig 17).

Pass the needle through the following nine beads of the frame to emerge from the same hole on the third A bead of the frame.

The three A beads support a feather motif below the L bead frame.

Repeat Steps 11 and 12 to make the feather motif.

Pass up through the 4G and 1F link to the central A bead of the trio on the foundation row. Pass through the outer hole of this A bead (fig 33).

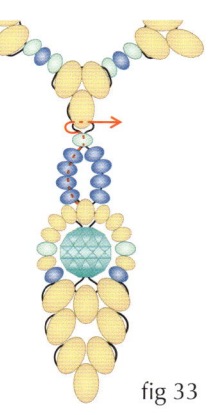

fig 33

20

Thread on 1E, 4D and 2C.

Pass through the outer hole of the last C bead and thread on 1C.

fig 34

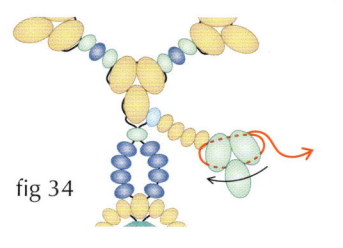

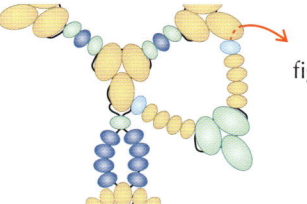

fig 35

Pass through the outer hole of the first C bead and the inner holes of the first 2C to make a 3C 'trio' (fig 34).

Thread on 4D and 1E. Pass through the outer hole of the next A bead trio around the foundation row (fig 35).

Repeat Steps 18 to 20 four times to complete five feather drops and five linking loops in total.

Finish off the thread ends neatly and securely.

21

Linking the Fans to the Loops - The top edges of the fans connect to the C bead trios on the row just made.

The fans are linked to one another with a series of swags.

Prepare the needle with 1.5m of single thread and tie a keeper bead 15cm from the end.

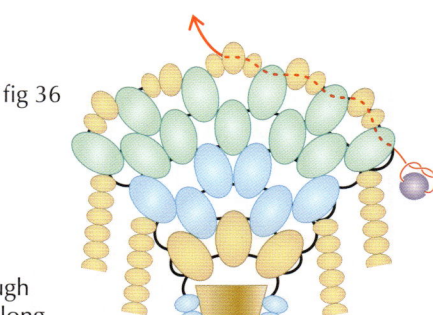

fig 36

Pick up the first fan motif from Steps 1-14.

Pass the needle through the first nine beads along the top edge of the fan (Row 6) to emerge from the central H bead (fig 36).

22 Thread on 1E, 1K, 1F and 2D.

Referring to fig 37, pass the needle through the outer hole of the central C bead of the C bead trio made in fig 34.

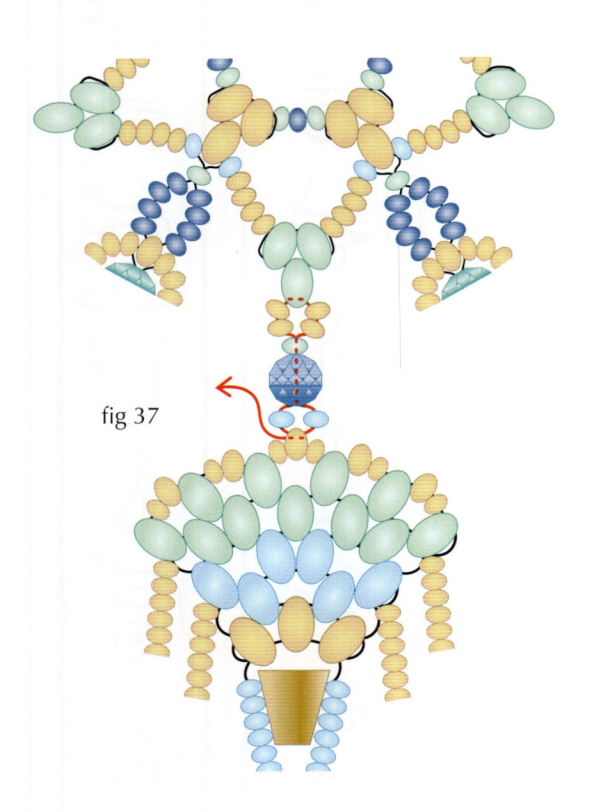

fig 37

Thread on 2D and pass back down the 1F and 1K beads.

Thread on 1E and pass through the H bead on the top of the fan in the same direction (fig 37).

Pass through the following eight beads along the top of the fan to emerge from the C bead at the other side of the fan.

23 Thread on 5D, 1F, 1G, 1E, 1H, 1K, 1H, 1E, 1G, 1F and 5D.

Pick up the next fan and pass the needle through the first nine beads along the top edge to emerge from the central H bead (as fig 36).

Tension the thread to allow the swag beads just added to fall as a gentle curve, without letting the thread show between the beads.

Repeat Step 22.

Repeat Steps 23 and 22 until all five fans are attached to the loops around the foundation row and all are linked together with swags.

Finish off the thread ends neatly and securely.

24 The Hanging Loop - Work Steps 1-5 to make a fan. Finish with the needle emerging from the end of row 5.

Pass the needle back through the first nine beads along the top edge of the fan (Row 6) to emerge from the central H bead (as fig 36).

Thread on 1E, 1K, 1F and 1H followed by nine repeats of 1D, 1E, 1D, 1G, 1D, 1F.

Thread on 1D and pass the needle back down the H, F and K beads to draw up the loop.

Thread on 1E and pass through the H bead on the top of the fan in the same direction (fig 38).

Pass the needle twice through all the beads just added to make the loop and the connection to the fan firm.

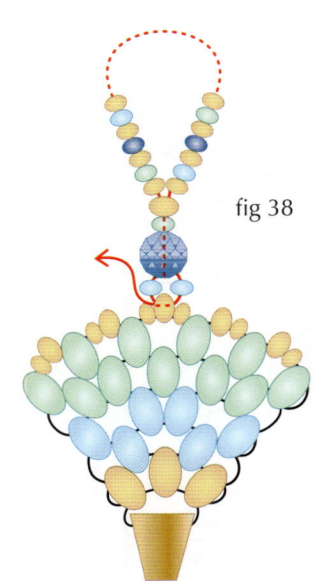

fig 38

Pass the needle through the holes of Row 5 and 6 of the fan one more time to stiffen the work.

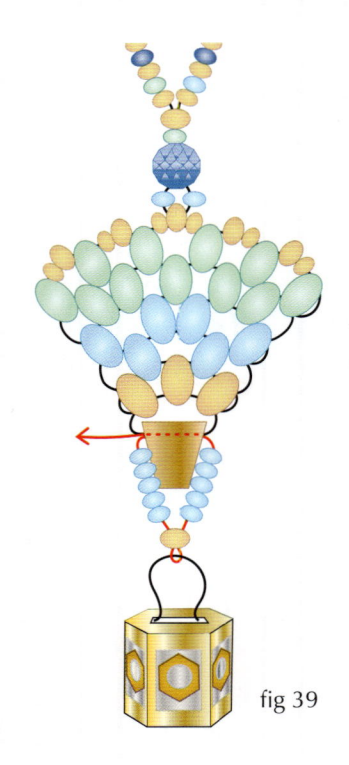

25 Pass the needle down through the beads of the fan to emerge from the hole at the wide end of the N bead.

Thread on 5E and 1H.

Pass the needle through the metal loop at the top of the bauble and back up through the H bead. Thread on 5E and pass through the same hole in the N bead again (fig 39).

Pass through the first 2E again and the narrow hole in the N bead.

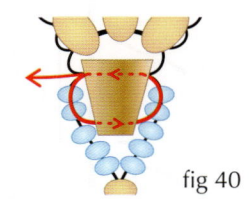

fig 39

Pass through the top 2E on the other 5E strap and through the wide hole of the N bead again (fig 40).

fig 40

Pass through the beads just added (especially the H bead and the bauble loop) several times to make the connection strong.

Finish off the thread ends neatly and securely.

62

Lotus Inspiration

Nubia Star

Five fans linked together to make a star

Materials

2.5g of metallic silver Twin beads A
2g of chalk white Twin beads B
1g of size 10 metallic silver seed beads C
1g of size 10 chalk white seed beads D
Five 6x5mm metallic silver Nib-Bit beads E
White size D beading thread

26 The First Fan

The fans in this design are worked from the widest row towards the E beads at the tip of each star point. Prepare the needle with 1.5m of single thread and tie a keeper bead 15cm from the end.

*Thread on 1A, 2D, 3B, 2D and 1A (fig 41).

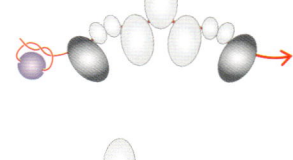

Pass through the outer hole of the last A bead and thread on 1B. Pass through the outer holes of the third and first B beads on the previous row. Thread on 1B and pass through the outer hole of the first A bead (fig 42).

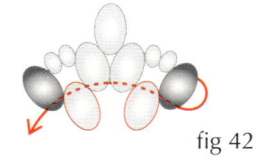

Thread on 1A and pass through the outer hole of the first B bead. Add 1A between the 2B added on the previous row and thread on 1A (fig 43).

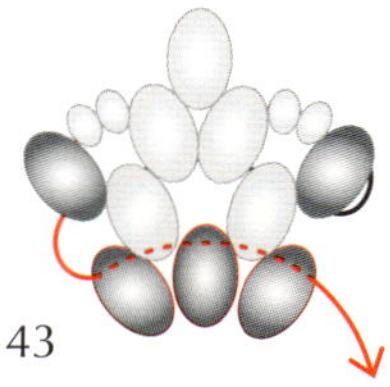

27

Referring to fig 44 reposition the needle through the bead holes of the previous row and the row just completed. Pass through the outer holes of the last 3A added (fig 44).

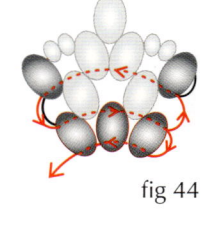

Pass through the wide end of 1E and the same holes on the last 3A beads again to make the point (fig 45). Reinforce this stitch.

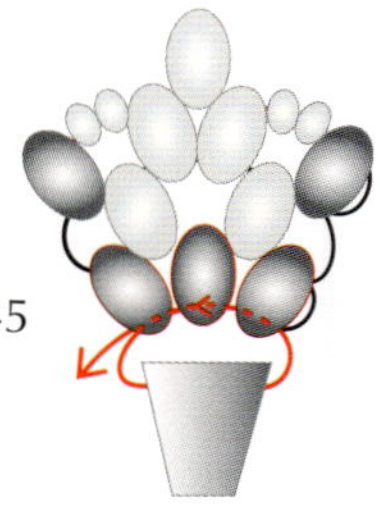

Reposition the needle to emerge at the end of the first row of the fan. Thread on 3C (fig 46).

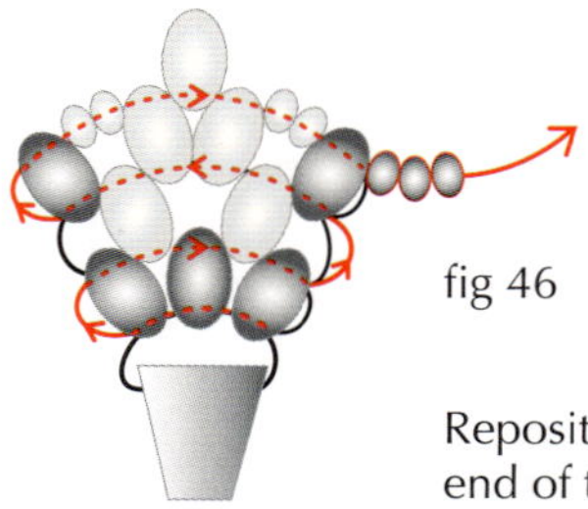

Repeat from * in Step 26 four times to make a linked row of five fans.

28 Create the Star

Starting at the first A bead, pass through all the top row bead holes to make a ring. Pass through the first A bead again (fig 47).

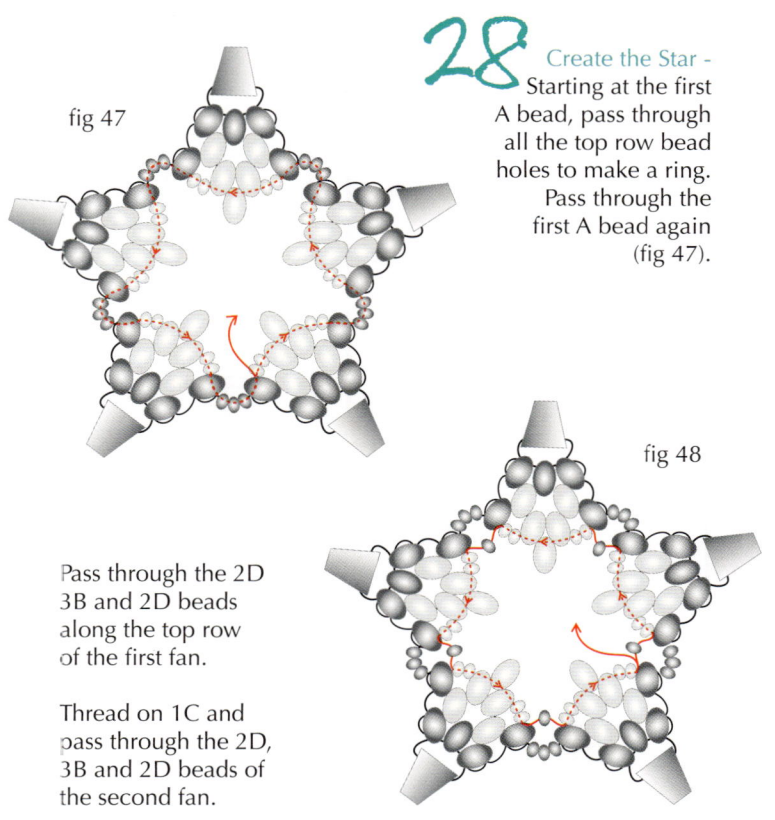

Pass through the 2D 3B and 2D beads along the top row of the first fan.

Thread on 1C and pass through the 2D, 3B and 2D beads of the second fan.

Repeat to add 1C between each pair of fans (fig 48).

30

Link the 5B beads pointing towards the centre space by adding 3D in each gap.

Reinforce the star where necessary with an extra pass of thread.

The Hanging Loop

Reposition the needle to emerge from the centre C bead along one side. Thread on 2D, 1A and 30C. Pass down the other hole on the A bead to draw up the loop. Thread on 1D. Pass down the first D bead and through the C bead on the star.
Finish off the thread ends neatly and securely.

Anastasia Bauble

You Will Need

Materials

One 60mm frosted purple glass bauble
3.5g of DB0791 opaque red Delica beads A
6g of size 15 semi-matt silver lined mulberry seed beads B
6g of size 10 scarab purple seed beads C
6g of size 8 transparent purple AB seed beads D
14g of size 10 silver lined gold seed beads E
8g of purple scarab Twin beads F
6g of size 3 silver lined red bugle beads G
Four 14mm dark amethyst rivoli stones H
Thirty-six 8x6mm amethyst crystal rondelle beads J
Forty-two 6x4mm red crystal rondelle beads K
Fifty-two 4mm amethyst crystal round beads L
One 12mm red faceted fire polished glass bead M
Purple size D beading thread

Tools

A size 10 beading needle
A pair of scissors to trim the threads

Romanov opulence is created with glittering crystals, deeply reflective rivolis and luxurious fringing. Sumptuous in jewel-like purple and ruby red, this design is equally stunning in frosty silver with diamond-clear crystals.

The Decoration is Made in Five Stages

Bezel settings for the four rivoli stones are made first.

An arched band is then constructed around the bauble body to link the bezels together.

A foundation row around the neck of the bauble is made and linked to the arched band.

The fringing is added to the lower edge of the arched band.

The hanging loop, with the crystal starburst motif, completes the design.

This design uses two-hole Twin beads. If you have not used Twin beads before see page 9 (Tips and Techniques) for more information.

1 The Bezel Settings – A bezel setting is a fitted collar around the edge of a stone which allows other attachments to be made. These bezels are made in Tubular Peyote stitch.

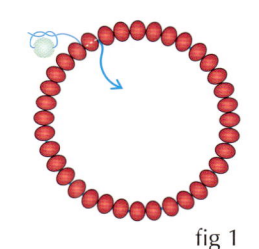

Prepare the needle with 1.2m of single thread and tie a keeper bead 15cm from the end.

Thread on 36A. Pass the needle through the first 1A again to make a ring (fig 1).

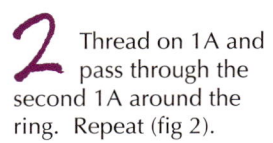

fig 1

2 Thread on 1A and pass through the second 1A around the ring. Repeat (fig 2).

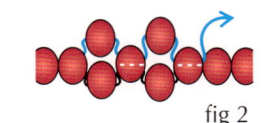

fig 2

Repeat to the end of the row (adding 18A in total) (fig 3).

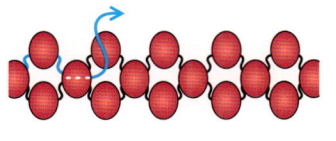

fig 3

You have made a series of keys and keyholes. In the next row the needle is passed through the key beads adding new beads into the keyholes. This is Tubular Peyote stitch.

The needle has to be repositioned to be in the correct place to start the next row.

Pass through the first bead of the new row (fig 4).

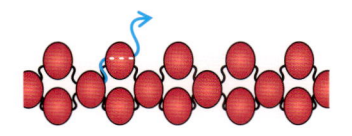

fig 4

This is called the "step-up" and needs to be made at the conclusion of each row.

3 Thread on 1A and pass through the second A bead along (the key bead) to draw the new bead into the keyhole (fig 5).

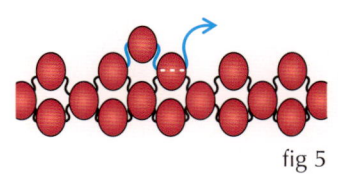

Repeat to the end of the row and step-up for the next row.

fig 5

Swap to B beads and work two rows - the smaller beads will reduce the diameter of the ring.

4 Weave the needle through the beadwork to emerge on the other edge of the band (Row 1). Add one Peyote-stitched row of B beads to this edge.

Place 1H face down into the ring and pull the thread firmly to close up the ring a little.

Work a final row in B beads (fig 6). Pull the thread firmly to make sure the rivoli stone is held in place.

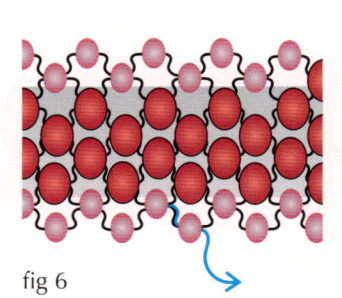

fig 6

65

5 Flip the bezel over to see the front of the rivoli stone.

Pass the needle through the bezel beads to emerge from an A bead on the fourth Peyote stitch row from the front of the H stone (fig 7).

Thread on 1A. Pass through the next bead around the bezel on the same A bead row to nestle the new bead into the gap (fig 8).

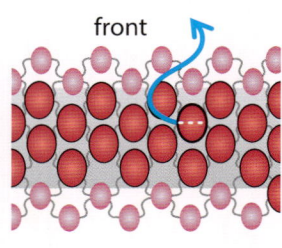

front

fig 7

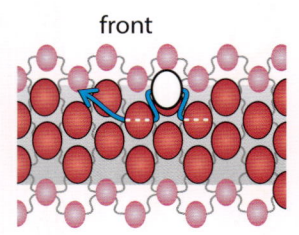

front

fig 8

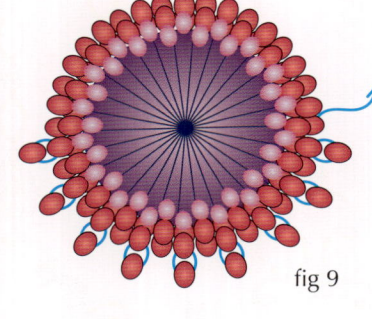

Repeat eight times, following the same row around the setting, to add nine 1A 'lugs' in total (fig 9).

fig 9

Finish off both thread ends without blocking the holes in the A beads.

Repeat from Step 1 to make three more identical units.

6 The Arched Band – There are eight arches to make: four curve downwards to support the bezels and four curve upwards to connect to the foundation row around the bauble neck.

Prepare the needle with 1.5m of single thread and tie a keeper bead 15cm from the end.

Thread on four repeats of 7D, 1F, 1D, 1F, 1D, 1F, 1D, 1F, 1D, 1F, 1D, 1F, 1D, 1F, 7D, 1F, 1C, 1F, 1C, 1F, 1C, 1F, 1C, 1F, 1C, 1F, 1C, 1F, 1C and 1F.

Pass the needle through the first 1D to make a ring (henceforth called the main ring). Pass through all the beads again to make the main ring more firm.

Pass through the first 20 beads of the sequence to emerge from the last F bead of the first block.

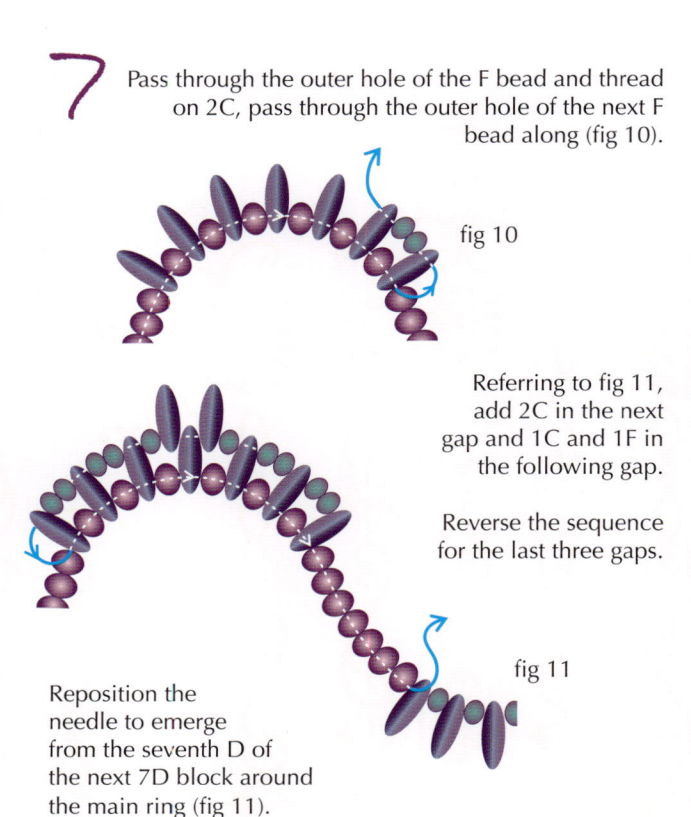

7 Pass through the outer hole of the F bead and thread on 2C, pass through the outer hole of the next F bead along (fig 10).

fig 10

Referring to fig 11, add 2C in the next gap and 1C and 1F in the following gap.

Reverse the sequence for the last three gaps.

fig 11

Reposition the needle to emerge from the seventh D of the next 7D block around the main ring (fig 11).

8 Attaching the Bezel – Line up the first A bead lug added in Step 5 with the current D bead.

Pass in the opposite direction through the A bead and back through the D bead to make a Square stitch. Pass through the following 1F and 1C around the main ring (fig 12).

Square stitch this C bead to the next 1A lug around the bezel (fig 13). Pass through the following 1F and 1C.

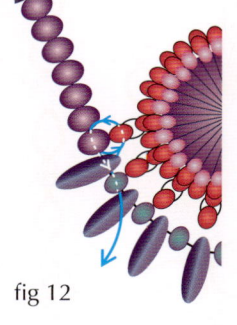

fig 12

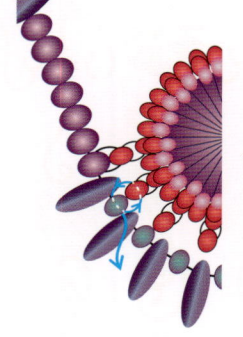

fig 13

Repeat to attach the remaining seven A bead lugs to the following 6C and 1D beads to curve the main ring around the edge of the bezel (fig 14).

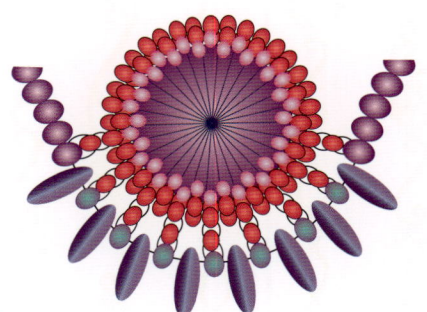

fig 14

66

fig 15

9 Pass the needle through the main ring beads to emerge from the last 1F of the next pattern block.

Repeat from Step 7 making sure that the bezelled rivoli is facing the correct way.

Repeat this sequence twice to create four 'up' and four 'down' arches (fig 15).

Pass the needle through the outer hole of the current F bead and the following 10 bead holes to emerge from the second F added in Step 7 (fig 16).

fig 16

fig 17

10 Referring to fig 17 pass though the outer hole of this F bead and thread on 1F.

Pass through the outer hole of the following F and back through the inner hole. Pass to the end of the row (fig 17).

This new F bead will connect to the foundation row around the bauble neck in Step 17.

11 Thread on 6C.

Count 7A beads' width up the side of the bezel from the closest A bead lug.

Choose the A bead closest to the front of the rivoli and pass through this seventh A towards the top of the bezel (fig 18).

fig 18

12 A finial is now added to the top of the bezel. Fig 19 shows a top view of the bezel edge - the needle has emerged from bead X. When complete the finial will be supported by beads W, X, Y and Z.

Thread on 4B, 1C, 1J, 1C, 1L, 1C and 1B.

Referring to fig 20 leave aside the last 1B bead to anchor the strand and pass back down the preceding 1C and the following 1L, 1C and 1J.

Thread on 1C and 4B.

front   back

fig 19

fig 20

Count 6A beads' width around the top of the bezel. Select the A bead closest to the front of the rivoli stone (see bead W on fig 19). Pass the needle through bead W to point away from the new finial (fig 20).

The finial is not stable and will tend to flop backwards and forwards. A second pair of support stitches needs to be added.

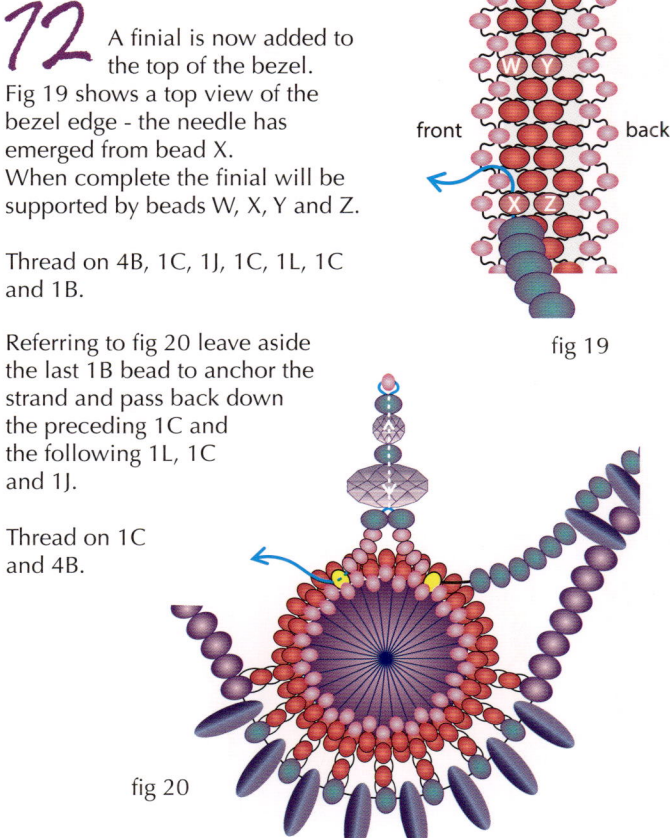

67

13 Referring to figs 19 and 21 pass back through bead Y (parallel to bead W).

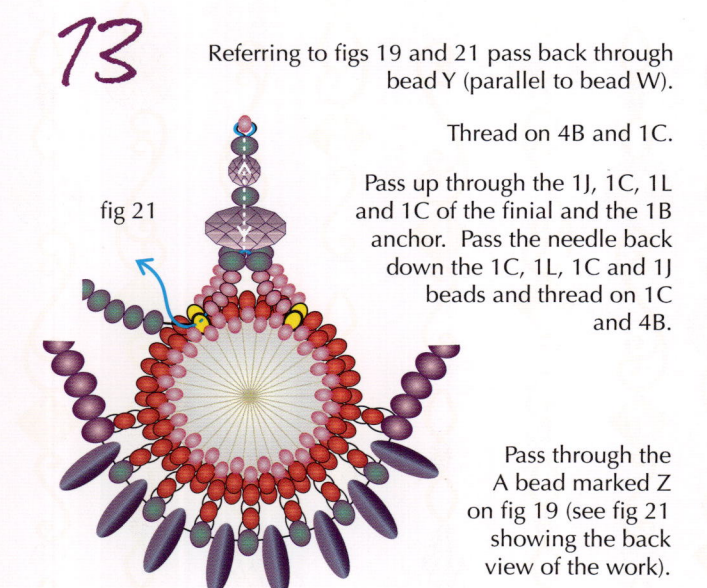

Thread on 4B and 1C.

Pass up through the 1J, 1C, 1L and 1C of the finial and the 1B anchor. Pass the needle back down the 1C, 1L, 1C and 1J beads and thread on 1C and 4B.

fig 21

Pass through the A bead marked Z on fig 19 (see fig 21 showing the back view of the work).

The finial will feel more firm, but is still a little unstable and the needle is pointing in the wrong direction.

14 Pass back through bead X on the bezel (see fig 19) and up through the following 4B and 1C to emerge below the J bead of the finial.

There are four C beads beneath the J bead of the finial - these are now stitched together to make a small drum which will support the top of the finial and tighten the threads.

Fig 22 shows a top view of these 4C beads (with the top of the finial removed for clarity). The letters W X Y Z correspond to the A beads on the bezel that these C beads connect to.

At present the needle is emerging from the C bead marked X.

Pass down Z and up Y.
Pass down W and up X.
Pass down W and up Y.
Pass down Z, up X and down W.
Pass down the following 4B and the A bead on the bezel.

fig 22

Thread on 6C and pass the needle through the outer hole of the next F bead around the ring (fig 23).

fig 23

15 Pass through the following 10 bead holes to emerge as in fig 16.

Repeat from Step 10 three times to complete the main ring.

Finish off the thread ends neatly and securely without blocking the holes in the C, D and F beads around the bottom row of the band.

16 The Foundation Row – Prepare the needle with 1.5m of single thread and tie a keeper bead 15cm from the end.

Thread on eight repeats of 1D and 2E. Pass the needle through the first 1D to make a ring.

fig 24

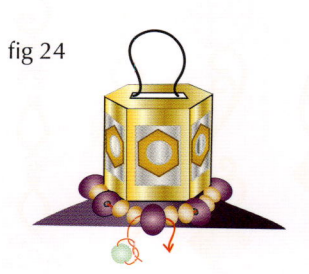

Place the ring over the neck of the bauble - it needs to fit snugly, so you may need to adjust the bead count.

If you need to make an adjustment, add or subtract E beads equally from all eight sections to keep the D beads evenly spaced around the ring (fig 24).

Remove the ring from the bauble and pass through the beads again to make it firm. Finish with the needle emerging from the first D bead of the sequence (as fig 24).

17 There are four connections to make between the foundation row and the single F beads along the top edge of the main ring. Take care not to twist the main ring as you make the connections or the work will not sit straight and you will need to start this step again.

Thread on 10E, 1C, 1D and 1L.

Pass through the top hole of one of the F beads added in Step 10.

Pass back up the 1L, 1D and 1C beads and thread on 10E.

Pass through the preceding 1D around the ring and the following E beads to emerge from the original D (fig 25).

fig 25

Pass through the following beads of the ring to emerge from the second D bead around.

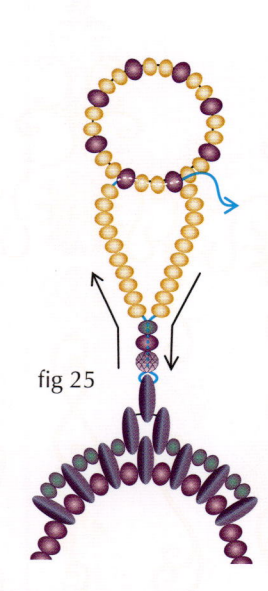

Repeat Step 17 three times to complete all four connections to the band.

Place the beadwork over the bauble to check nothing is twisted. Remove the beadwork from the bauble and finish off the thread ends neatly and securely within the beads of the neck ring.

18
The Fringing - Prepare the needle with a new 1.5m single thread and tie a keeper bead 15cm from the end. Pass through 8-10 beads along the lower row of the main ring to emerge from the D bead just before the first F bead below a bezel.

*Pass the needle through the outer hole of the F bead to emerge between this F and the next 1F along (fig 26).

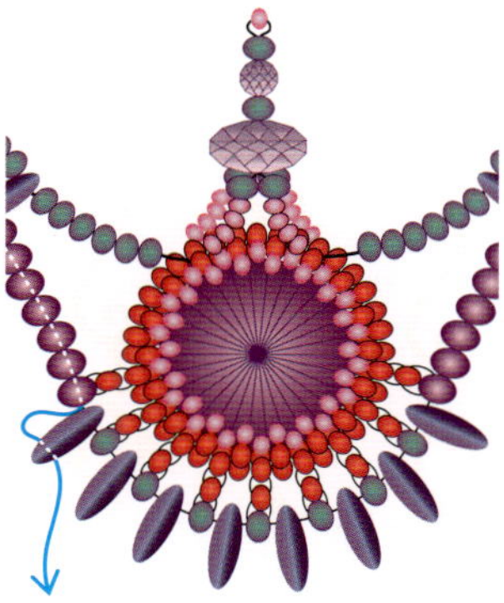

fig 26

Strand 1 - Thread on 15E, 1G, 1E, 1L, 1E, 1G, 2E, 1C, 1J, 1D, 1K, 1C and 3B. Leaving aside the last 3B threaded to anchor the strand, pass back up the last C and the following beads to emerge 2E from the top of the strand. Thread on 1E and pass through the outer hole of the next 1F around the bezel (fig 27).

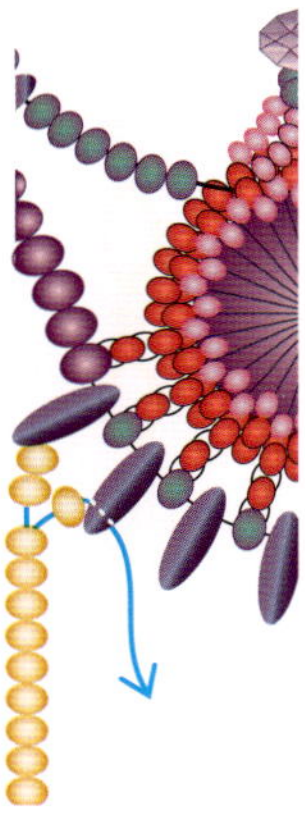

fig 27

Strand 2 - Thread on 21E, 1G, 1E, 1L, 1E, 1G, 2E, 1C, 1J, 1D, 1K, 1C and 3B. Leaving aside the last 3B threaded to anchor the strand, pass back up the last C and the following beads to emerge 1E from the top of the strand. Thread on 1E and pass through the outer hole of the next 1F around the bezel (fig 28).

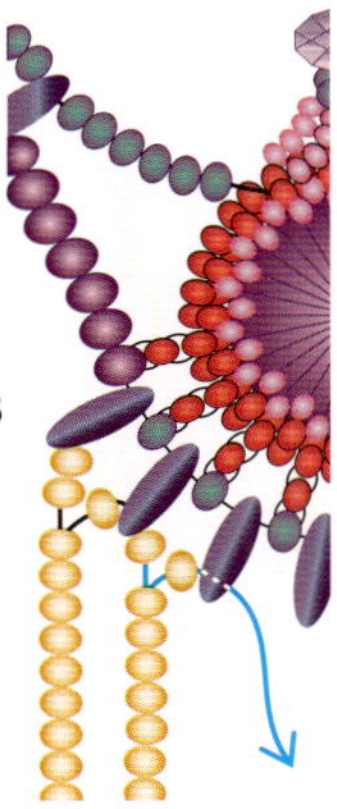

fig 28

Strand 3 - Thread on 33E, 1G, 1E, 1L, 1E, 1G, 2E, 1C, 1J, 1D, 1K, 1C and 3B. Make the 3B anchor as before and pass back up the strand beads to emerge 1E from the top of the strand. Thread on 1E and pass through the outer hole of the next 1F around the bezel (as fig 28).

Strand 4 - Thread on 15E, 1C, 1E, 1L, 1E, 1C, 23E, 1G, 1E, 1L, 1E, 1G, 2E, 1C, 1J, 1D, 1K, 1C and 3B. Make the 3B anchor as before and pass back up the strand beads to emerge 1E from the top of the strand. Thread on 1E and pass through the outer hole of the next 1F around the bezel (as fig 28).

Repeat Strand 3 and Strand 2.

Strand 7 - Thread on 14E, 1G, 1E, 1L, 1E, 1G, 2E, 1C, 1J, 1D, 1K, 1C and 3B. Make the 3B anchor as before and pass back up the strand beads to emerge 1E from the top of the strand. Thread on 2E and pass through the outer hole of the next 1F around the bezel (see fig 29).

Pass the needle through the following 7D and 1F around the bottom row of the arched band (fig 29).

fig 29

19
Strand 8 - Thread on 8E, 1C, 1E, 1L, 1E, 1C, 2E, 1G, 1E, 1L, 1E, 1G, 2E, 1C, 1J, 1D, 1K, 1C and 3B. Leaving aside the last 3B to anchor the strand, pass the needle back up the last C and the following beads to emerge from the top of the first G bead.

Thread on 2E, 1C, 1E, 1L, 1E, 1C and 8E. Pass the needle through the lower hole of the last F on the current arch (fig 30).

Pass through the following 7D ready to start the next fringe section.

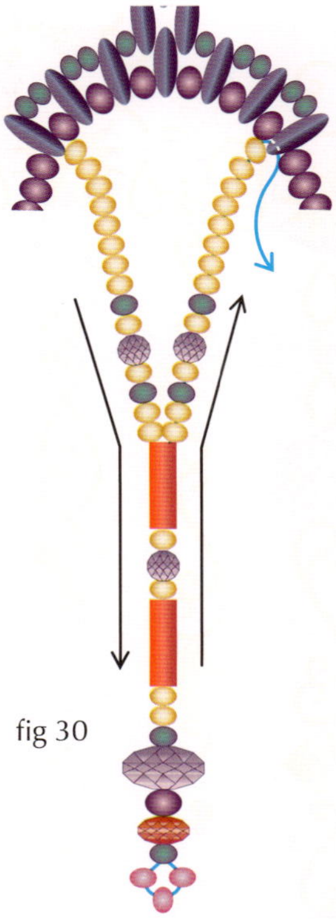

Repeat from the * in Step 18 three times to complete four sets of fringe strands.

Finish off all remaining thread ends neatly and securely. Place the beading over the bauble.

fig 30

69

20 The Hanging Loop - This is decorated with a large sunburst of crystal beads. The 'rays' of the sunburst are supported on a bezel of A and B beads around the M bead.

Prepare the needle with 1.5m of single thread and tie a keeper bead 15cm from the end.

Thread on 1M and 14A. Pass through the M bead to bring the 14A into a strap on the side (fig 31).

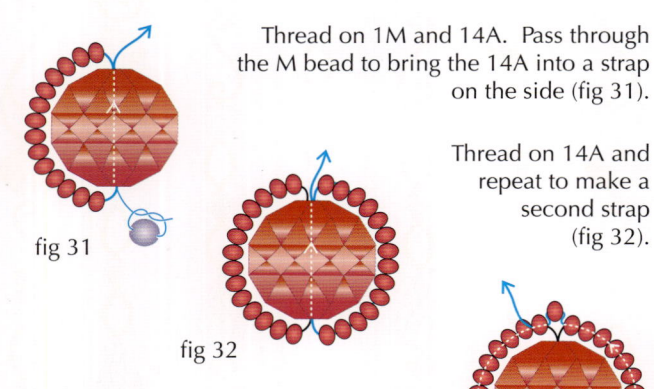

Thread on 14A and repeat to make a second strap (fig 32).

fig 31

fig 32

Pass through the first 14A and thread on 1A. Pass through the second 14A and thread on 1A. Pass through the following 1A (fig 33).

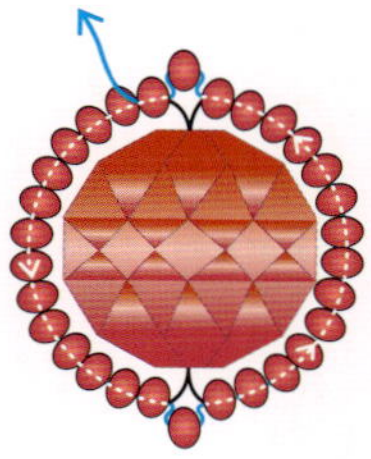

This is the first row of the bezel.

fig 33

21 Thread on 1A and pass through the second A bead around. Repeat fourteen times to complete the first row of Peyote stitch. Step up for the next row (as in Step 2).

Work one row of Peyote stitch in A beads as before.

Pass the needle to the other edge of the A bead band and add one Peyote stitch row in A beads on this edge.

Extra Info....
As the M bead is much more rounded than the H rivoli stones there is a tendancy for the bezel to over-tighten on the working edge and pull back from the M bead on the other.
To help to prevent this from happening, the needle is swapped from one edge of the Peyote stitch band to the other several times.

*Add one Peyote stitch row in B beads to this edge.

Pass the needle to the other edge of the band and repeat to add a row of B beads.

Reposition the needle to emerge on the other side of the band and repeat from * to add one more row of B beads on each edge of the band.

22 Adding the Crystal Bead Rays - To make the rays stand firm they are added on two rows of stitching.

The first row around the 'front edge' of the A bead band is made in Steps 22-24. The second row around the 'back edge' of the band is made in Step 26.

The hanging loop and the connection to the bauble are also created as the rays are added to the bezel.

Look at the bezel band - the A bead zone down the centre alternates between 3A and 2A wide (fig 34).

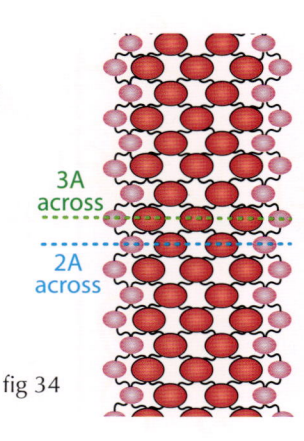

front back

3A across
2A across

fig 34

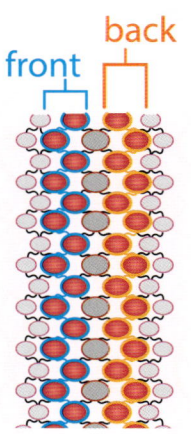

The stitches to support the rays are taken through the beads along both edges of the A bead zone (fig 35).

fig 35

23 Pass through the front edge A beads to emerge from the next '3A wide' section past the hole in the M bead (fig 36).

Thread on 1B, 1K, 1C and 3B.

Pass back down the 1C and 1K beads and thread on 1B.

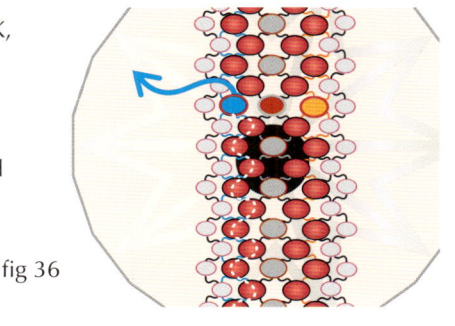

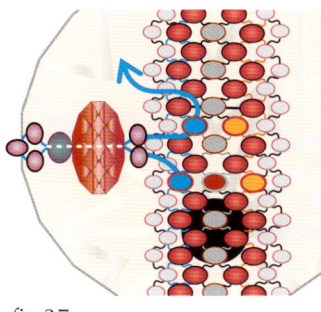

fig 36

Count 3A around this edge of the bezel band and pass the needle through this bead (fig 37) - note the needle has passed through an A bead on a '2A wide' section.

fig 37

Repeat Step 23, noting that the needle passes through an A bead on a '3A wide' section to complete the sequence. Repeat these two rays.

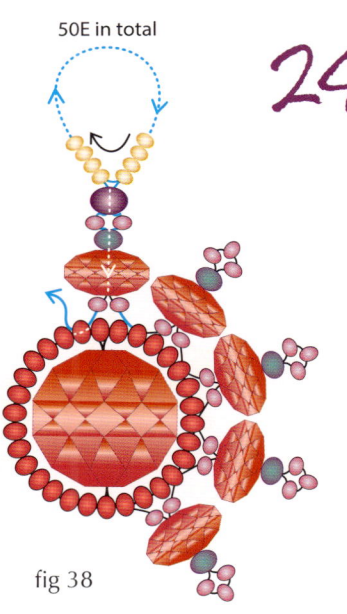

50E in total

24 Adding the Loop - Thread on 1B, 1K, 1C, 1B, 1D and 50E. Pass the needle through the 50E again to make a ring.

Pass back down the D bead and thread on 1B. Pass back down the 1C and 1K beads.

Thread on 1B and complete the ray as before (fig 38).

Add four more standard rays following Step 23.

fig 38

25 Making the Connection to the Bauble - The last (tenth) ray makes the connection to the bauble.

Thread on 1B, 1K, 1C, 1B and 1D.
Pass through the metal loop at the top of the bauble and back through the 1D, 1B, 1C and 1K beads just added.

Thread on 1B and complete the ray as before to finish the first row of stitching.

26 The needle should emerge from the A bead where this ray row began (see fig 39).

Pass the needle in the opposite direction through the 1A on the other edge of the band at this position (fig 39).

The final row of stitching links this edge of the A bead band to the rays made in Steps 23-25.

Thread on 1B.
Pass back up through the 1K of the ray just made and the following beads of the connection to the bauble loop. Pass through the bauble loop and back down the ray beads to emerge below the K. Thread on 1B and pass through the third A bead around this edge of the band.

fig 39

The ray (and the connection to the bauble) is now supported across the width of the A bead band.

Repeating this technique, work around this edge of the band to connect it to each ray in turn (this also facilitates an extra reinforcing pass of thread through the 50E loop made in Step 24).

Pass the needle through the beads of the ray that connect to the metal bauble loop once more to reinforce the stitch through this loop and the connection to the bezel.

Finish off all thread ends neatly and securely.

Peacock Bauble

You Will Need

Materials

One 60mm frosted gold glass bauble
14g of size 10 transparent teal AB seed beads A
7g of size 10 silver lined dark gold seed beads B
6g of size 10 scarab purple seed beads C
6g of size 6 frost silver lined blue AB seed beads D
6g of size 8 frost silver lined turquoise AB seed beads E
6g of size 3 transparent purple AB bugle beads F
6g of size 3 silver lined teal bugle beads G
4g of size 15 frost cobalt blue AB seed beads H
3g of size 15 transparent capri blue AB seed beads J
2g of size 15 lustre transparent teal AB seed beads K
0.3g of size 15 sparkling light bronze lined seed beads L
0.3g of size 15 chalk white seed beads M
0.3g of size 15 frost black seed beads N
10g of size 10 silver lined gold seed beads P
0.1g of size 8 frost metallic bronze seed beads Q
One 10mm turquoise fire polished glass bead R
One 8mm turquoise fire polished glass bead S
Five 8x6mm scarab blue oval crystal beads T
Nine 8x6mm turquoise AB oval crystal beads U
One 6mm teal round crystal bead V
Two 4mm turquoise round crystal beads W
One 8x6mm turquoise AB crystal rondelle bead X
One 6x4mm teal crystal rondelle bead Y
5g of size 8 silver lined gold seed beads Z
15cm of 0.8mm half-hard gold plated wire
Blue size D beading thread

Tools

One size 10 and one size 13 beading needle
A pair of scissors to trim the threads
Wire cutters and round-nosed pliers

Proud and perfectly poised, sitting atop a crystal encrusted decoration, this very elegant gentleman has a glorious tail that envelops the back of the bauble. Lots of detail means more instructions but he is definitely worth the investment.

The Decoration is Made in Ten Stages

A foundation row is fitted around the neck of the bauble.

The plain section of the bauble net is made first.

The tail fringe strands are added to the back of the bauble net.

The crystal detail is added to the front of the bauble net.

The body of the peacock is made.

The neck is made using Tubular Herringbone stitch.

The head is made and the top plume added.

The head, neck and body are assembled onto a sturdy ring which will fit over the bauble neck.

The wings are made and attached to complete the peacock.

The hanging loop is added to complete the design.

Extra Info....

Two sizes of needle are required for this project.

The thicker needle is used for the plain netting and the tassel strands of the tail where the extra stiffness is useful for passing back through long lines of beads.

The finer needle is used for the crystal detail at the front of the bauble net and weaving the head and neck in the smaller size 15 seed beads.

1 The Foundation Row -
Prepare the thicker needle with 1.5m of single thread and tie a keeper bead 15cm from the end.

Thread on 1Z, 3P, 1E, 3C, 1E, 3C, 1E, 3P, 1Z, 3P, 1Z, 3P, 1Z and 3P.

Pass the needle through the first 1Z to make a ring (fig 1).

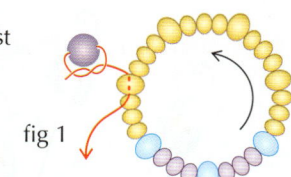

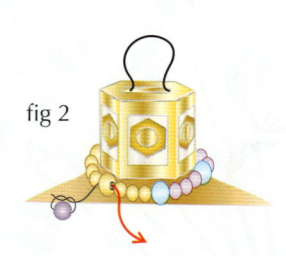

fig 2

fig 1

Place the ring over the neck of the bauble (fig 2) - it needs to fit snugly so you may need to adjust the bead count.

If you need to make an adjustment, add or subtract C and P beads equally from the appropriate sections leaving the 4Z and 3E seed beads evenly spaced around the ring.

Pass the needle through the beads again to make the ring firm. Make sure you finish with the needle emerging from the first 1Z pointing toward the first E bead (as fig 1). Remove the ring from the bauble.

2 The Plain Netting -
Corresponding to the foundation row: the netting is divided into two zones. The front of the net is made with P and Z beads. The back of the net (under the tail strands) is worked with C and E beads.

Row One - Thread on 2P, 1Z and 3P. Pass back up the Z bead to make a 3P picot.

Thread on 2P and pass through the first E bead around the ring (fig 3).

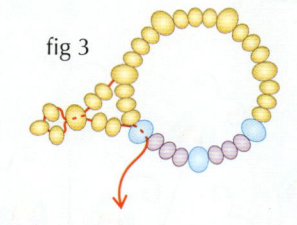

fig 3

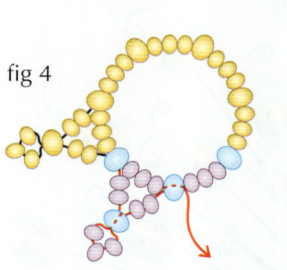

fig 4

Thread on 2C, 1E and 3C. Pass back up the E bead to make a 3C picot.

Thread on 2C and pass through the next 1E around the ring (fig 4).

Repeat the stitch shown in fig 4 once.
Repeat the stitch shown in fig 3 four times (see fig 5).

Pass through the first 2P, 1Z and 2P added on Row One (fig 5).

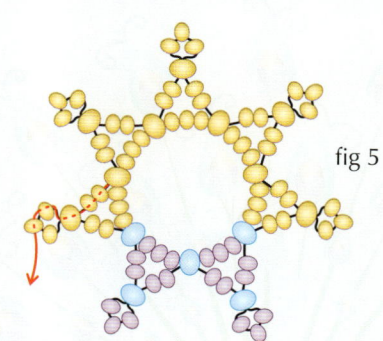

fig 5

3 Row Two - Thread on 5C, 1E and 3C. Pass back up the E bead to make a 3C picot.

Thread on 5C and pass through the middle 1C of the next Row One picot around the work (fig 6).

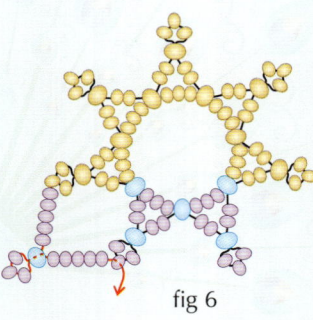

fig 6

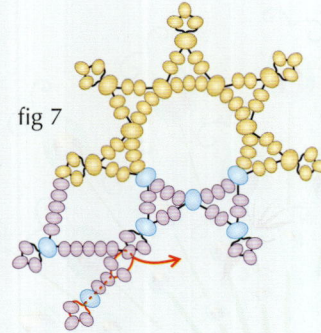

fig 7

Thread on 3C, 1E and 3C. Pass back up the E bead and the following 2C.

Thread on 1C and pass through the middle 1C of the same Row One picot again (fig 7).

Repeat Step 3 up to fig 7 once, then repeat Step 3 up to fig 6 (passing through the middle 1P of the next Row One picot to complete the stitch). The remainder of the row is worked in P and Z beads.

4 Thread on 3P, 1Z and 3P. Pass back up the Z bead and the following 2P. Thread on 1P and pass through the middle 1P of the same Row One picot again (as fig 7)*.

Thread on 5P, 1Z and 3P. Pass back up the Z bead to make a 3P picot. Thread on 5P and pass through the middle 1P of the next Row One picot around the work (as fig 6).

Repeat Step 4 three times. Repeat Step 4 to * once to complete the row.

Pass the needle down through the first 5C, 1E and 2C of Row Two to be in the correct position to start Row Three (fig 8).

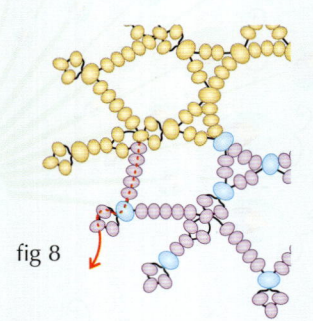

fig 8

5 Row Three - Thread on 5C, 1E and 3C. Pass back up the E bead to make a picot. Thread on 5C and pass through the middle 1C of the next picot around the netting (fig 9).

Repeat three times - the third repeat will finish at the last C bead picot of Row Two.

Swap to P and Z beads and repeat the same technique ten times - the last repeat will complete the row.

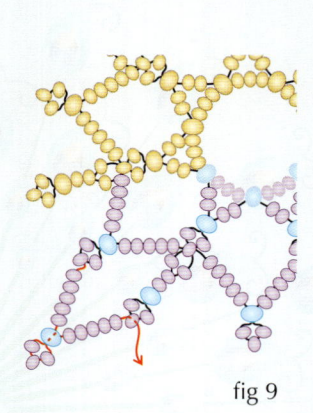

fig 9

Pass the needle down through the first 5C, 1E and 2C of Row Three to be in the correct position to start Row Four (as fig 8).

6 Row Four - Thread on 5C, 1E and 3C. Pass back up the E bead to make a picot.
Thread on 5C and pass the needle through the middle 1C of the next picot around the netting (as fig 9).

Repeat twice.

Swap to P and Z beads and repeat five times only.

This is the centre front of the netting and the sequence needs to be adjusted to leave a space for the crystal decoration.

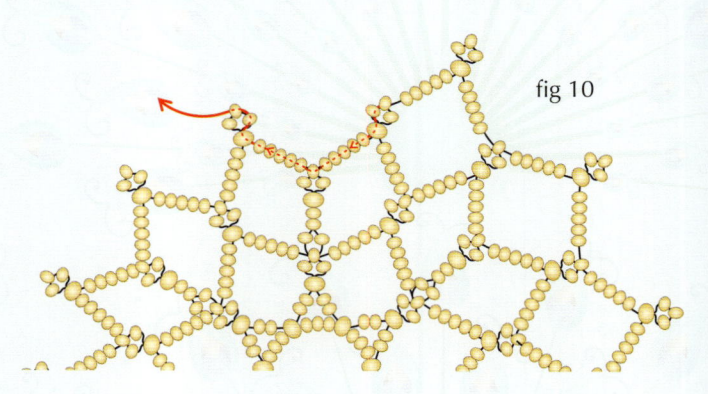

fig 10

7 Referring to fig 10, pass through the following 1P of the picot and the following 1Z and 5P to the next picot around (from Row Two).

Pass through the 1P at the bottom of this picot and the following 5P, 1Z and 2P of the next Row Three loop (fig 10).

This creates a centre-front arched space ready for the crystal decoration made in Steps 17 to 22.

Repeat the P and Z stitch from Step 6 five times to complete the row.

Pass down through the first 5C, 1E and 2C of Row Four to be in the correct position to start Row Five (as fig 8).

The remainder of the netting is worked in C and E beads only to add two short rows across the bottom of the existing C and E bead section.

74

8 Row Five - Thread on 5C, 1E and 3C. Pass back up the E bead to make a picot. Thread on 5C and pass the needle through the middle 1C of the next picot around the netting (as fig 9).

Repeat once. This completes Row Five.

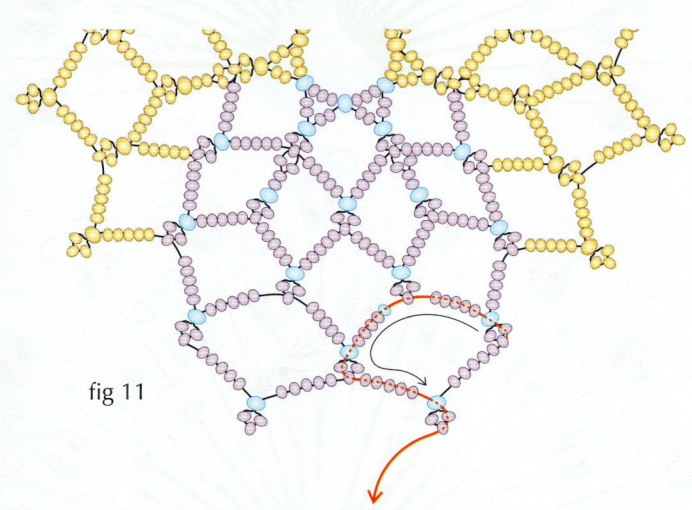

fig 11

Referring to fig 11 reposition the needle to emerge from the middle C bead of the last picot made. Note the needle is now pointing in the opposite direction.

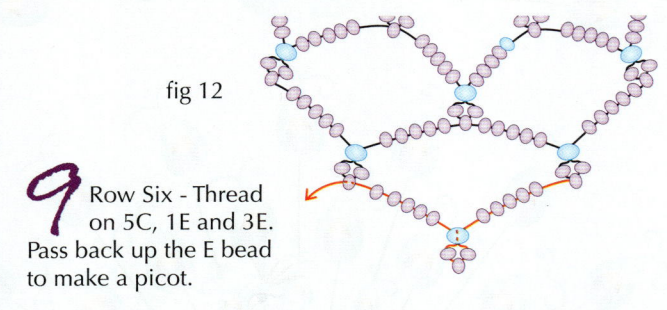

fig 12

9 Row Six - Thread on 5C, 1E and 3E. Pass back up the E bead to make a picot.

Thread on 5C and pass the needle through the middle 1C of the other picot of Row Five (fig 12).

The netting is complete.

Weave the needle through the netting to the top ring, if necessary trim the thread end to 20cm, and remove the needle - do not tie any knots (as you may block the bead holes).

10 The Tail Fringe Strands - One fringe strand attaches to each C bead picot on the netting. The main part of each fringe strand is identical to the next.

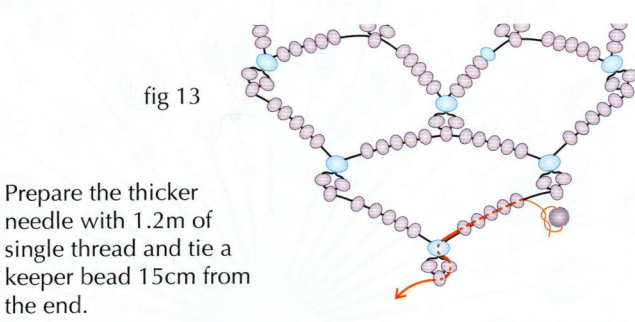

fig 13

Prepare the thicker needle with 1.2m of single thread and tie a keeper bead 15cm from the end.

Pass the needle through the first 5C, 1E and 2C of the last netted loop to emerge from the middle C bead of the last picot made (fig 13).

11 Thread on 2C, 1F, 1A, 1G, 2A, 1E, 1D and 3B. *Pass the needle through the D bead again make a strap of 3B on the side of the D bead (fig 14).

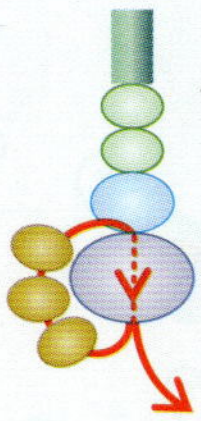

Thread on 3B and pass through the D bead again to make a second strap (fig 15).

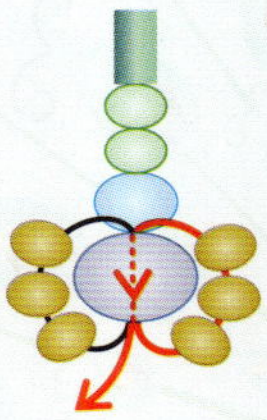

fig 14

fig 15

Thread on 3B and pass through the D bead in the opposite direction to make a picot of 3B at the bottom (fig 16).

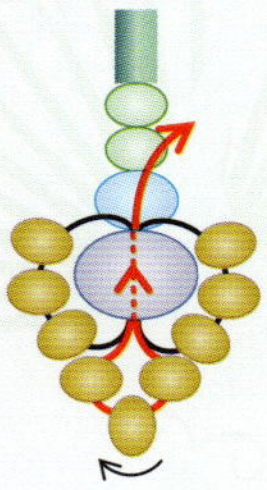

fig 16

fig 17

Pass through the first 3B, the 3B of the picot and the second 3B (fig 17).

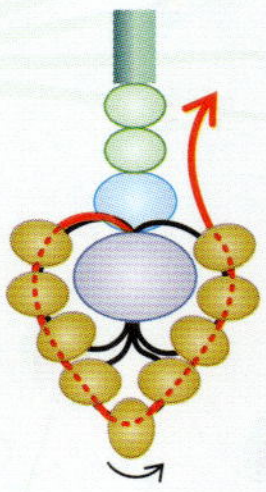

Thread on 1A. Pass through the previous 1B and back through the A bead (fig 18). This is Square stitch.

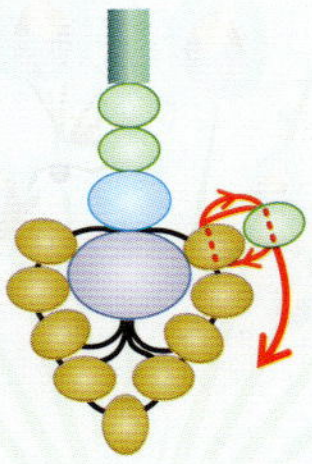

fig 18

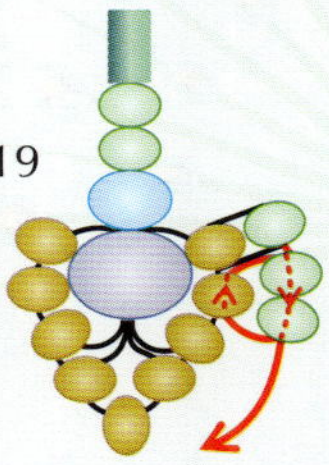

fig 19

Thread on 2A. Pass through the next 1B along and back through the new 2A (fig 19). This is an increase Square stitch.

Repeat the increase Square stitch twice to add 2A to each of the next 2B beads (fig 20).

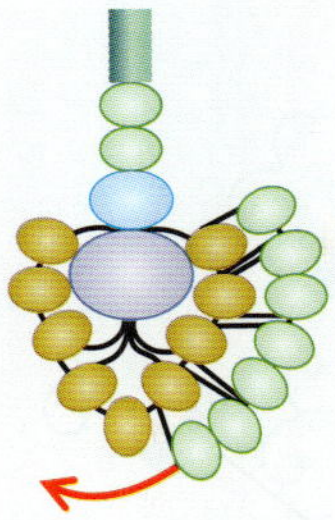

fig 20

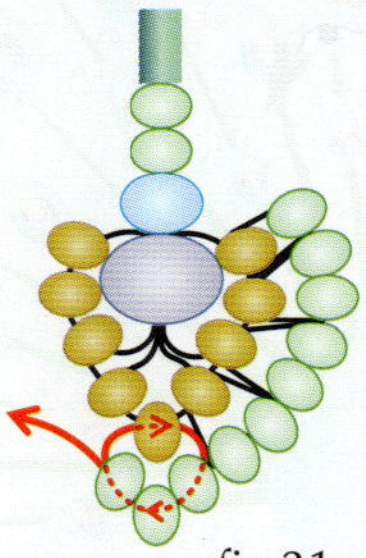

Thread on 3A. Pass through the B bead at the tip of the picot and back through the new 3B to make a triangular tip (fig 21).

fig 21

Make a 2A increase stitch to the each of the next 3B beads along and finish the sequence with a 1A Square stitch (fig 22).

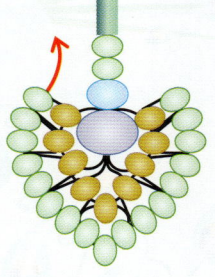

fig 22

12
Thread on 2A. Pass down the 1E and 1D beads at the centre of the motif and through the 3B of the picot. Pass back up the 1D and 1E beads (fig 23).

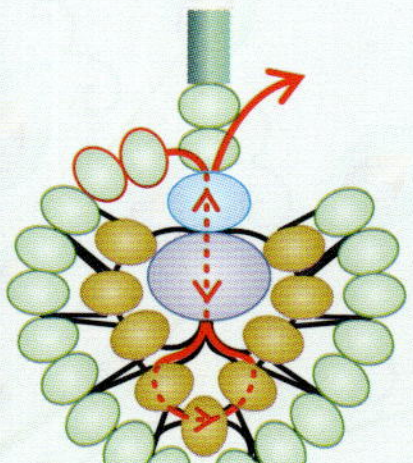

fig 23

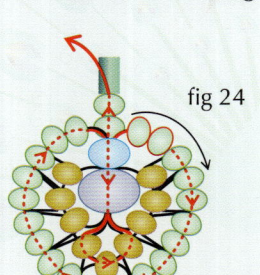

fig 24

Thread on 2A and pass through the first 1A added in fig 18, the following A beads added in Step 11 and the 2A added in fig 23.

Pass down through the 1E and 1D beads, through the 3B of the picot and back up the 1D, 1E and 2A beads added at the start of Step 11 (fig 24).

The eye motif is complete.

13
Pass back up the following 1G, 1A, 1F and 1C. Thread on 1C and pass through the middle 1C of the picot to centre the strand beneath the picot (fig 25).

The fringe strand is complete.

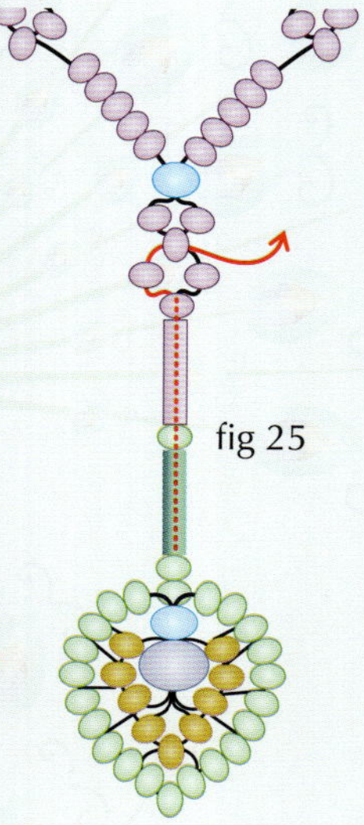

fig 25

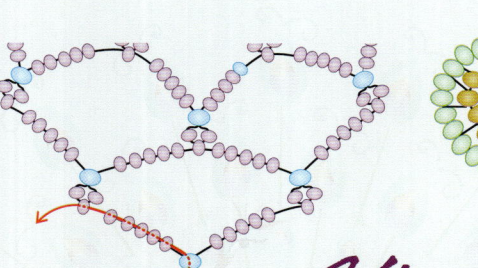

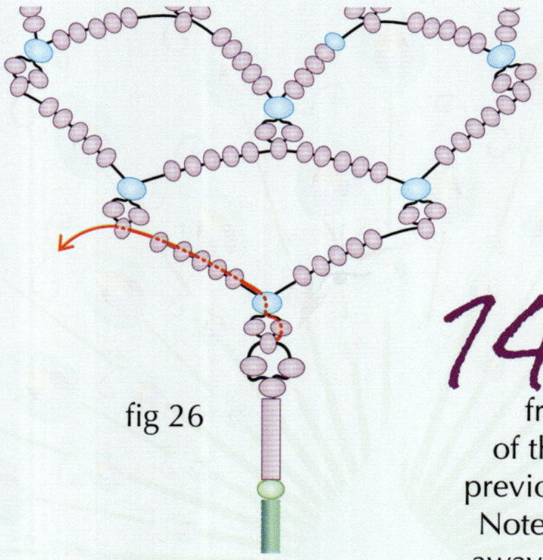

fig 26

14
Reposition the needle to emerge from the middle C bead of the second picot on the previous netted row (fig 26). Note the needle is pointing away from the main section of C bead netting.

Repeat Steps 11 and 12 to add the fringe strand and complete the second eye motif.

15
Pass back up the following 1G, 1A, 1F and 1C to the underside of the picot.

Referring to fig 27 pass through the top 1C of the adjacent 5C link and the 1C at the bottom of the picot where the strand started.

This centres the new strand below the picot (adding an extra 1C as in fig 25 would twist the strand and make it stick out awkwardly). This variation at the top of the strand is needed on the remaining seven edge strands (see fig 28).

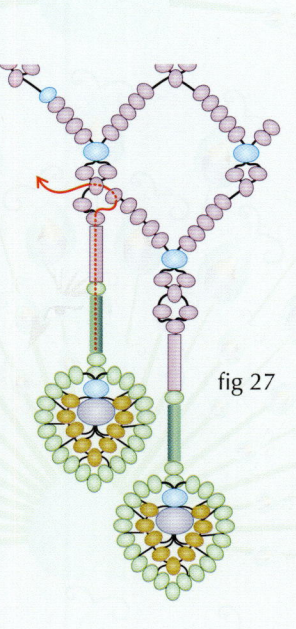

fig 27

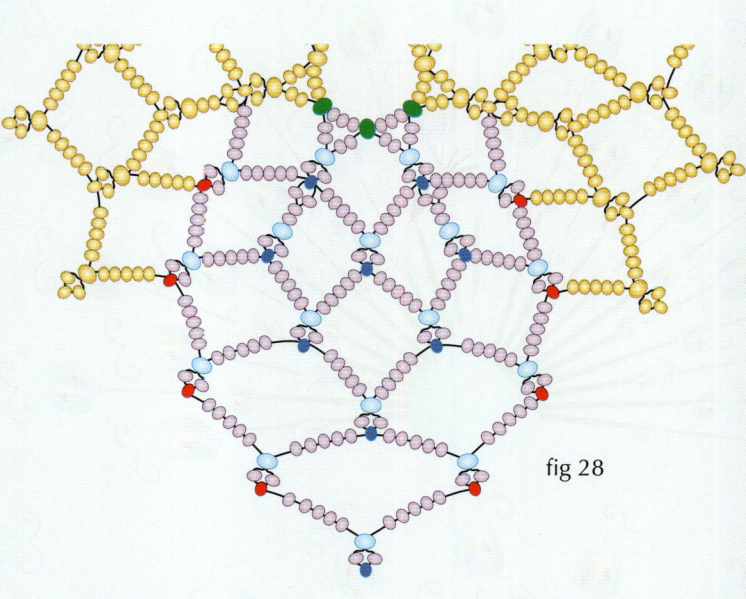

fig 28

16
Fig 28 shows the positions for the remaining fringe strands highlighted in blue, red and green.

You will need to carefully pass the needle through the netting to emerge from the middle 1C of the picots at these positions. Do not skip across a connection or you will pucker the net - follow a previous thread path.

At the positions marked in blue - work the fringe strand as Steps 11-13 inclusive. Make sure all these fringe strands sit on the top surface of the netting.

At the positions marked in red (along the edges of the C bead zone) make the fringe strands as in Steps 14 and 15. Work a mirror image of figs 26 and 27 at the red positions along the right-hand edge of the tail.

The top three positions are marked in green. These fringe strands attach to the 3E beads on the foundation row - make these strands following Steps 11-13 (see fig 29 showing the top connection to an E bead rather than the picot on previous strands).

When all the strands are complete, leave the thread end loose and remove the needle.

76

fig 29

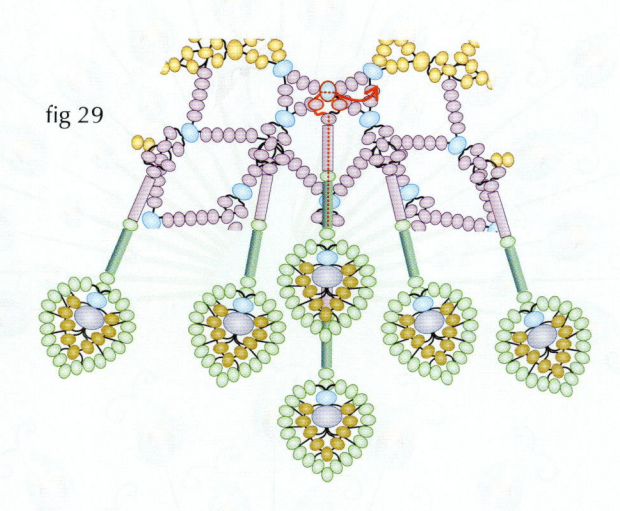

17 The Crystal Decoration
The Crystal Centrepiece at the front of the decoration is made as a separate motif. The less complex crystal strands are added directly to the net.

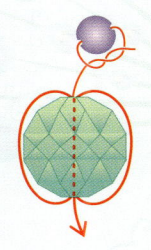

The Crystal Centrepiece - Prepare the fine needle with 1.5m of single thread and tie a keeper bead 15cm from the end.

Thread on 1V. Pass the needle through the V bead again to make a strap of thread around the side of the bead.

Repeat to make a second strap on the other side (fig 30).

fig 30

18
A frame of B beads is added to the V bead using Circular Brick stitch.

Thread on 2B. Referring to fig 31 pass the needle under the first thread strap close to the V bead hole. Pass back up the second B to bring the two B beads side-by-side on the thread strap with the holes parallel (fig 31).

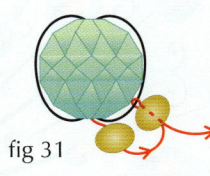

fig 31

Thread on 1B. Pass the needle under the thread strap and back up the new B bead to position it alongside the previous B (fig 32).
This is Circular Brick stitch.

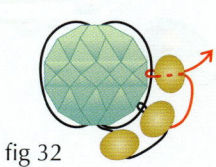

fig 32

Repeat fig 32 to add two more 1B Brick stitches along this thread strap and five 1B stitches along the second strap.

Pass down through the first 1B of the row to complete the circle (fig 33).

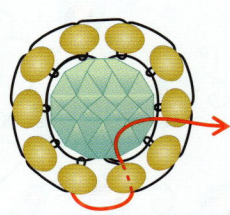

fig 33

Pass the needle through the V bead and out through one of the B beads closest to the hole at this end of the bead (fig 34).

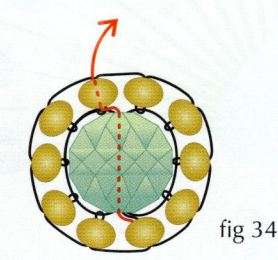

fig 34

19
Thread on 2J, 1T and 4J. Pass back through the first 1J of the 4J and the T bead (fig 35).

Thread on 1J and pass through the second J and the first J beads of Step 19 and back up through the T bead (fig 36).

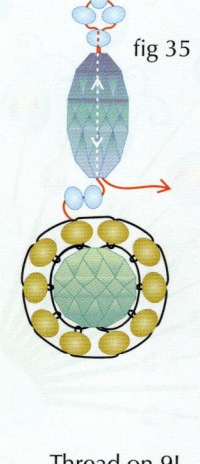

fig 35

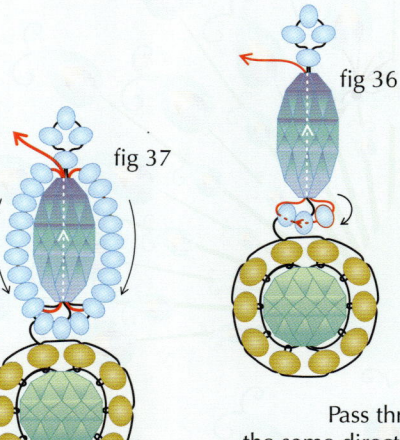

fig 36

fig 37

Thread on 9J. Pass through the T bead in the same direction to make a strap on the side of the T bead.

Repeat to add a second 9J strap (fig 37).

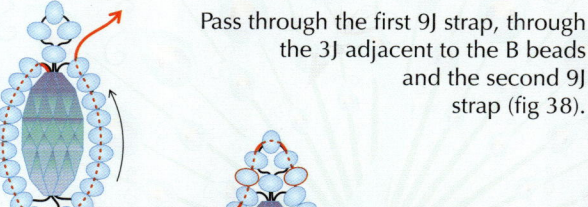

Pass through the first 9J strap, through the 3J adjacent to the B beads and the second 9J strap (fig 38).

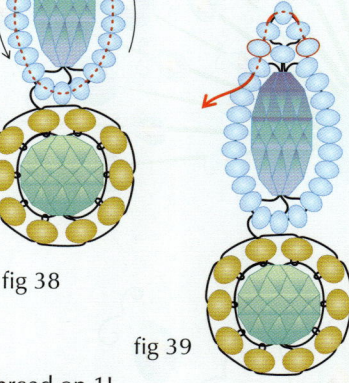

fig 38

fig 39

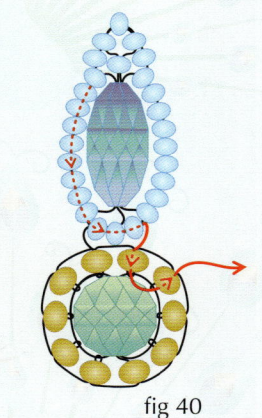

Thread on 1J. Pass through the 3J of the picot. Thread on 1J and pass through the first 1J of the following strap (fig 39).

fig 40

Pass through the following 8J of the strap, the 3J at the base of the T bead and the <u>next</u> B bead around the V bead. Pass up the following 1B around the B bead frame (fig 40).

Repeat from the beginning of Step 19 up to fig 39 to add a T bead with a J bead frame (see fig 41).

The two frames need to be linked together.

Pass through the following 6J of the 9J strap and locate the third J bead up the adjacent 9J strap.

Referring to fig 41 pass up through this 1J and down through the J on the second frame (fig 41).

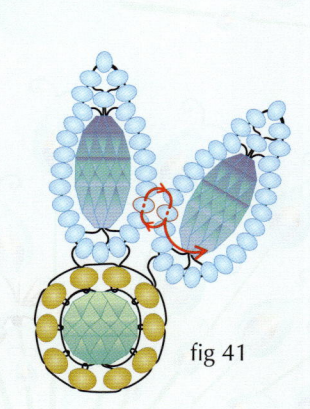

fig 41

77

20 Pass through the following 5J and the B bead below it (fig 42).

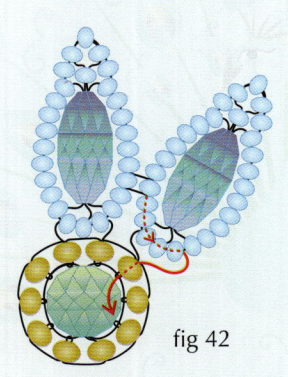

fig 42

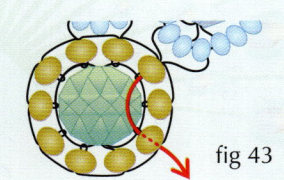

fig 43

Pass up through the second B bead around the B bead frame to emerge in the correct position to start the first tassel strand (fig 43).

21 Thread on 4J, 1B, 1J, 1F, 1J, 1B, 1D, 1A, 1U, 1A, 1B and 3K.

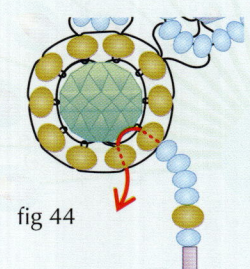

Pass back up the last 1B to draw the 3K into an anchor.

Pass up through the following beads just added and the same B bead on the B bead frame*.

Pass down the next 1B around the frame (fig 44).

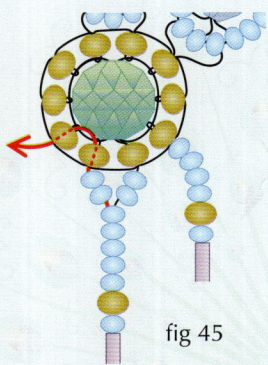

fig 44

22 Thread on 7J, 1B, 1J, 1F, 1J, 1B, 1D, 1A, 1U, 1A, 1B and 3K.

Pass back up the last 1B to draw the 3K into an anchor.

Pass up through the following beads just added to emerge 2J below the B bead frame.

Thread on 2J and pass up through the next 1B around the B bead frame. Pass down the following 1B (fig 45).

fig 45

Repeat Step 21 up to * to make the third tassel strand.

Pass up through the second B bead around the V bead frame (as fig 43) to emerge in the correct position to add the third framed T bead.

Repeat Step 19 up to fig 39.

Repeat fig 41 to mirror the link between the last framed T bead and the first (fig 46).

Remove the keeper bead and finish off both thread ends on this motif. Set aside for the moment.

fig 46

23 Fig 47 shows the front of the bauble net with the attachment positions of the crystal dangles numbered along the edge.

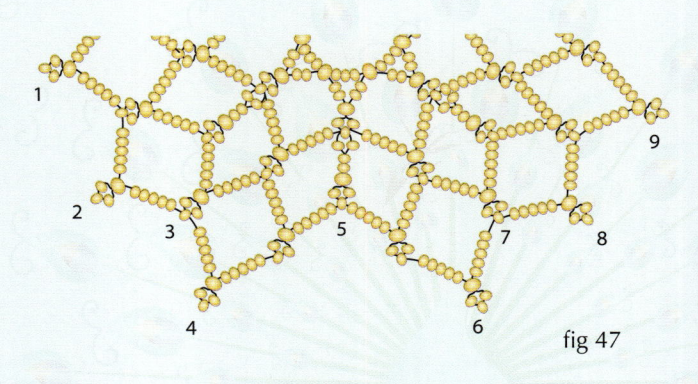

fig 47

The dangles attach to the P bead picots at these positions.

Prepare the fine needle with 1.5m of single thread and tie a keeper bead 15cm from the end.

Pass the needle through a few beads of the net to emerge from the middle P bead of the picot at position 1 on fig 47.

24 Thread on 3J, 1B, 1D, 1A, 1B and 3K.

Pass back up the last 1B and the following 1A, 1D, 1B and 1J.

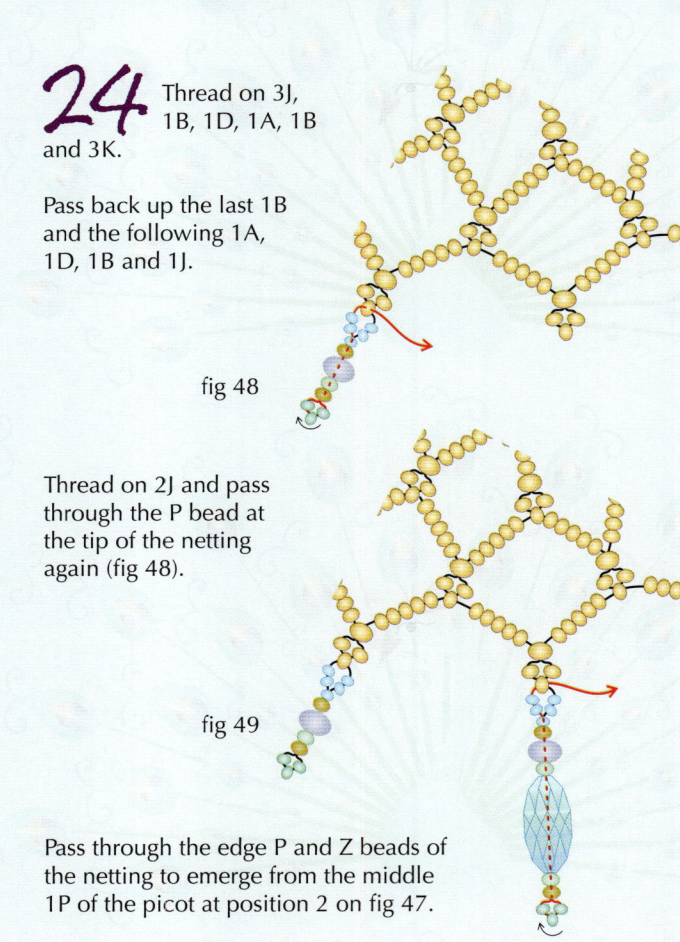

fig 48

Thread on 2J and pass through the P bead at the tip of the netting again (fig 48).

fig 49

Pass through the edge P and Z beads of the netting to emerge from the middle 1P of the picot at position 2 on fig 47.

*Thread on 3J, 1B, 1D, 1A, 1U, 1A, 1B and 3K.
Pass back up the last 1B and the following 1A, 1U, 1A, 1D, 1B and 1J.
Thread on 2J and pass through the P bead at the tip of the netting again (fig 49).

78

25 Pass the needle through the P and Z edge beads of the netting to emerge from the middle 1P of the picot at position 3 on fig 47 - note this picot is more difficult to identify as a P bead row of the netting already connects through this position.

Repeat from * in Step 24 to add a matching crystal dangle at this position.

Reposition the needle to emerge from the middle P bead of the picot at position 4 on fig 47.

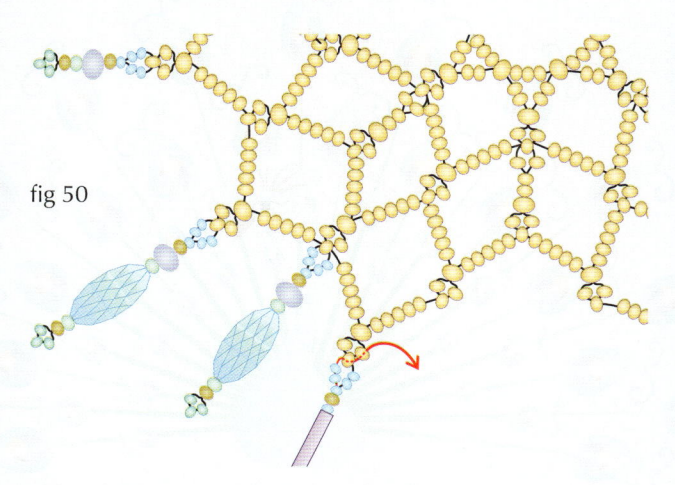

fig 50

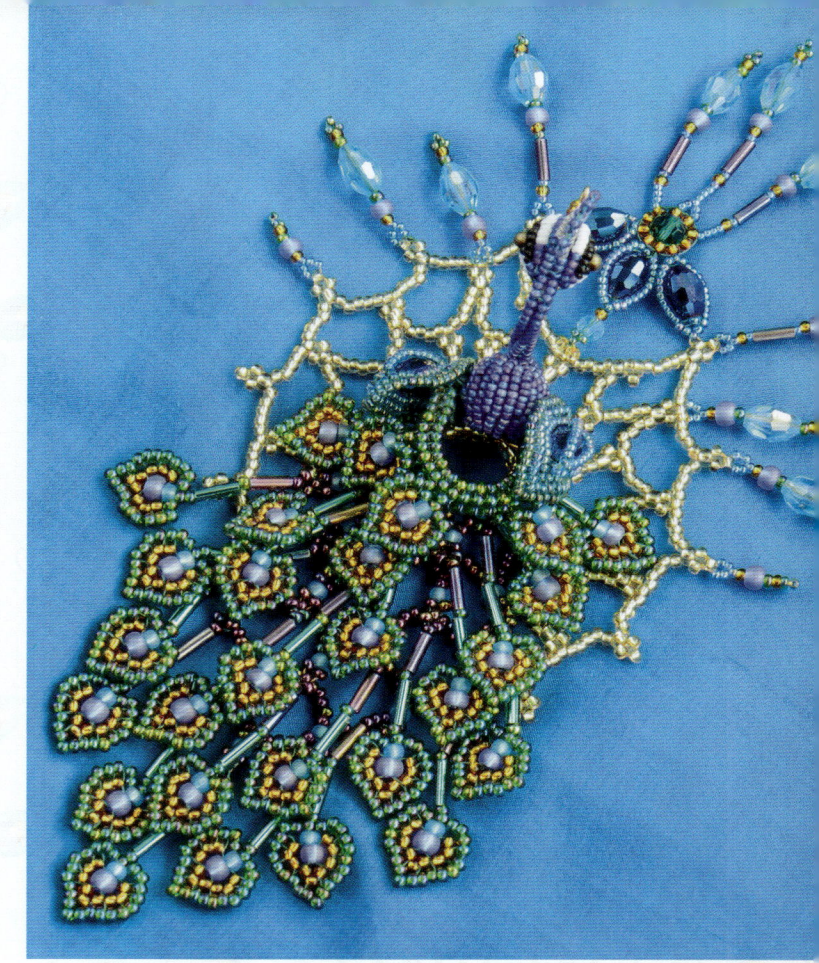

26 Thread on 3J, 1B, 1J, 1F, 1J, 1B, 1D, 1A, 1U, 1A, 1B and 3K.

Pass the needle back up the last 1B to draw the 3K into an anchor. Pass up through the following beads just added to emerge 2J below the P bead picot.

Thread on 2J and pass through the P bead in the middle of the picot and the following 1P (fig 50) - this is the first attachment point for the Crystal Centrepiece.

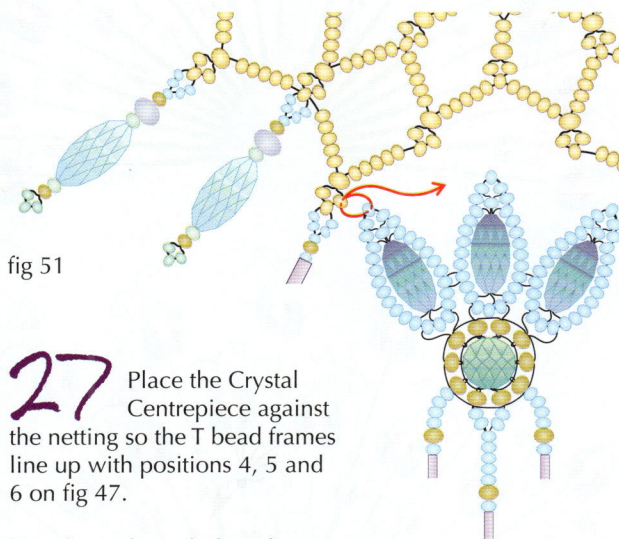

fig 51

27 Place the Crystal Centrepiece against the netting so the T bead frames line up with positions 4, 5 and 6 on fig 47.

Pass down through the adjacent 1J at the tip of the closest T bead frame and up the P bead on the picot (fig 51).

Pass the needle through the netting to emerge from the middle P of the picot at position 5 on fig 47 - again, make sure you have located the correct picot P bead as a P bead row of the netting already connects through this position.

28 Referring to fig 52 throughout, thread on 1P, 2J, 1W and 1B. Pass through the 1J at the tip of the central T bead frame and back through the 1B and 1W beads.

Thread on 1J. Pass through the first 1J in the same direction and thread on 1P. Pass through the picot P bead to centre the attachment below position 5 (fig 52).

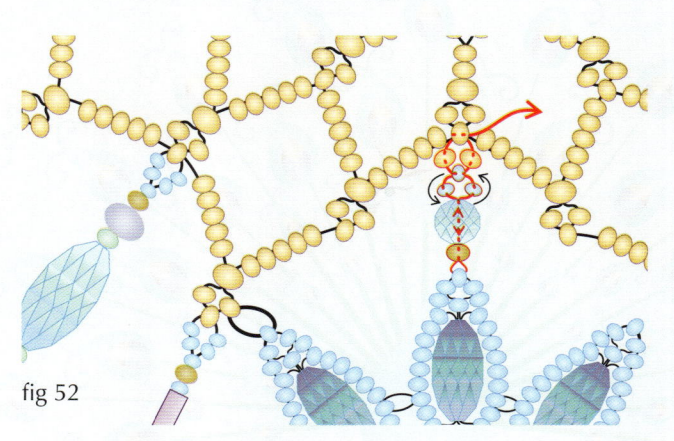

fig 52

29 Reposition the needle to emerge from the first P of the picot at position 6 and make the connection to the third T bead frame of the Crystal Centrepiece (a mirror image of fig 51).
Pass through the next 1P (the middle 1P) of the same picot and repeat the crystal dangle made in Step 26.

Work back along the last three positions marked on fig 47 to complete a symmetrical pattern.

Finish off the thread ends neatly and securely. Place the net over the bauble.

30 The Body
Prepare the fine needle with 1.2m of single thread and tie a keeper bead 15cm from the end.

Thread on 1R and 12H. Pass through the R bead to make a strap on the side.

Thread on 12H and pass through the R bead again to make a second strap (fig 53).

Repeat twelve more times to add fourteen 12H straps in total.

fig 53

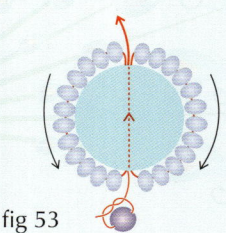

fig 54

31
Although the R bead is quite well covered, there are gaps. A series of short straps is added to fill in the gaps around the widest part of the R bead.

Pass through the first 3H of the nearest 12H strap. Thread on 6H and pass through the last 3H of the same strap (fig 54).

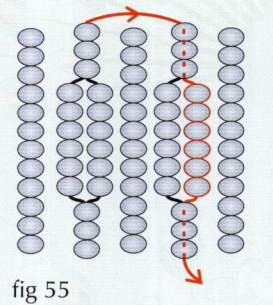

Pass through the first 3H at this end of the second 12H strap along and thread on 6H. Pass through the last 3H of the same strap (fig 55).

Repeat this technique five more times to make seven short straps in total (fig 56).

fig 55

fig 56

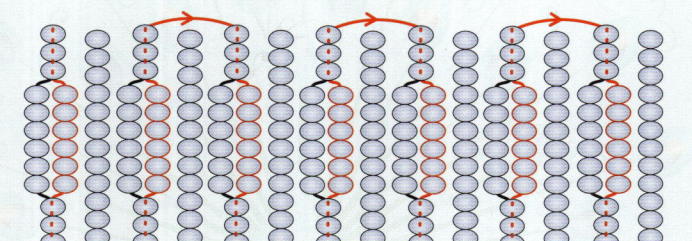

Pass through the R bead and remove the needle. Set aside for the moment.

32 The Neck
This is made using Tubular Herringbone stitch to produce a hollow rope.

Prepare the fine needle with 2m of single thread and tie a keeper bead <u>80cm</u> from the end.

Begin with a foundation row of Ladder-stitched beads.

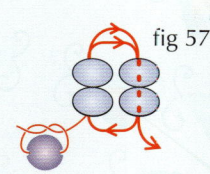

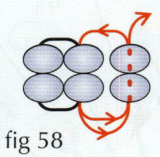

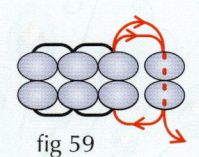

fig 57   fig 58   fig 59

Thread on 4H. Pass up the first 2H and down the second 2H to make two columns of 2H (fig 57).

Thread on 2H. Pass down the previous 2H and up the new 2H (fig 58). Repeat once to complete a strip of four columns (fig 59).

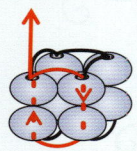

fig 60

Roll the strip so Column 1 is adjacent to Column 4.
Pass up Column 1, down Column 4 and up Column 1 to make a small drum (fig 60).
This completes the foundation row.

Tubular Herringbone stitch adds two beads per stitch.

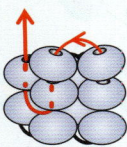

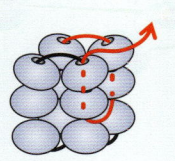

fig 61

Thread on 2H. Pass down the top 1H of Column 2 and up the top 1H of Column 3 (fig 61).

fig 62

Thread on 2H. Pass down the top 1H of Column 4 and up the top <u>2H</u> of Column 1 (fig 62) - this last stitch completes the row and repositions the needle for the start of the next row.

Repeat both stitches (fig 63).

Repeat until you can count 22 rows in total (20 rows of Tubular Herringbone and the 2H depth of the Ladder stitch foundation).

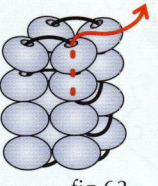

Work one 2H stitch only (half a row) and remove the needle leaving the thread end loose.

fig 63

33 The Head

Employing the same technique as the body, the head is made from an S bead covered with straps of seed beads. This time more colours are used - a plan of the first eight straps is shown in fig 64.

Remove the keeper bead from the foundation end of the neck and attach the needle to this 80cm thread end.

Thread on 1S and push up to the end of the neck. Take care not to catch the threads or beads at the end of the neck as you make the following straps.

fig 64

needle emerges this end of the S bead

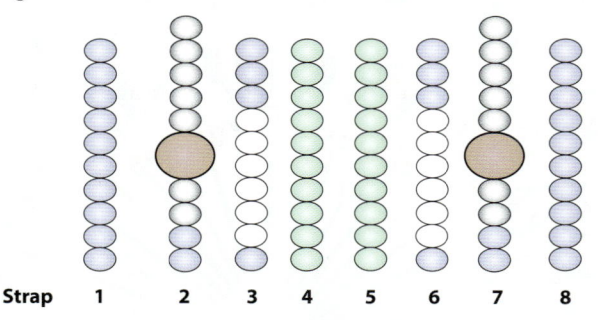

Strap   1   2   3   4   5   6   7   8

this end adjacent to neck

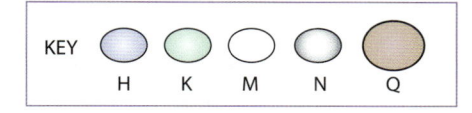

KEY   H   K   M   N   Q

Referring to fig 64 add the straps to the S bead in the order shown:-
Be sure to add the sequences the right way around - note the end of the neck is at the bottom of fig 64.
Pass through the S bead after each strap has been added.

       Strap 1 - 10H
       Strap 2 - 5N, 1Q, 2N and 2H
       Strap 3 - 3H, 6M and 1H
       Strap 4 - 10K
       Strap 5 - 10K
       Strap 6 - 3H, 6M and 1H
       Strap 7 - 5N, 1Q, 2N and 2H
       Strap 8 - 10H

34

Fig 65 shows the additional short straps needed. It is important that the main S bead hole does not become blocked with thread so the needle is not passed through the S bead after each short strap is added.

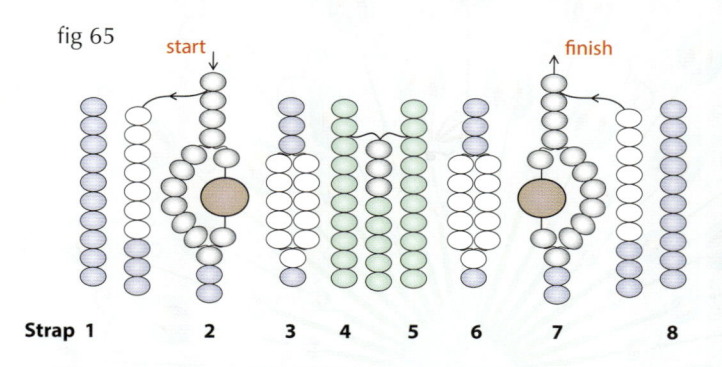

fig 65   start   finish

Strap   1   2   3   4   5   6   7   8

Refer to fig 65 throughout to make sure you position the new additions on the correct side of the existing eight straps.

(i) Pass through the first 1N of Strap 2 and thread on 7M and 3H. Pass through the S bead to draw the new strap between Straps 1 and 2.

(ii) Pass through the first 4N of Strap 2 and thread on 6N. Pass through the last 1N and 2H of the same strap. Position the new short strap as shown in fig 65. Do not pass through the S bead.

(iii) Pass through the first 1H and 1M at this end of Strap 3 and thread on 5M. Pass through the last 3H of the same strap. Do not pass through the S bead.

(iv) Pass through the first 3H at this end of Strap 6 and thread on 5M. Pass through the last 1M and 1H of the same strap. Do not pass through the S bead.

(v) Pass through the first 2H and 1N at this end of Strap 7 and thread on 6N. Pass through the last 4N of this strap. Pass through the S bead. Make sure the new short strap pulls into the correct position between Straps 7 and 8 (see fig 65).

(vi) Thread on 3H and 7M. Pass through the last N bead of Strap 7 pulling the new strap between the previous short strap and Strap 8 (see fig 65). Do not pass through the S bead.

The short strap between Straps 4 and 5 is added in Step 38.

35 Pass the needle through the 10H of Strap 8 to emerge adjacent to the near end of the neck.

Examine the far end of the neck. In Step 32, one 2H stitch was added before removing the needle, this means that Columns 1 and 2 are each one bead longer than Columns 3 and 4. Identify the shorter Columns 3 and 4.

Trace Columns 3 and 4 up the neck to the back of the head and line up these two columns with the ends of Straps 1 and 8 on the head.

Pass the needle down and up the first 3H of these two columns to attach them to the ends of Straps 1 and 8.

Finish with the needle emerging from the fifth H bead along Strap 1 (S1 in fig 66).

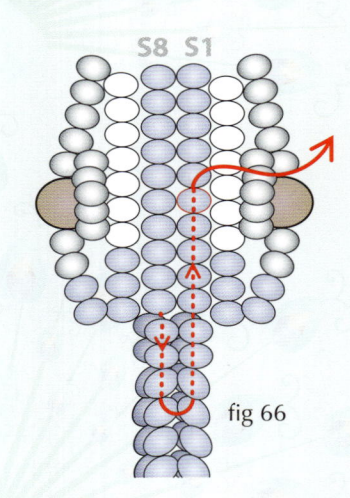

fig 66

36 The Plume - The top of the head is decorated with a fan of beads. It is supported by Straps 1 and 8.

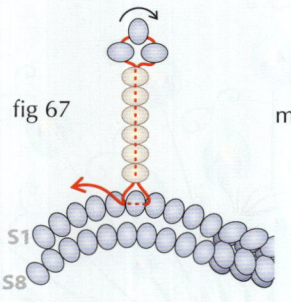

fig 67

Thread on 6L and 3H. Pass back down the 6L beads to make a 3H picot at the top of the stem. Pass through bead 5 on Strap 1 (S1 in fig 67).

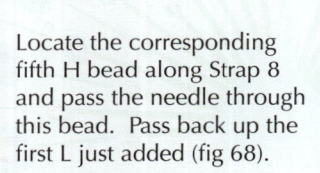

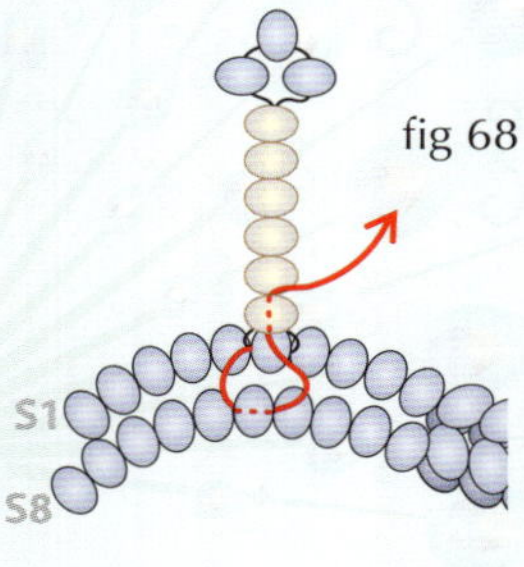

Locate the corresponding fifth H bead along Strap 8 and pass the needle through this bead. Pass back up the first L just added (fig 68).

fig 68

Thread on 6L and 3H. Pass back down the 6L just added and the 1L at the base of the previous stem. Pass through the fourth H bead of Strap 1 (1H towards the junction with the neck) (fig 69).

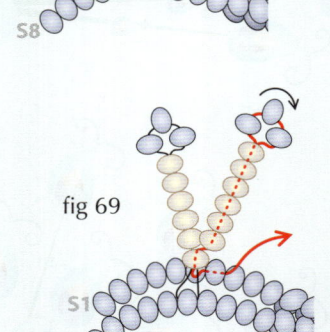

fig 69

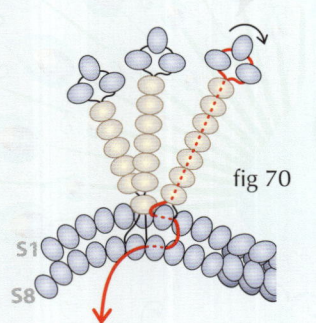

fig 70

Thread on 7L and 3H. Pass back through the 7L beads and the fourth H bead on Strap 1.

Pass through the fourth H bead on Strap 8 (fig 70).

37 Pass back up the first L of the previous stem and thread on 6L and 3H.

Pass back down the 6L and the 1L at the base. Pass through the H bead on Strap 8 and back up the same 7L (fig 71).

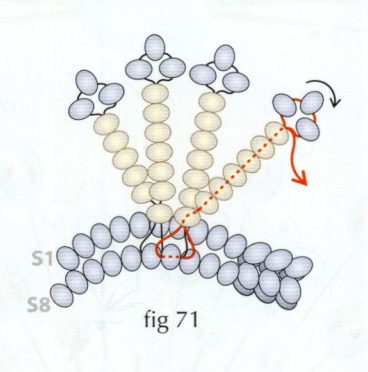

fig 71

Pass through the first 1H of the picot.

Line up this H with the adjacent 1H of the previous stem and Square stitch together (fig 72).

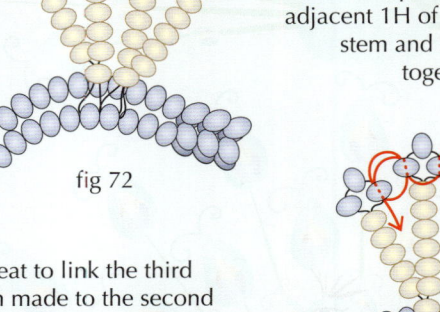

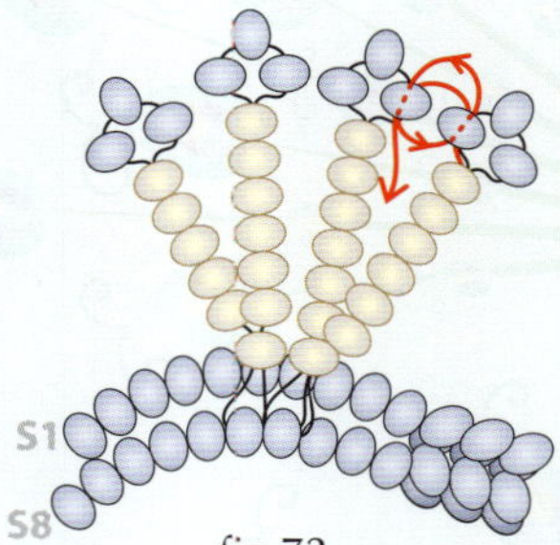

fig 72

Repeat to link the third stem made to the second stem and this stem to the first (the shortest stem) (fig 73).

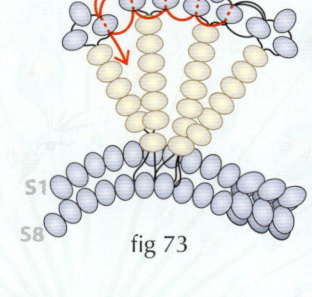

fig 73

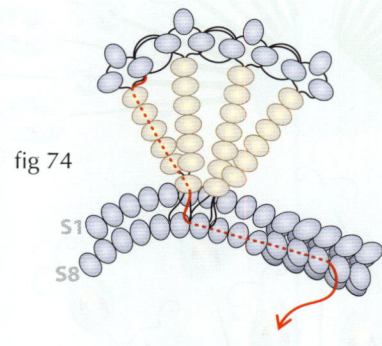

fig 74

Pass the needle down the L beads of the first plume stem and through the following H beads towards the neck end of Strap 8. Pass through the following 3H of the neck rope (fig 74).

Pass through the corresponding 3H of Column 1 of the neck to emerge adjacent to the end of Strap 5 on the underside of the head.

82

38 Thread on 5K and 3N. Referring to fig 75 pass through the last 2K of Strap 5 to pull the new short strap between Straps 4 and 5. Do not pass through the S bead.

Pass back through the first 2K beads at this end of Strap 4 and back through the 3N and 5K just added.

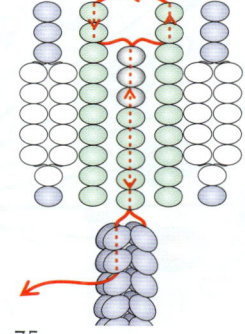

fig 75

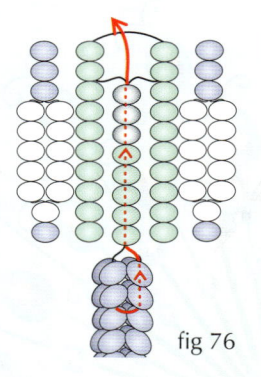

Pass through the first 2H of Column 2 on the rope (fig 75).

Reposition the needle to emerge from the N bead at the end of the short strap just added (fig 76).

fig 76

39 Adding the Beak - Smooth the 0.8mm wire removing any kinks. Make sure the end is trimmed neatly.

The wire needs to pass through the S bead and the hollow neck rope. At present there are a lot of crossed threads inside the S bead which can form a plug. Poke the thicker needle in and out of the S bead hole 10-15 times to make a clear channel for the wire.

Pass the wire through the S bead and the neck carefully - don't use too much force - it will fit with a little wiggle and push. Take care at the junction of the S bead and the neck to pass down the centre space of the rope. Leave 25mm of wire showing at the head end ready to make the beak.

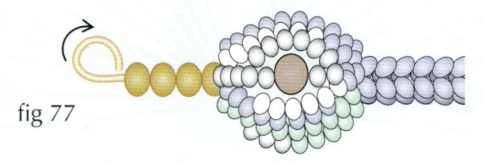

fig 77

Thread 4B onto the beak end of the wire. Trim the wire to 8mm and roll a loop towards the top of the head to suggest a slightly upturned tip to the beak (fig 77).

Pick up the needle (attached to the end of the short strap made in Step 38) and thread on 2N and 2B.

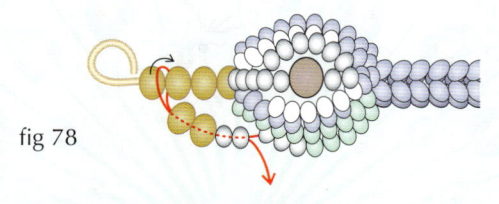

fig 78

Referring to fig 78, wrap the thread over the wire beak between the end 2B beads and pass back through the 2B and 2N just added (fig 78).

Pass back through the 3N and 5K beads of the short strap and finish off the thread end neatly and securely.

40 Assembling the Neck and Body - Reattach the needle to the thread tail at the other end of the neck.

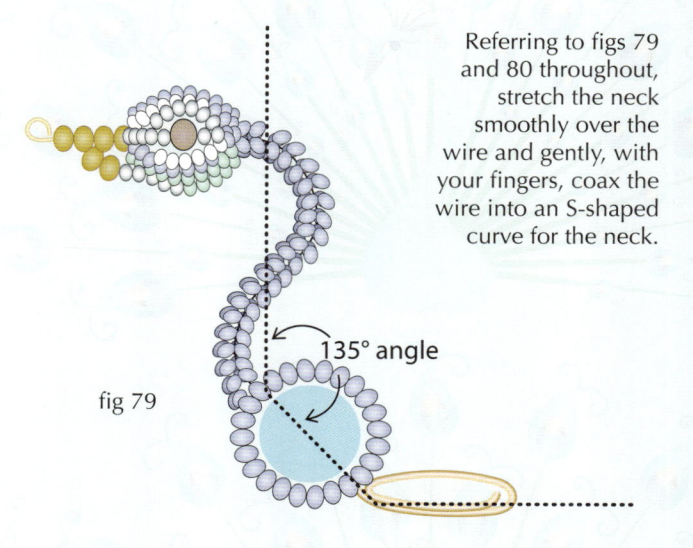

Referring to figs 79 and 80 throughout, stretch the neck smoothly over the wire and gently, with your fingers, coax the wire into an S-shaped curve for the neck.

fig 79

135° angle

Straighten the end of the wire a little and thread on the R bead at the centre of the body so it sits at 135° to the main axis.

If necessary, adjust the neck rope so the two shorter columns (attached to the top of the head) run down the back of the neck and the two slightly longer columns (attached to the underside of the chin) run down the front of the neck. The extra 2H beads added at the end of Step 32 will help to conceal the wire as it passes into the R bead of the body.

Stitch the end of the neck rope to the front of the body so the two longer H bead columns line up with the H bead rows at the front of the body to make a smooth join.

Remove the needle leaving the thread end loose.

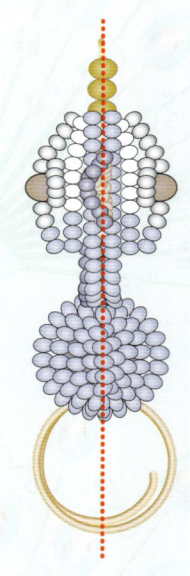

fig 80

83

41 As shown in figs 79 and 80, the long end of the wire needs to be manipulated into a ring. This ring will fit over the bauble neck.

Do not bend the wire directly around the bauble neck or the bauble will break. Find a cylindrical mould 12-18mm in diameter - a chunky pen or wooden spoon handle is ideal. Compare your potential mould to the width of the bauble neck - it needs to be approximately the same diameter or a little bit bigger than the base of the bauble neck.

Roll the full length of the wire end around the mould to come right up against the base of the body, making a neat, compact coil (the wire should make 1.5 - 2 turns around the mould). Make sure the coil reaches right up to the hole in the R bead core of the body. Remove the mould.

Adjust the coil so it is in line with the body, neck and head (as fig 80).

Carefully bend the wire (use your fingers), at the junction of the coil with the body, so the R bead hole in the body is at an angle of 135° to the flat plane of the coil (see fig 79). Note the coil is tucked slightly underneath the base of the body.

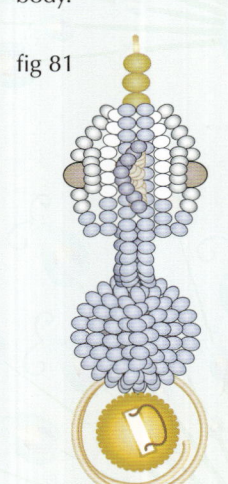

fig 81

Check the coil for size over the bauble neck - the back of the body will slightly overhang the central space of the coil so you may need to make it a little larger. A 2mm margin all around the bauble neck is required (fig 81).

When the coil is in place the peacock head and neck should be in the correct attitide for the finished design as fig 79. If necessary adjust the angle of the coil behind the body so the body, neck and head stand as in fig 79 and in line with the centre back of the tail strands (as fig 80).

Only one turn of the wire coil is required. Very carefully (make sure you are cutting the correct part of the wire) trim the excess length away leaving a single ring of wire attached to the base of the body.

Set aside for the moment.

42 At present, the wire ring is too insubstantial and unstable to make a firm connnection to the beadwork at the top of the netting. A hollow rope, made in Tubular Herringbone stitch, will cover the wire so it can be securely fixed to the foundation row around the bauble neck.

Prepare the thick needle with 1.5m of single thread and tie a keeper bead 40cm from the end.

Referring to Step 32, and using A beads, make a four column foundation row in Ladder stitch for a new length of Tubular Herringbone stitch.

Work 20 rows of Tubular Herringbone stitch (22 rows in total including the 2A deep foundation row).

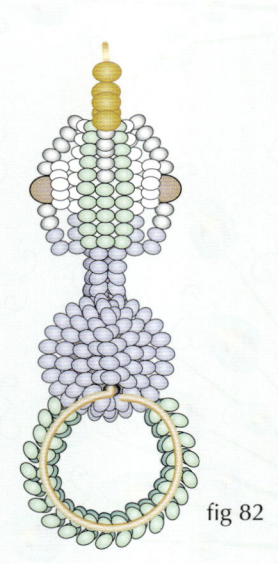

43 Compare the rope to the wire ring. It needs to be long enough to cover most of the wire ring with the rope ends just making contact with the H beads at either side of the body - see fig 82 showing the underside of the ring with the rope held against the ring for the comparison to be made. The beaded rope will form a horseshoe shape.

If necessary, adjust the row count to achieve a fit as shown in fig 82.

fig 82

44 A flat, fan-shaped tab, three rows deep is now added to each end of the rope. These tabs will make it easier to connect the rope to the body.

Work one 2A Herringbone stitch of a new row (columns 1 and 2 only). Pass the needle back up the last 1A added (fig 83).

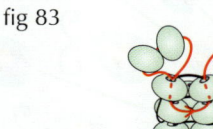

fig 83

Thread on 2A. Pass back down the first 1A and up the second 1A of the previous row (fig 84).

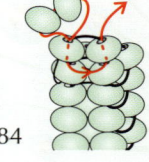

fig 84

Thread on 2A and pass down and up through the 2A of the last row (fig 85).

fig 85

Pass through the new 4A to neaten (fig 86).

Square stitch 2A to the last 1A of the previous row to start a new row (fig 87).

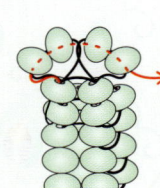

fig 86

Make two 1A Square stitches and one 2A Square stitch to complete the row (fig 88).

Pass the needle back through the 4A of the previous row and the 6A of the new row to neaten the work and remove the needle.

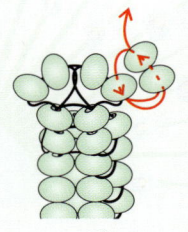

fig 87

Remove the keeper bead from the far end of the rope and attach the needle to this end.

Identify the two columns that support the first tab at the other end of the rope (Columns 1 and 2) and add an identical tab to the same two columns at this end of the rope.

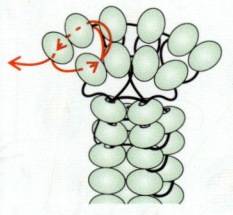

fig 88

45 Straighten out the last 1cm at the cut end of the wire ring ready to thread on the beaded rope - this end will be trimmed so don't worry about making a slight kink.

Referring to fig 89, pass the end of the wire between the 2A beads of the last row of Tubular Herringbone stitch at the base of the first tab and into the central channel of the rope.

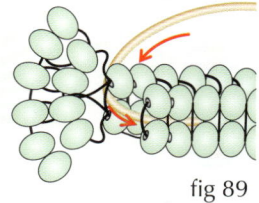

fig 89

Gently ease the rope along the wire. Don't allow the rope to spiral around the wire - keep the columns smooth.

Continue until the tab comes up against the side of the body (fig 90) - note columns 3 and 4 of the rope are on the outside of the ring allowing the tab (attached to columns 1 and 2) to fit snugly on either side of the body).

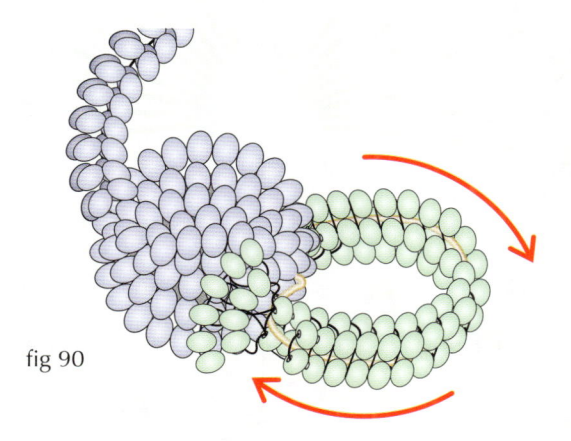

fig 90

Hold the second tab against the other side of the body and check that the rope-covered ring makes a good fit over the bauble neck - it will be awkward, as there is still an extra length of wire poking out of the other end of the rope, but it is important to check the fit.

When you are confident that the ring will fit the bauble, and the tabs make neat contact with the body, trim the excess wire length away so the cut end is level with the end of the rope cavity.

Stitch the tabs to the sides of the body.

46 Place the complete ring over the bauble neck lining up the front of the body with the front of the crystal decoration on the net.

The wired ring needs to be stitched to the foundation row around the top of the net.

Make a note of which A bead of the rope lines up with the centre-back E bead of the net ring. Pass the needle through the rope beads to emerge from this A bead. Remove the net and ring from the bauble and stitch the ring to the rope at this position.

47 Replacing and removing the bauble as necessary, carefully work around the seam attaching the E beads of the foundation row to the correct A beads on the rope.

At the centre-front the bottom of the body will be just above the middle Z bead picot on Row One of the netting (made in Step 2). Make a stitch to secure the picot to the underside of the body - you may need to add a P bead (or two) to the stitch to avoid distorting the netting.

48 Place the decoration over the bauble. The top of the tail fringe strands are quite exposed. Three eye motifs are added to the rope ring to conceal the seam between the rope and the net and to fill out the top of the tail.

Reposition the needle to emerge from the top edge of the rope at the the centre-back position.

Thread on 2A, 1E, 1D and 3B to start an eye motif. Work Steps 11 and 12 to complete the eye motif. Pass through the same A bead on the rope to make the connection neat.

Repeat to add an identical eye motif 7A beads to the right along the rope and a third, identical motif 7A beads to the left. Finish off the thread ends neatly and securely.

49 The Wings - Prepare the fine needle with 1.5m of single thread and tie a keeper bead 15cm from the end.

Thread on 1T and 9J. Pass the needle through the T bead to make a strap of J beads on the side. Thread on 9J and pass through the T bead again to make a second strap (fig 91).

Thread on 4J. Pass back through the first 1J just added and the T bead to make a picot (fig 92).

fig 91

fig 92

fig 93

Pass through the first 9J and thread on 1J. Pass through the 3J of the picot and thread on 1J. Pass through the second 9J (fig 93).

Thread on 3J and pass through the first 1J of the following strap to complete a frame around the T bead (fig 94).

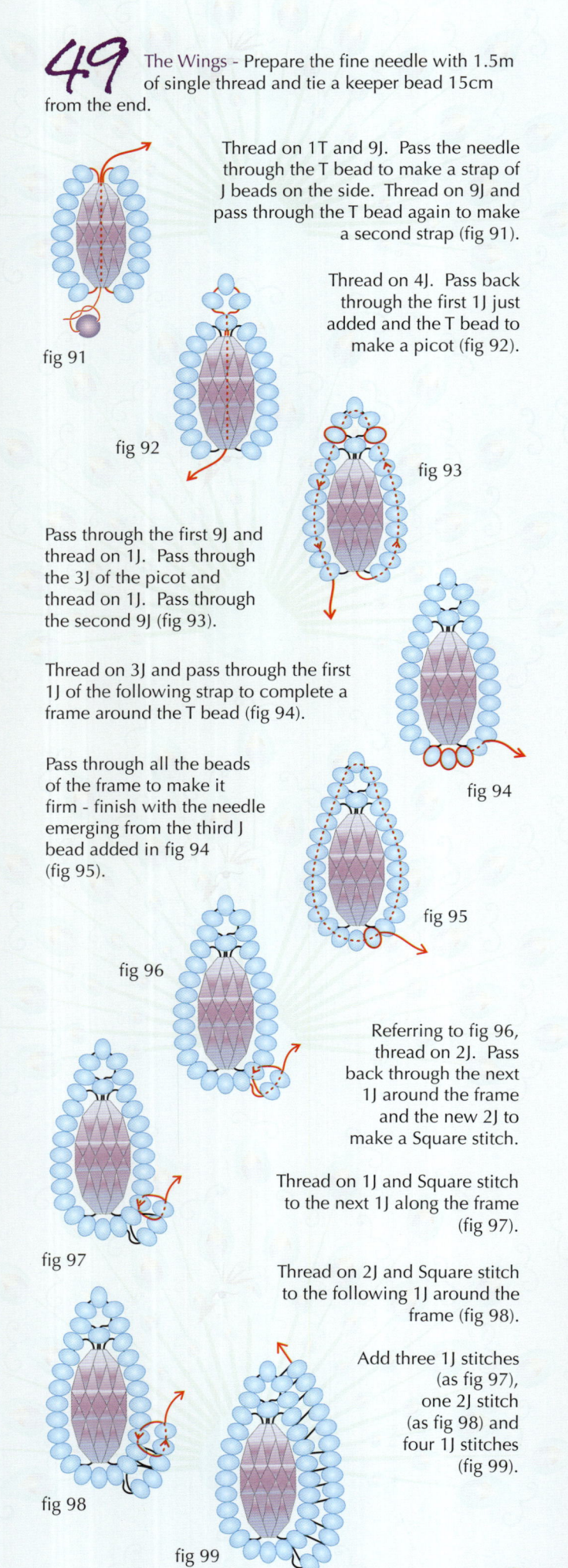

Pass through all the beads of the frame to make it firm - finish with the needle emerging from the third J bead added in fig 94 (fig 95).

fig 94

fig 95

fig 96

Referring to fig 96, thread on 2J. Pass back through the next 1J around the frame and the new 2J to make a Square stitch.

Thread on 1J and Square stitch to the next 1J along the frame (fig 97).

Thread on 2J and Square stitch to the following 1J around the frame (fig 98).

Add three 1J stitches (as fig 97), one 2J stitch (as fig 98) and four 1J stitches (fig 99).

fig 97

fig 98

fig 99

50 Thread on 4J. Pass back through the J bead at the tip of the picot and the last 3J just added (fig 100).

Thread on 2J. Square stitch the second J bead just added to the next 1J along the frame (fig 101)*.

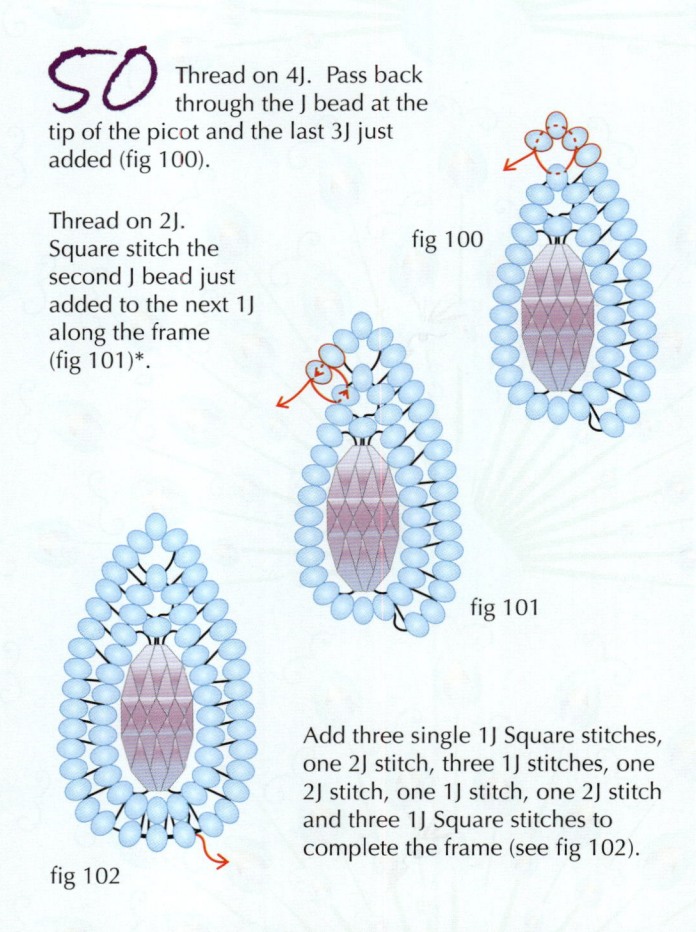

fig 100

fig 101

Add three single 1J Square stitches, one 2J stitch, three 1J stitches, one 2J stitch, one 1J stitch, one 2J stitch and three 1J Square stitches to complete the frame (see fig 102).

fig 102

Pass the needle through all the beads just added to neaten the outline. Finish with the needle emerging from the last 1J added (fig 102).

51 Swap to K beads for the outermost row.

Thread on 2K and make the first stitch as fig 97 attaching the new 2K to the next 1J around the frame.

Working towards the wing tip and referring to figs 97 and 98 add the following stitches - two 1K, one 2K and twelve 1K.

Using K beads repeat Step 50 to *.

Add the following stitches - eleven 1K, one 2K, two 1K, one 2K and three 1K. This completes the frame.

Pass the needle through all the K beads just added and pull firmly - the wing frame will curve (a little) popping the T bead outwards 2-3mm (which enhances the shape of the wing).

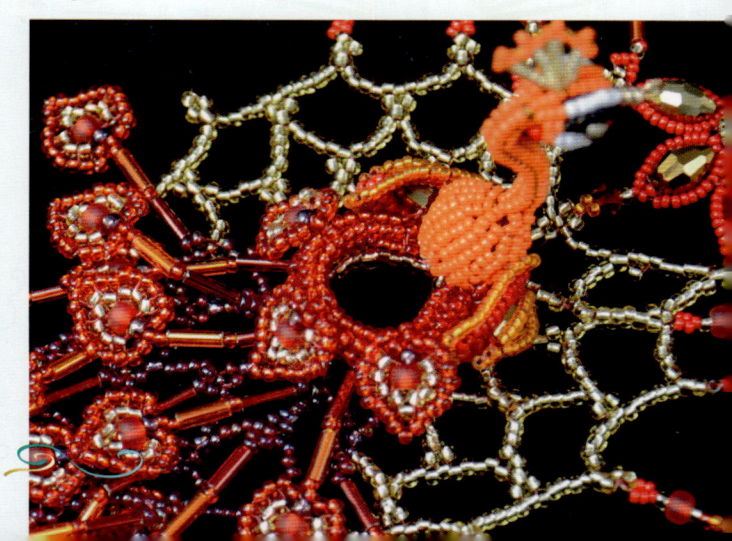

86

52 Weave the needle through the J beads at the rounded end of the frame to emerge at the T bead hole.

Pass through the T bead to emerge on the outside of the wing 'curve'.

Thread on 9J and, as before, pass through the T bead again to make a strap.

Repeat to make a second strap of 9J (fig 103).

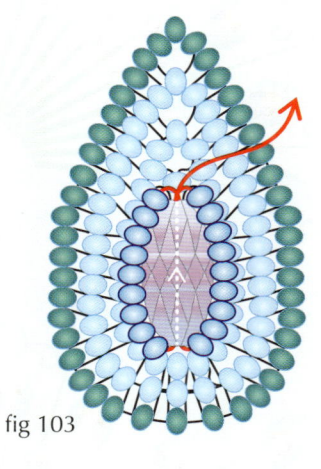

fig 103

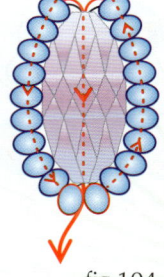

fig 104

Pass through the 9J beads of one of the new straps and thread on 2J. Pass through the 9J of the other strap and down through the T bead (fig 104).

Thread on 9J and pass through the T bead again to make a central strap (fig 105).

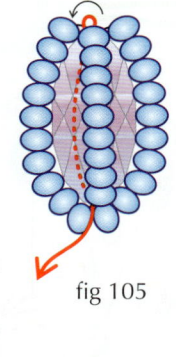

Pass through the first of the three new 9J straps and thread on 5J.

fig 105

Pass the needle back through the second J bead just added (to make a picot) and thread on 1J. Pass through the second 9J strap (fig 106).

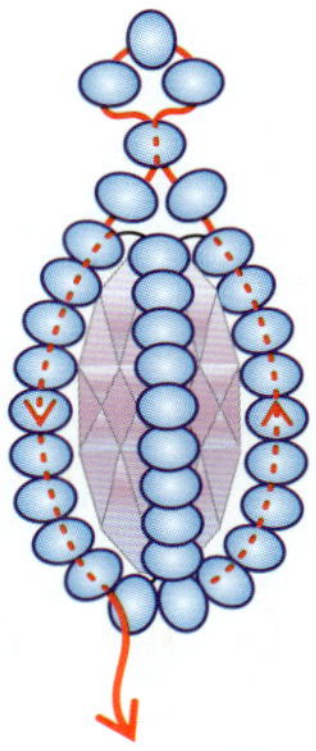

fig 106

This completes the wing.

Pass the needle through the closest 1J of the original 3-row frame and remove the needle.
Repeat to make a second wing.

53 Attaching the Wings - Place the rounded end of each wing over the tab connections on either side of the body. The wings should arch backwards concealing the tabs and the sides of the rope-covered wire. The rounded ends of the wings should be approximately 18-20mm apart across the front of the body.

Use the thread ends to stitch the front end of each wing to the body and the tabs. Leave the long wing edges and the points unattached so they can 'swell' out over the underlying structures.

54 The Hanging Loop - Prepare the thick needle with 1.2m of single thread and tie a keeper bead 15cm from the end.

Thread on 1X and 1A. Pass through the wire loop at the top of the bauble and back up the 1A and 1X just added.

Thread on 1A, 1Y, 1A, 1D, 2B, 1W, 1A, 1B, 1C and 50P.

Pass down the 1C and the following nine beads to emerge alongside the keeper bead (fig 107).

Reinforce the connections by passing through all the beads twice more - repeat again if the needle will pass.

Finish off the thread ends neatly and securely.

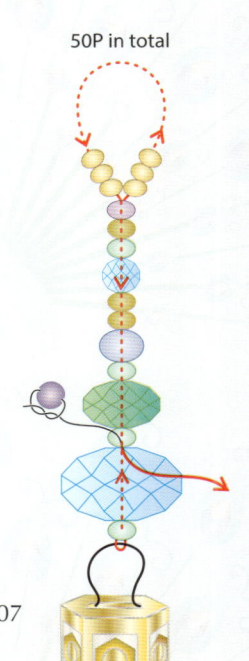

50P in total

fig 107

Nutcracker Soldier

You Will Need

Materials

4.5g of DB0723 opaque dark cranberry Delica beads A
2.5g of DB1832F duracoat galvanised matt gold Delica beads B
0.3g of DB0010 chalk black Delica beads C
1g of DB0354 matt light rose Delica beads D
1g of DB0351 matt white Delica beads E
2g of size 15 matt white seed beads F
7g of size 2 chalk white bugle beads G
6g of size 2 chalk black bugle beads H
Fourteen 2.5mm gold plated metal beads J
One 12mm black fire polished glass bead K
One 10mm black fire polished glass bead L
One 6mm black fire polished glass bead M
One 8x4mm black fire polished glass washer bead N
Two 5mm gold plated filigree bead cups P
Two DB0760 matt opaque periwinkle Delica beads Q
10cm of 1.0mm gold plated wire
20cm of monofilament thread
Red, black, pale pink and white size D beading thread

Tools

A size 10 beading needle
A pair of scissors to trim the threads
Wire cutters, flat-nosed pliers and round-nosed pliers

a completed Nutcracker Soldier measures approximately 11.5 x 3.5cm

We're going to the ballet for a magical Christmas treat where a handsome nutcracker soldier leads a band of tin toys in a fight against the Mouse King and his hoard of gingerbread-eating, miscreant mice.

The Decoration is Made in Six Stages

The main section of the tunic is made first using Peyote stitch.

The tunic arms and the hands are made next.

The legs and feet are constructed as a separate unit.

The head is woven in Brick stitch and the hair is added.

The hat is worked upwards from the top of the head.

The soldier is assembled and a wire hanging loop is added to the top.

The construction requires Peyote stitch, Square stitch and Brick stitch techniques. If you are not familiar with these three stitches please see Beadwork Basics on pages 10 and 11.

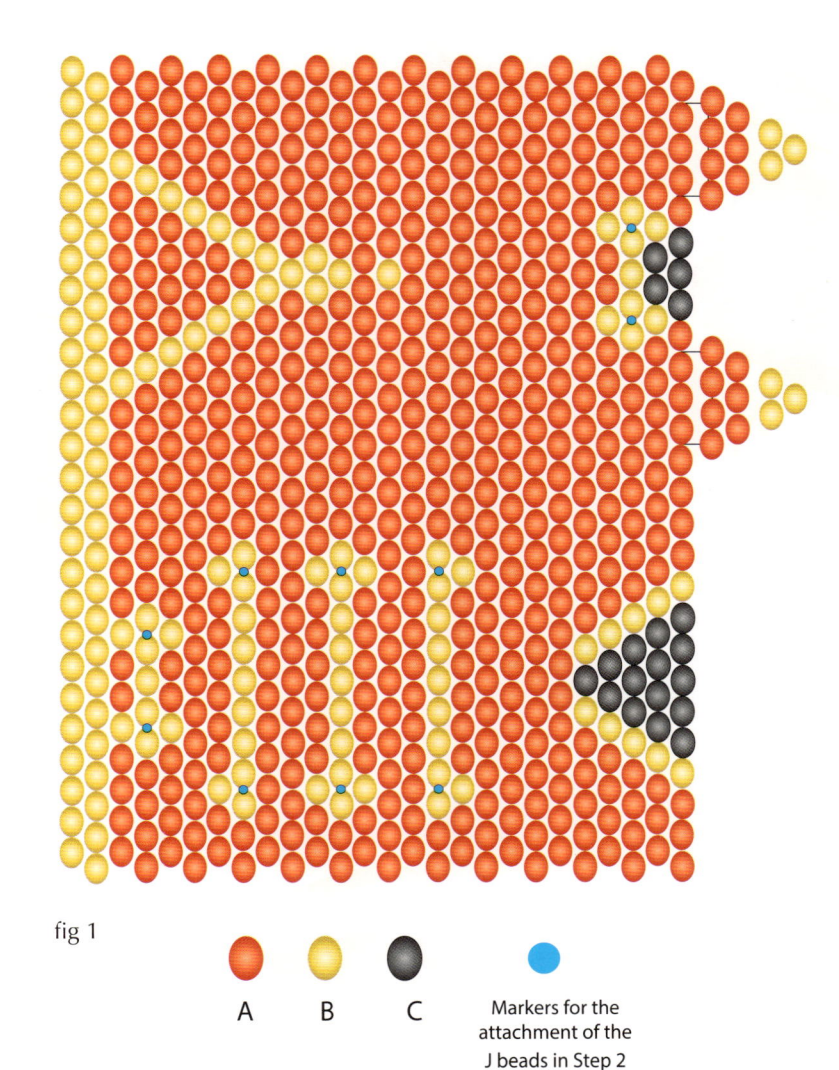

1 **The Tunic** - Fig 1 shows a Peyote stitch grid for the main section of the tunic.

On the right of the grid are two ten-bead triangles which form the tails of the tunic. These are added in Brick stitch when the larger block is complete.

Prepare the needle with 1.5m of single red thread and tie a keeper bead 15cm from the end. Thread on 2B and 24A as shown at the bottom of the grid.

Work in Peyote stitch to the top of the grid ignoring the two ten bead triangular sections on the right. When a new thread is required leave the old thread end loose and add the new length using a keeper bead stopper - do not tie any knots within the work.

When the main Peyote stitch section is complete, turn the work so the right-hand edge is at the top. Reposition the needle and add the two triangular sections in Brick stitch.

fig 1

A B C Markers for the attachment of the J beads in Step 2

2 Repositioning the needle through the beadwork as necessary, add 1J bead to the front surface at the positions marked with a blue dot. A single straight stitch will suffice at each location.

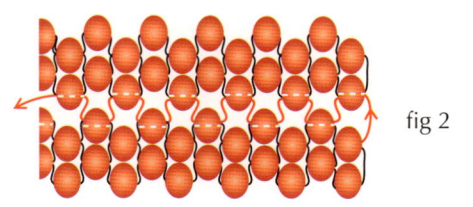

fig 2

Interlock the two key and keyhole edges of the work and stitch the seam to form a tube (fig 2).

Finish off all the thread ends neatly and securely without blocking the B bead holes along the top edge of the tunic. Set this section aside.

3 The Arms - Fig 3 shows a Peyote stitch grid for one arm.

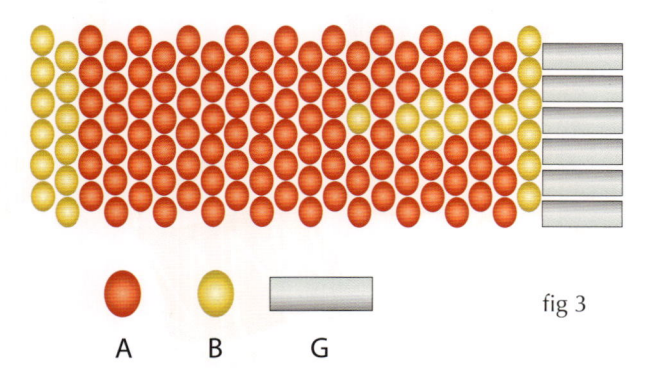

fig 3

A   B   G

Prepare the needle with 1.5m of single red thread and tie a keeper bead 15cm from the end. Thread on 2B, 18A, 1B and 1G as shown along the bottom of the grid.

Work in Peyote stitch to the top of the grid.

Interlock the key and keyholes along the two long sides of the rectangle to make a long tube and stitch the seam firmly to secure. Finish with the needle emerging at the B bead end of the tube.

4 Adding an Epaulette - Using flat pliers, gently squash a bead filigree bead cup flat.

Pass the needle through the centre hole of the flattened filigree and thread on 1J. Pass back down the central filigree hole and the B bead on the opposite side of the tube end to pull the filigree across the end of the tube (fig 4).

Pass up through an adjacent B bead and one of the holes around the edge of the filigree.

fig 4

fig 5

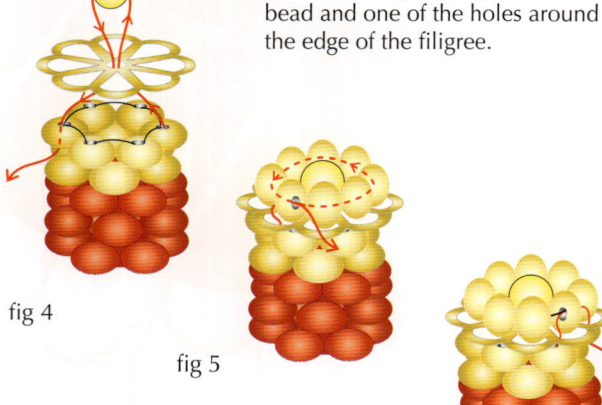

Thread on 8B. Pass the needle through the first 1B to make a ring. Position the ring around the central J bead (fig 5).

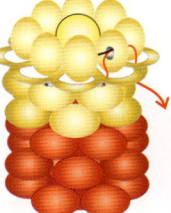

fig 6

The B bead ring and the filigree need to be secured.

Passing the needle through the outer filigree holes, work around the 8B ring to make four small stitches between alternate beads on the ring and the top row of B beads around the tube (fig 6).

Remove the needle and set aside.

5 The Hand - The hands are made in Square stitch. Prepare the needle with 1m of single, pale pink thread and tie a keeper bead 15cm from the end.

Thread on 6D for the first row.

Thread on 1D. Pass the needle through the last bead of the first row and back through the new 1D to bring the two beads together with the holes parallel (fig 7).

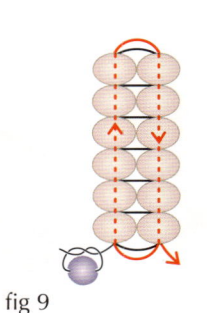

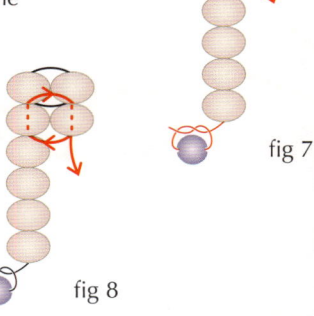

fig 7

fig 8

fig 9

Thread on 1D. Pass the needle through the next bead along the first row and back through the new bead (fig 8). This is Square stitch.

Repeat to the end of the row to add 6D in total. Pass the needle through the 6D of the first row and the 6D of the second to neaten the work (fig 9).

Add a third row of 6D using the same technique.

6 Pass the needle up the middle row of 6D and thread on 1D. Pass back down the last 2D of the same row, skip past the next 1D and pass through the first 3D (fig 10). Pull the thread to curve the beadwork a little to create the palm.

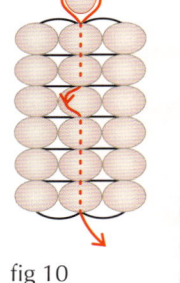

Pass the needle up the adjacent 3D of the third row and thread on 2D. Pass back through the first 1D just added to make the tip of the thumb.

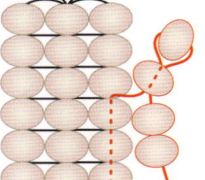

Thread on 2D to complete the thumb (the fourth row) (fig 11).

fig 10

fig 11

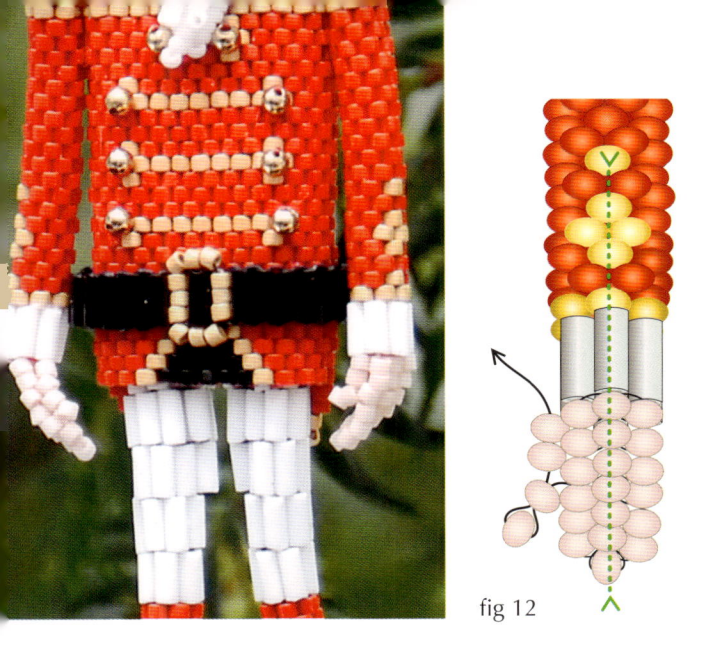

fig 12

fig 14

fig 15

fig 16

fig 17

9 Adding the Foot - Thread on 3H for the first row. Thread on 1H and Square stitch to the last 1H of the previous row (fig 14).

Repeat twice to complete a row of 3H.

Pass the needle down the corresponding H bead on the end of the leg tube and back out of the next (fig 15).

Add a row of 3H Square stitches to the side of the previous row to make a block of 3H x 3H (fig 16).

Thread on 3C and pass down the end 2H of the first row (fig 17).

7 Position the hand at the end of the arm so the longest (centre) finger is in line with the G bead at the base of the decorative pattern on the arm (fig 12). Note - the pattern sits on the outer edge of the arm so make sure the palm of the hand is facing the opposite way.

Passing the needle up and down across the gap, connect the ends of the four hand rows to the corresponding 4G beads at the end of the arm.

Finish off the pink thread ends neatly and securely.

Repeat from Step 3 to make the second arm and hand. Note - when adding the thumb on the second hand attach it to the first row of 6D to make it a mirror image of the first hand. Set both arms aside.

8 The Legs and Feet - The legs are made in Peyote stitch and extend up into the tunic to create the body. The feet are added in Square stitch.

Fig 13 shows the Peyote stitch grid for the first leg. Prepare the needle with 1.5m of black thread and tie a keeper bead 15cm from the end.

Thread on 3H, 1B, 3A and 11G as shown along the bottom of the grid. Work in Peyote stitch to the top of the grid.

Roll the work into a long tube interlocking the first and last rows and stitch the seam firmly to secure. Finish with the needle emerging at the H end of the tube.

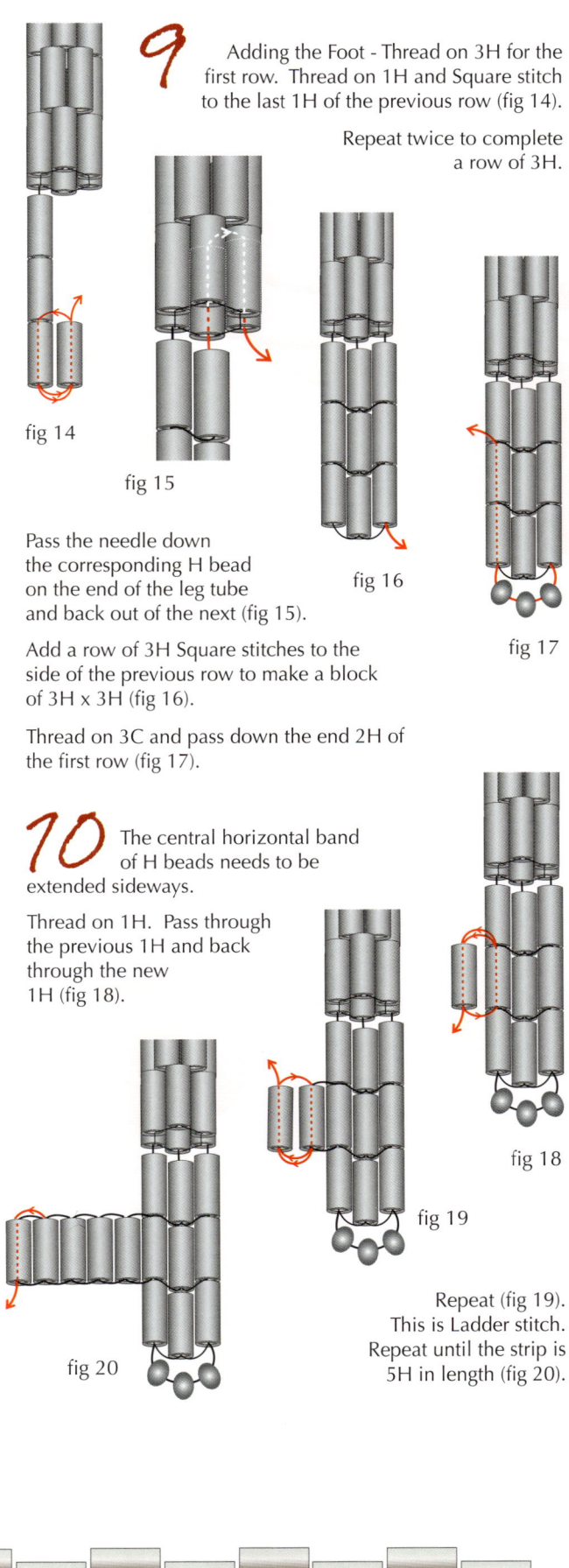

10 The central horizontal band of H beads needs to be extended sideways.

Thread on 1H. Pass through the previous 1H and back through the new 1H (fig 18).

fig 18

fig 19

fig 20

Repeat (fig 19). This is Ladder stitch. Repeat until the strip is 5H in length (fig 20).

fig 13

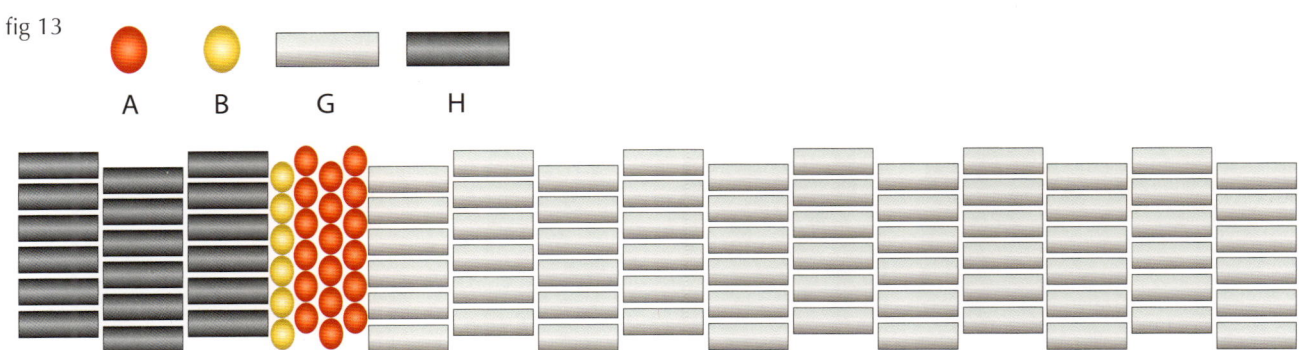

A B G H

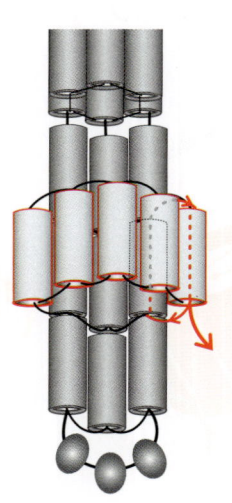

11
Bend the new strip into an arch to meet the middle H on the other side of the 3H block (to correspond to the profile of the leg section).

Square stitch the two touching H beads together (fig 21) - note the needle is emerging from the lower edge of the last H added.

This 5H arch is now linked to the 3C beads to make the top of the foot.

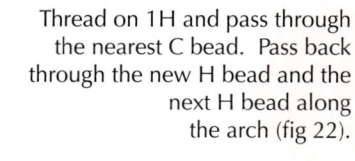

fig 21

Thread on 1H and pass through the nearest C bead. Pass back through the new H bead and the next H bead along the arch (fig 22).

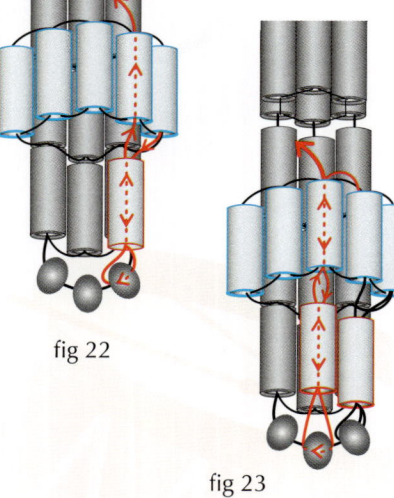

fig 22

fig 23

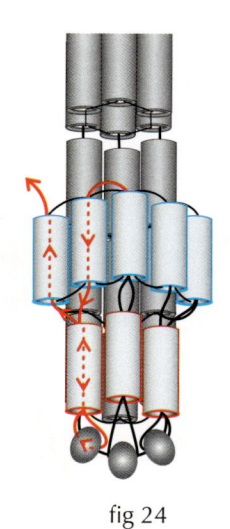

Pass down the middle 1H of the arch and thread on 1H. Pass through the middle C and back through the new H and the middle H on the arch (fig 23).

Pass down the following H of the arch and thread on 1H. Pass through the last 1C, back through the new H and the next 1H along the arch (fig 24).

Reposition the needle to emerge from the top of the middle 1H of the arch (fig 25).

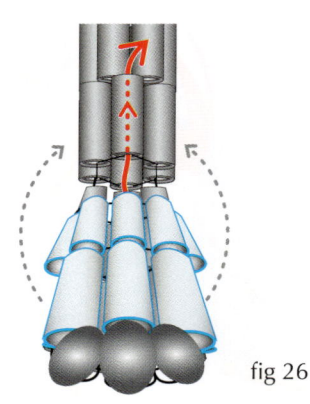

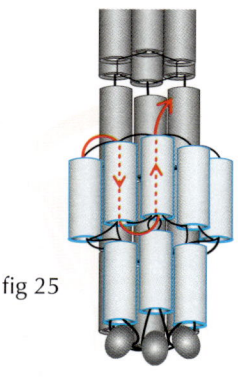

fig 24

fig 25

12
Pass up the middle H at the bottom of the leg to draw the foot up (fig 26).

Repeat to connect the adjacent H beads on the base of the leg to the corresponding second and fourth H beads of the arch.

fig 26

Reposition the needle to emerge from the end of an H bead at the ankle position (to one side of the foot crease). Thread on 7B.

Referring to the photo below, lay the 7B beads across the top of the foot crease and secure with a stitch at the ankle position on the other side of the foot to suggest a spur strap. Finish off the thread ends neatly and securely.

Repeat from Step 8 to make a matching leg and foot.

13
Fig 27 shows the Peyote stitch grid for a third bugle bead tube. This tube will connect the two legs together to form the body and is made in G beads.

Prepare the needle with 1.2m of black thread and tie a keeper bead 15cm from the end.

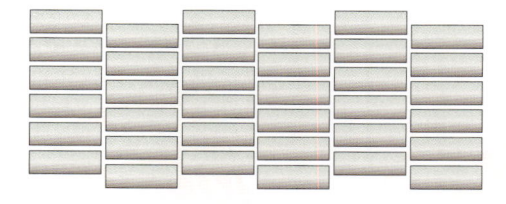

fig 27

Thread on 6G as shown along the bottom of the grid. Work in Peyote stitch to the top of the grid.

Roll the work into a tube and stitch the seam as before.

92

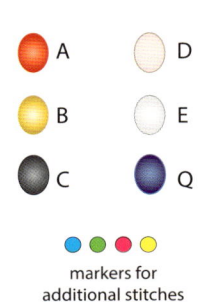

A	D
B	E
C	Q

markers for additional stitches

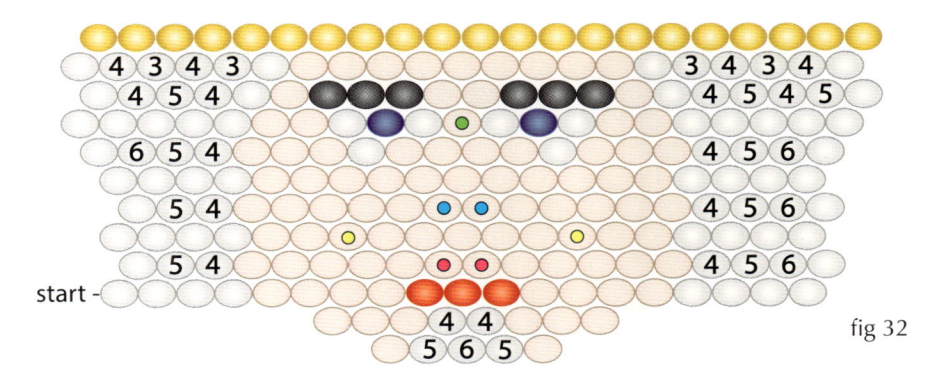

fig 32

14 Arrange the new tube between the two leg tubes as shown in fig 28. The top of all three tubes are in a line and the feet are facing forwards.

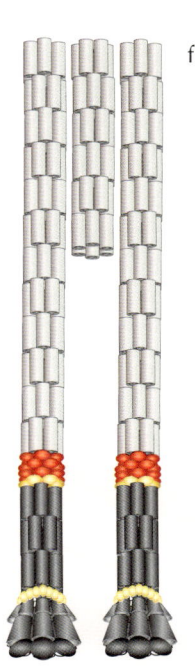

fig 28

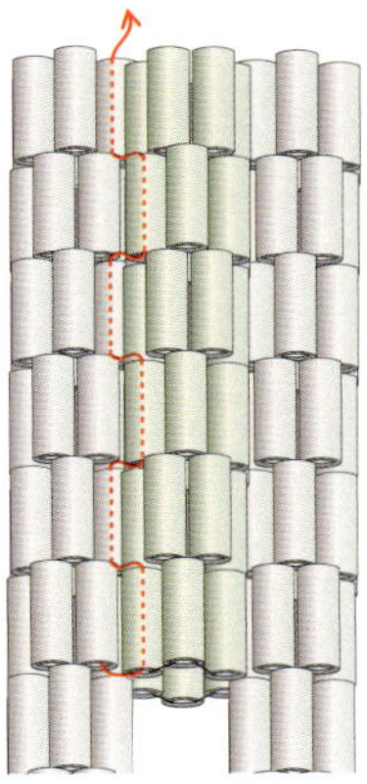

fig 29

Referring to fig 29 stitch the three tubes together, front and back, to make an oblong block (the body).

fig 30

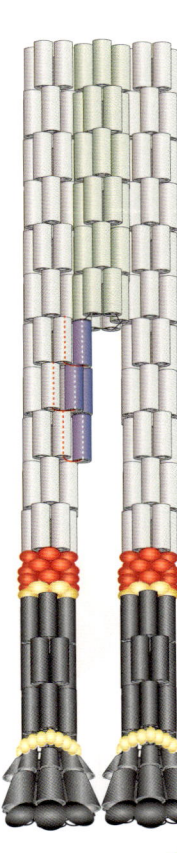

The G bead sections of the legs need a slightly thicker profile.

Referring to fig 30, extra G beads have been added to the inner thigh of the left leg. The new beads nestle neatly into the V-shaped depressions between the G beads of the Peyote stitch tube (see fig 31 showing the top view).

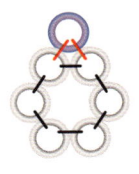

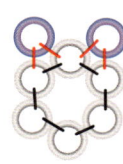

fig 31

Repositioning the needle as necessary, Square stitch sufficient G beads to the inner edge of the top three rows of the left thigh to taper the leg.

Repeat to make the other leg match.

Finish off the thread ends neatly and securely. Set aside.

15 The Head - The base layer of the head is made in Brick stitch. Fig 32 shows the grid with coloured dots and numbers indicating the attachment positions of the 3D features.

Prepare the needle with 1.5m of single, pale pink thread and tie a keeper bead 40cm from the end.

Starting at the row indicated make a Ladder stitch foundation row and work up to the top of the grid in Brick stitch.

Remove the keeper bead. Attach the needle to this short thread end and work the two part-rows below the foundation row. Leave the thread end loose and reattach the needle to the longer thread end on the top row of the work.

16 The Nose - Reposition the needle to emerge pointing upwards from the bead marked in green on fig 30 (between the eyes).

Thread on 1D and Square stitch the new D bead to the marked bead (fig 33).

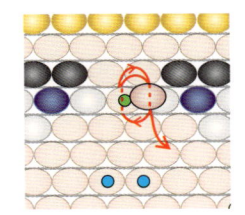

fig 33

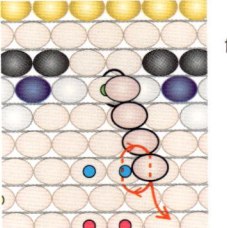

fig 34

Thread on 3D. Pass up through one of the beads marked in turquoise and Square stitch the last 1D to the marked bead (fig 34).

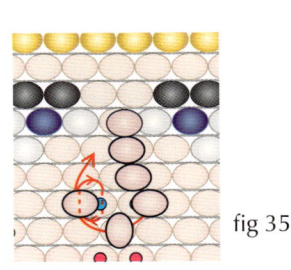

Thread on 2D. Pass down the second bead marked in turquoise and Square stitch the last 1D added to this marked bead (fig 35).

fig 35

Pass up the first 3D of the nose (fig 36).

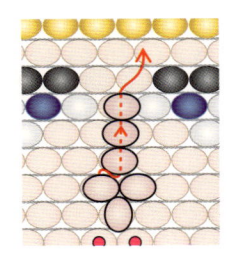

fig 36

93

19 The Hair and Beard - Fig 32 shows the E bead sections of the grid overlaid with numbers. These numbers give the bead counts for the hair and beard strands. The strands are made in F beads.

Prepare the needle with 1.2m of single white thread and tie a keeper bead 15cm from the end. Pass the needle through a few beads of the head to emerge pointing downwards from the E bead marked 5 in the bottom left-hand corner of the grid.

Thread on 5F. Leave aside the last 1F to anchor the strand and pass back up the previous 4F and the E bead on the head (fig 38). Pass down the adjacent E bead (marked 4) ready to start the next strand.

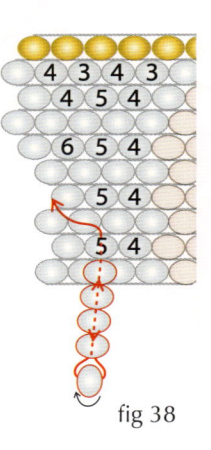

Following this technique work the remainder of this hair section adding strands of the correct length. Make sure each strand points downwards as in fig 38.

fig 38

Repeat to complete the beard and the remaining hair section.

Remove the needle and let the thread end hang loose. Remove the keeper bead and finish off this thread end neatly and securely.

17 Pass up and down the two face beads between the eyebrows to reverse the direction of the needle and pass back down the first three nose beads.

Thread on 1D. Pass through the single D bead at the bottom of the nose and back up through the new D bead (fig 37).

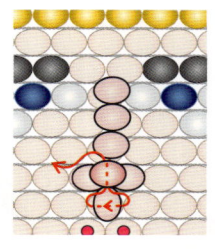

Secure this new D bead to the nose beads to the left and the right with Square stitches.

The nose is complete.

fig 37

20 The Hat - This is made in Brick stitch using H beads and a black thread. It is worked upwards from the top B bead row of the head.

Prepare the needle with 1.2m of single black thread and tie a keeper bead 15cm from the end. Pass the needle up through the first B bead along the top edge of the face.

Start the row with a 2H Brick stitch picking up the first loop of thread along the top edge of the head (fig 39).

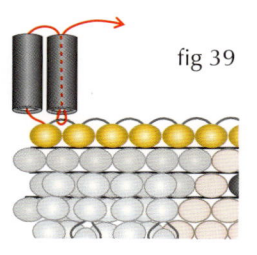

fig 39

Work single Brick stitches across the row to add 1H to each thread loop (21H).

At the end of the row thread on 1H and pass down the end B bead of the head row.

Reverse the needle direction by passing through the beads in the row below and pass back through last H bead added (fig 40).

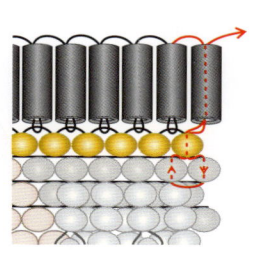

This end of the row now overhangs the previous row by half a bead's width. The row is 22H long.

18 The Moustache - Reposition the needle through the nose beads and the face to emerge pointing downwards from one of the beads marked in yellow shown on fig 32.

Thread on 4C and pass down the closest bead marked in cerise. Pass up the adjacent marked bead and thread on 4C. Pass up the remaining bead marked in yellow.

The moustache needs catching down into place.
Pass the needle down the adjacent D bead of the face and back through the last 2C added.
Gently pull this side of the moustache into a curve, secure with a small stitch to the threads between the beads of the face and pass through the following 2C of the moustache to emerge below the nose.

Repeat, in reverse, across the other half of the moustache to make the two halves match.

Finish off both pale pink thread ends neatly and securely without blocking any holes in or around the E bead sections of the work.

fig 40

Using the same technique at the start and end of each row, add two more rows of H beads (23H and 24H respectively).

21 The Seam - Roll the head and hat sections into a (slightly cone-shaped) tube.

The head seam is joined first using the white thread; the hat seam is stitched in black.

The Head Seam - The beads interlock well at the top and the bottom of the head seam. In the middle section the row ends butt up against one another rather than interlock - this part of the seam will need to be Square-stitched.

Attach the needle to the white thread and stitch the white head seam only. Add hair strands of appropriate lengths to conceal the join and finish off the white thread end neatly and securely.

The Hat Seam - Reattach the needle to the black thread and Square stitch the hat seam to complete.

22 Finishing the Hat - The hat needs a swag, a plume and a peak.

The Swag - Pass the needle up and down through the top row of H beads to emerge pointing down from the eighth H bead along from the seam. Thread on 17B.

Referring to fig 41 pass up the corresponding H bead on the other side of the centre front (to emerge on the top edge) to make a swag.

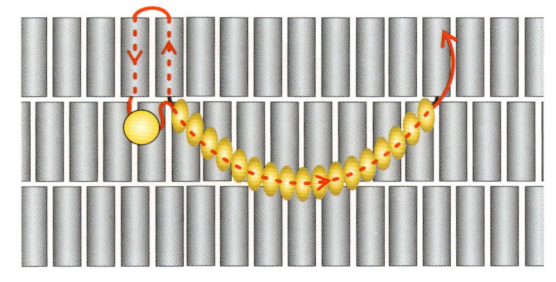

fig 41

Pass down the next H bead along the top edge and thread on 1J. Pass back through the swag beads to pull the J bead into place at this end of the swag and to emerge at the other end (fig 41).

Thread on 1J and pass up the next H bead back around the top row on this side of the hat.

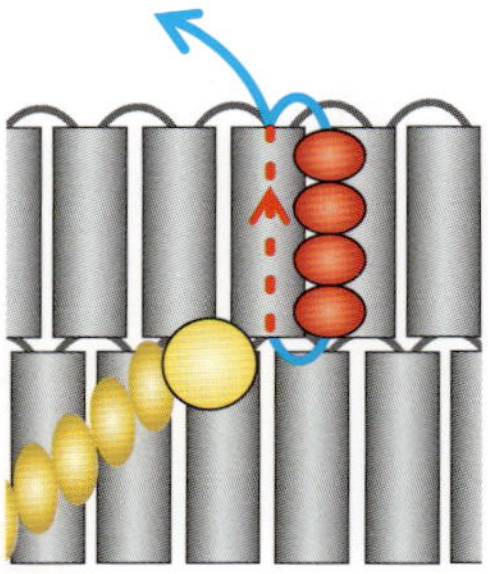

24 The Peak - Referring to fig 46 locate the two B beads highlighted in red on the top row of the head. Pass the needle through the hat beads to emerge from the closest of these two B beads.

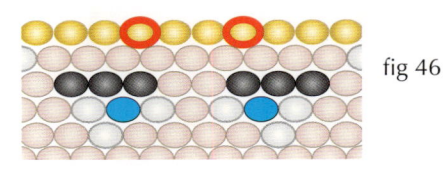

fig 46

Thread on 5B and pass through the other marked B bead on fig 46 to make an arch. Pass back through the 5B and the first marked B bead on fig 46.

Pass the needle back and forth through the 5B beads again to make the arch firm.

Slip 1B into the gap between the arch and the centre of the B bead row and secure with a Square stitch to the inside of the arch to complete the peak.

Finish off any remaining thread ends, on the head and hat, neatly and securely.

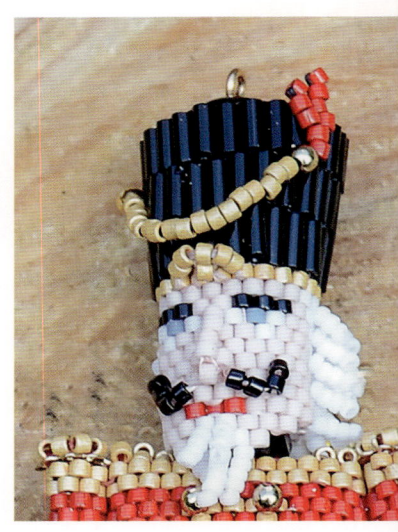

23 The Plume - Thread on 4A. Pass up through the same H bead again to make a strap of 4A on the outside of the hat (fig 42).

Pass the needle down the 4A. Use the tip of the needle to pick up a thread adjacent to the J bead (to anchor the turn) and pass back up the bottom 2A beads (fig 43).

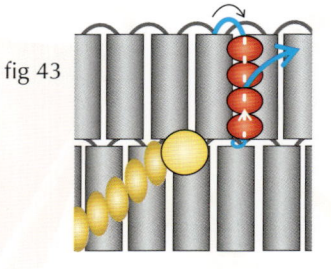

fig 42

fig 43

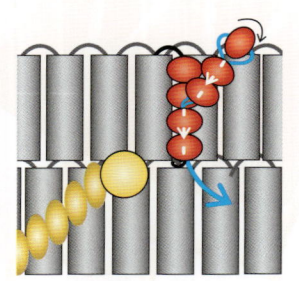

fig 44

Thread on 3A. Pass back down the first 2A just added and the bottom 2A of the 4A strap (fig 44).

Pick up a thread loop with the needle tip (to anchor the turn) and pass back up the first 4A of the plume.

Thread on 2A. Pass back down the first A just added and the following 4A to complete the plume (fig 45).

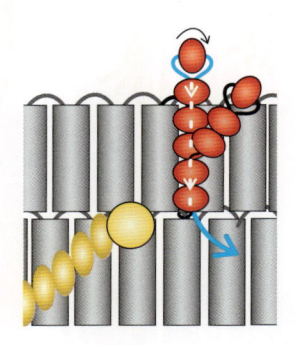

fig 45

25 Assembling the Soldier - Prepare the needle with a 1m length of single red thread and tie a keeper bead 15cm from the end.

Push the body section at the top of the legs into the main tunic tube. Flatten the tunic tube around the body section so the button bars are central at the front of the work and the V-pattern is central at the back.

Adjust the leg length so four rows of G beads are visible below the bottom edge of the tunic. The four thicknesses of beadwork are now stab-stitched together (see fig 47).

Carefully push the needle between the A beads at the very centre of the tunic front, between the G beads of both layers of the body and out between the beads at the centre back of the tunic.

Pass the needle through 2-3A beads on the back of the tunic and repeat the stab stitch from the back to the front of the work.

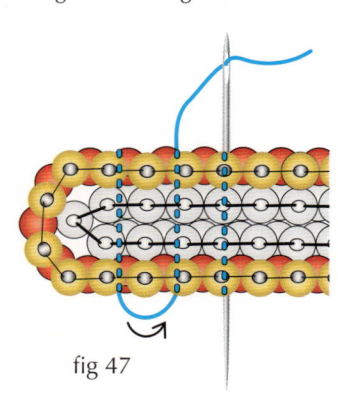

fig 47

Repeat these stitches twice more in different locations, to stop the body section from moving out of place.

26 The Shoulders - Look along the top edge of the tunic - the B beads should pair up across the gap between the front and back of the tunic. The shoulder stitches are attached to the last three pairs on each side.

Reposition the needle to emerge from the the top of the last B bead on the front of the tunic (fig 48).

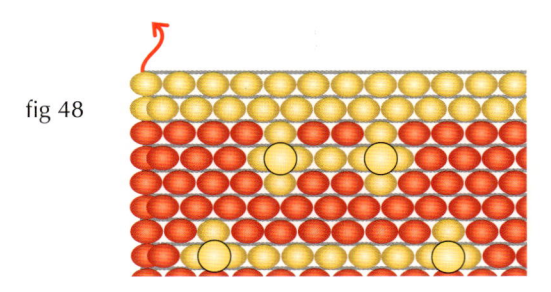

fig 48

fig 49

Thread on 2B. Pass down the corresponding B bead on the back edge and up the next 1B along (fig 49). The 2B stitch should sit across the top of the shoulder.

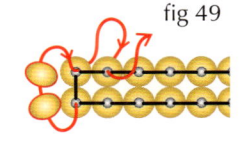

fig 50

Thread on 3B. Pass down the corresponding B bead on the front and up the next B bead along the top edge (fig 50). The 3B stitch should sit parallel to the previous 2B stitch.

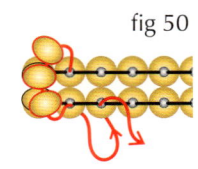

Repeat to add a second parallel 3B strap linking the next pair of B beads along the tunic top row. This shoulder is complete. Repeat to create the second shoulder at the other side of the tunic.

27 Place the arms on either side of the tunic so the double row of B beads at the top is level with the same two rows on each arm. Make sure the pattern on the sleeves is on the outer edge of each arm and the hands are facing palm inwards to the bottom of the tunic.

Carefully observe which beads at the top of the arm and the tunic are in contact.

The top four or five horizontal rows of each arm need to be Square-stitched to the matching beads on the edge of the tunic. Use the attached thread ends to make the necessary stitches.

Finish off all remaining thread ends on the tunic and the arms.

28 The Belt - The belt completes the tunic. It is made in Ladder stitch.

Prepare the needle with 1m of doubled black thread and tie a keeper bead 15cm from the end.

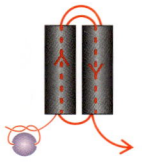

fig 51

Thread on 2H. Pass up the first 1H and down the second to bring the two beads parallel (fig 51).

Thread on 1H. Pass down through the previous 1H and up the new H bead (fig 52).
Work twelve more 1H stitches.

fig 52

The Belt Buckle - Thread on 3B to make the next Ladder stitch, 1H for the second and 3B for the third Ladder stitch (fig 53).

Thread on 3B. Pass up the previous 3B stitch. Thread on 3B and pass down the last 3B Ladder stitch (fig 54).

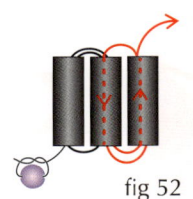

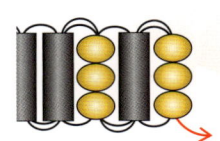

fig 53

Continue with single 1H stitches until the belt fits around the tunic just below the lowest J beads on the front of the design.

Link the two ends of the belt together with a Square stitch.

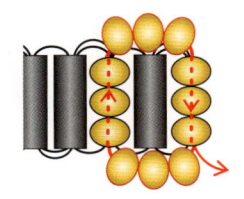

fig 54

To make sure the belt cannot slip, make two stab stiches through the full depth of the work (see fig 47). Make the stitches carefully and pass through at least 2H after each stitch to spread the connections across the width of the work. Finish off the thread ends neatly and securely.

29 Attaching the Head - Make a 4mm hook at one end of the wire. Pass the other end of the wire between the legs, up through the hole in the centre of the small G bead tube in the middle of the body and out between the shoulders at the top of the tunic.

Thread on 1N and 1M.

Thread on the head so the bottom row sits on the N bead and the M bead is concealed inside the lower section of the head.

Thread the L and the K beads onto the wire and push down into the head and hat cavity. The K bead will sit just proud of the top of the hat. Trim the excess wire length to 8mm and turn a neat loop with round-nosed pliers.

Suspend the completed Nutcracker Soldier on a length of clear monofilament thread.

Tin Drum

You Will Need

Materials

6g of size 3 transparent blue AB bugle beads A
6g of size 2 silver lined gold bugle beads B
4g of size 10 transparent blue AB seed beads C
3g of size 10 silver lined red seed beads D
Four size 8 metallic gold seed beads E
Two 5cm squares of 150gsm Pergamano ™ parchment
One 25x250mm strip of dark blue cartridge paper or thin card
One wooden cocktail stick
Navy blue size D beading thread
Craft glue and sticky tape

Tools

A size 10 beading needle
A pair of scissors to trim the threads
Seven fine dressmakers' pins

drum measures 35x25mm plus hanging loop

A *young male dancer, dressed as a drummer boy, weaves in and out of the battle scene in The Nutcracker ballet. This smart, shiny drum made with a bugle bead shell, parchment skins and wooden sticks, would do him proud.*

The Decoration is Made in Four Stages

A bugle bead shell is made first.

A parchment skin is stitched to each end of the shell.

The rims are added to the top and bottom of the shell.

The cording is attached between the two rims.

A hanging loop and the drum sticks are added to complete the decoration.

Extra Info....
The core of the drum shell is made from a band of Peyote-stitched bugle beads. Two lengths of bugle beads are used in the same weave.

It is important to monitor the tension in the thread as tiny differences in the diameter of the bugle beads can cause the band to distort if the thread is pulled too tight.

The band should be flexible and completely flat. If the shorter bugle beads, along the edges of the band, are being pulled out of alignment it may suggest that the tension is a little too tight at the turn of the rows.

Also see the Extra Info box on page 41 for general notes regarding bugle beads.

1 The Drum Shell - This is made in Peyote stitch.

Prepare the needle with 1.5m of doubled thread and tie a keeper bead 15cm from the ends. The first layer is made in Peyote stitch.

Thread on 1B, 2A and 1B for the first row.

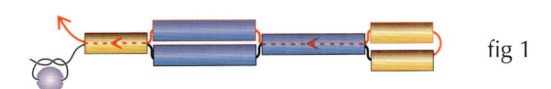

fig 1

Add 1B and 1A for the next row to start the Peyote stitch (fig 1) and add a Peyote stitch row of 1B and 1A (fig 2).

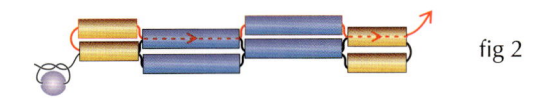

fig 2

Repeat the last row until you have 40B along each edge.

Bring the first and last rows together, interlock the A and B beads and stitch the seam to make a tube.

2 Roll up the strip of card gently, so it retains its springiness, and fit it into the bugle tube (fig 3).

Make sure the edges of the card do not stand proud of the beadwork - trim to fit if necessary.

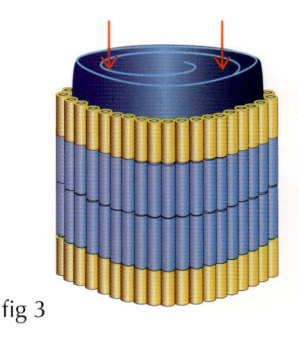

fig 3

To fully expand the drum shell, remove and increase the diameter of the card cylinder by 1-2mm. Secure the overlap with a tab of sticky tape before carefully returning to the bugle tube.

The drum shell is complete.

Extra Info...
Pergamano ™ parchment is a robust, translucent, vellum-like paper product which resists tearing.

It is more conventionally used in paper crafting to create delicate embossed and pierced designs.

3 The Skins - These are made with the Pergamano parchment and attached using an adaptation of Ladder stitch.

Place a parchment square over the end of the drum shell. The B bead holes will be visible through the parchment.

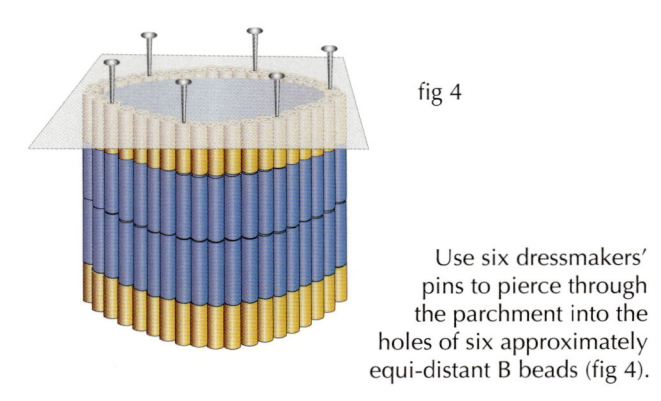

fig 4

Use six dressmakers' pins to pierce through the parchment into the holes of six approximately equi-distant B beads (fig 4).

Use a separate pin to prick holes in the parchment directly above each of the remaining 34B bead holes.

With the six pins still in place, carefully trim the parchment into a neat circle no more than 1mm outside the pricked circle.

4 Each B bead corresponds to a parchment hole - this pairing must be maintained throughout.

The parchment holes will be referred to as H.

Continuing with the doubled thread, reposition the needle to emerge from the top of a B bead and pass up through the corresponding H to emerge above the parchment skin.

Remove the six pins.

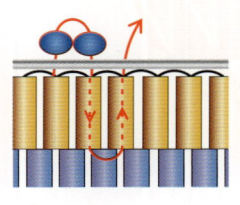

fig 5

5 Thread on 2C. Pass down the next H along and the corresponding 1B.

Pass up the next B bead and the corresponding H (fig 5).

Thread on 1C. Pass down the previous 1C and the corresponding H and B bead.

Pass up the following 1B, H and the new C (fig 6).

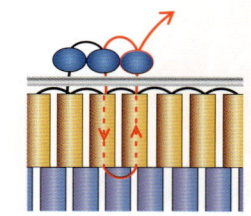

fig 6

Thread on 1C. Pass down the next H and 1B along. Pass up the following 1B and H (fig 7). This is modified Ladder stitch.

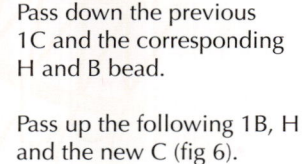

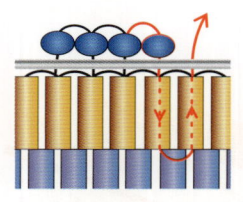

fig 7

Repeat the stitches as in figs 6 and 7 until the row is complete (40C in total).

Link the first and last C beads with a Square stitch (fig 8).

Remove the needle leaving the double thread end loose.

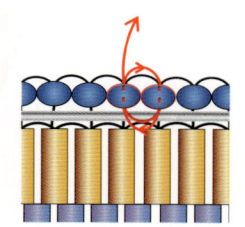

fig 8

6 The Rim - An extra row of Ladder-stitched B and C beads is added around the outside of the B and C end of the drum shell to create a rim.

As the new rim row will have a larger circumference than the drum shell itself; the overall length of the rim row and the connections to the shell will need to be adjusted as you work to get a good fit.

Prepare the needle with 1.5m of single thread and tie a keeper bead 15cm from the end. Pass down through 1C, H and 1B of the previous row.

Thread on 1B and 1C. Pass down the previous 1C, H and 1B and back up the new beads to make a Ladder stitch (fig 9).

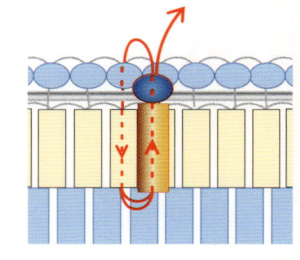

fig 9

Add two Ladder stitches to extend the new row to three stitches (fig 10).

fig 10

Wrap these new stitches around the edge of the shell matching up the last stitch made with the nearest B/C stitch on the edge of the shell (see fig 11 showing the best connection as a top view).

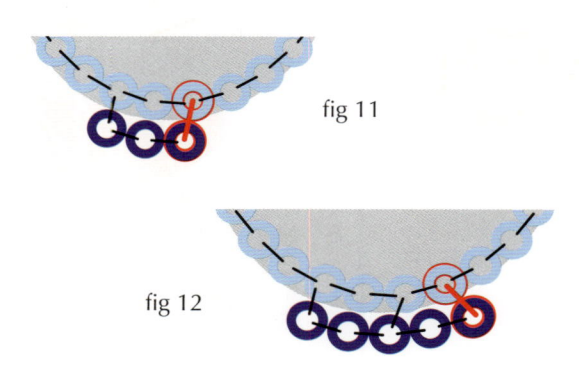

fig 11

fig 12

Pass down the 1C, H and 1B on the drum shell and up the 1B and 1C of the new rim row (as fig 9).

Add two Ladder stitches as before and connect to the drum shell easing the fit by connecting to the most appropriate B and C beads - see fig 12 showing the best connection is now only one bead's width around the shell.

Repeat to the end of the row making adjustments as necessary to fix every second Ladder stitch of the rim to the most appropriate B and C shell beads (approx 48 stitches).

100

7 The B beads just added around the rim require a second pass of thread to pull them into a neat alignment.

Work in Ladder stitch passing up and down the B beads of the rim only (fig 13). Repeat all around the rim.

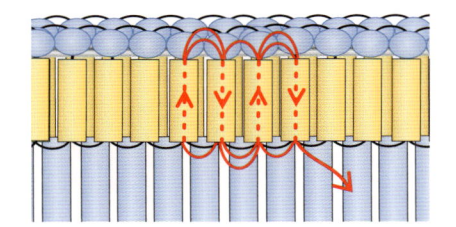

fig 13

Remove the needle leaving the thread end loose.

Repeat Steps 3 to 7 on the other end of the drum shell.

Extra Info....
The following instructions to add the cording assume a rim of 48B has been added to each end your drum shell.

However as the two rims were made in situ, and eased into the best possible fit around the drum shell, you may find that your rims do not match these numbers.
Indeed, the rim at the top of the drum may contain a different number of B beads to the rim at the bottom.

If this is the case, you will have to make a slight adjustment, or two, to keep the zig-zag spacing neat. If you keep the adjustments small, to one bead at a time, they will not be noticeable on the finished drum.

As you work the cording watch carefully how taut the cording stitches are pulling between the two rims - you may get a better fit with one more, or one less D bead on some stitches.

Alternatively you may need to select the sixth or the eighth B bead along the rim to complete the stitch.

8 The Cording - The zig-zag decoration around the drum passes from one rim to the other.

Reposition the needle to emerge from the inner edge of the rim and thread on 10D.

Pass the needle down the third B bead around the opposite rim and up the next B along (fig 14).

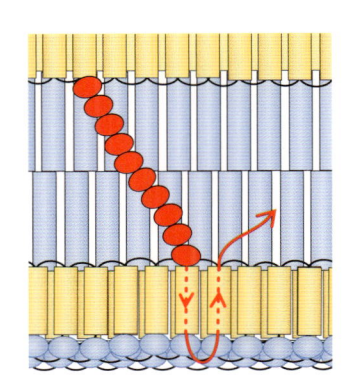

fig 14

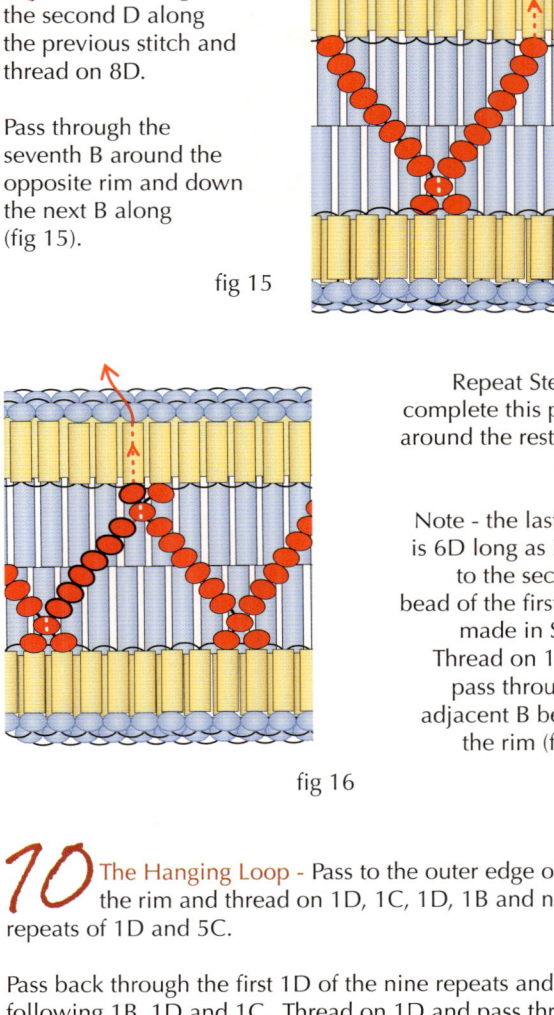

9 Thread on 1D. Pass through the second D along the previous stitch and thread on 8D.

Pass through the seventh B around the opposite rim and down the next B along (fig 15).

fig 15

Repeat Step 9 to complete this pattern around the rest of the drum.

Note - the last stitch is 6D long as it links to the second D bead of the first stitch made in Step 8. Thread on 1D and pass through the adjacent B bead on the rim (fig 16).

fig 16

10 The Hanging Loop - Pass to the outer edge of the rim and thread on 1D, 1C, 1D, 1B and nine repeats of 1D and 5C.

Pass back through the first 1D of the nine repeats and the following 1B, 1D and 1C. Thread on 1D and pass through the adjacent C bead on the edge of the rim.

Reinforce the loop and finish off all remaining thread ends neatly and securely.

The Sticks - Cut 3.5cm from each end of the cocktail stick. Glue 2E onto the pointed ends of each piece.
Using a thread to tone with the stick colour, attach the sticks to the rim with two or three firm stitches. Apply a little glue to the stitches to stop the sticks from slipping out.

Sugar Plum Fairy

You Will Need

Materials

4g of DB2189 semi-frost silver lined honeysuckle Delica beads A
3.5g of DB2174 semi-frost silver lined dyed pink Delica beads B
1.5g of DB0041 silver lined crystal Delica beads C
4g of DB0354 matt light rose Delica beads D
4.5g of DB0351 matt white Delica beads E
0.1g of DB0755 matt opaque light blue Delica beads F
2.5g of size 15 silver lined crystal seed beads G
One 8mm white pearl round bead H
One 9x7mm through-hole drop glass bead J
30cm of 0.8mm silver plated half-hard wire
Pale pink and white size D beading thread

Tools

A size 10 beading needle
A size 12 beading needle
A pair of scissors to trim the threads
Wire cutters, flat-nosed and round-nosed pliers

Sugar Plum Fairy measures 9.5 x 3.5cm plus hanging loop

Sparkling perfection dancing to tinkling bells, the Sugar Plum Fairy's solo entrances even the most fidgety member of the audience. Lots of techniques and small details mean this is a project for more experienced beaders.

The Decoration is Made in Six Stages

The main body and the tutu (skirt) are made first.

The arms are made and attached at the shoulders.

The legs are made as a separate unit.

The head, complete with tiara, and the neck are made next.

The wings are made.

A wire armature is used to assemble the legs, body and head. The tutu and wings are added and the final pose is secured.

This decoration is made in a combination of Brick stitch, Square stitch, Peyote stitch and Tubular Herringbone stitch. If you require more information about these techniques please see Beadwork Basics on pages 10 and 11.

Use the size 10 needle for all steps unless stated otherwise.

fig 1

A
B
C
D

1 The Body and Tutu -
Fig 1 shows a Brick stitch grid for the main body section.

Prepare the needle with 2m of single pink thread and tie a keeper bead 50cm from the end.

Starting at the row indicated on fig 1 make the 15A foundation row in Ladder stitch.

Work in Brick stitch upwards from the foundation row making shaping stitches where necessary. Finish with the needle emerging from the bead marked W.

Remove the needle leaving the thread end loose. Remove the keeper bead and attach the needle to this thread end.

As shown in fig 1 work the shaping rows below the foundation row.
Remove the needle leaving the thread end loose and reattach it to the thread end at W.

2
Roll the beadwork into a cone so bead W meets bead X and bead Y meets bead Z - this is the centre-back seam.

Pass down bead X and up bead W. Pass down bead X and the following 1D along the seam to make a Square stitch (fig 2).

Pairing up the beads across the seam continue in Square stitch to secure the join down to beads Y and Z.

Finish with the needle emerging downwards from bead Y (fig 3).

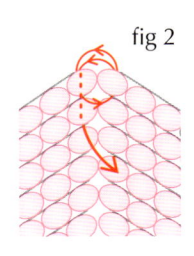

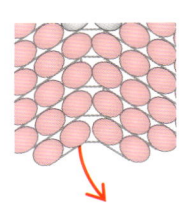

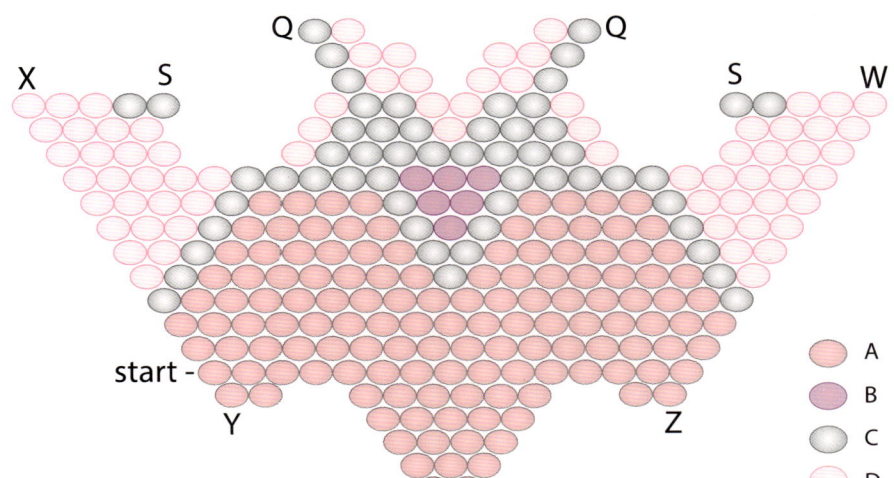

fig 2

fig 3

3
Add a centralised 3A Brick stitch row across the four A beads at the base of the centre back seam (fig 4).

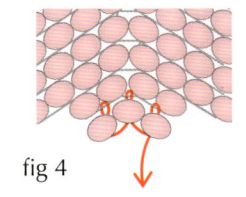

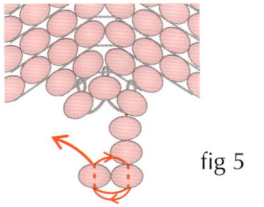

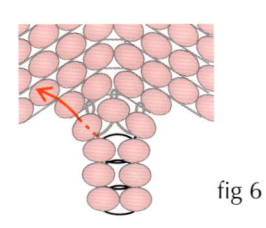

fig 4

fig 5

Thread on 3A. Thread on 1A and Square stitch to the previous A bead (fig 5).

Thread on 1A and Square stitch to the middle 1A of the 3A. Repeat to add a third 1A Square stitch. Pass the needle up through the following edge A bead (fig 6).

fig 6

Reinforce the 6x2 block just made with an extra pass of thread. Remove the needle leaving the thread end loose. Set the body section aside.

103

4 The Tutu - Prepare the needle with 1.5m of single pink thread and tie a keeper bead 15cm from the end.

Thread on 30G. Pass the needle through the first G bead to make a ring (fig 7).

fig 7

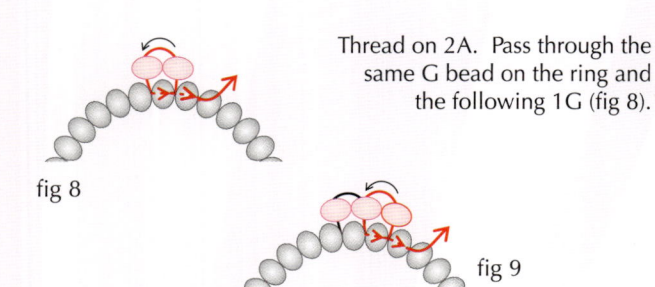

Thread on 2A. Pass through the same G bead on the ring and the following 1G (fig 8).

fig 8

fig 9

Thread on 1A. Pass down the previous A bead, the new G bead on the ring and the following 1G (fig 9).

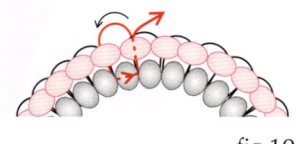

fig 10

Repeat this stitch 27 times.

Link the first and last A beads of the ring together to emerge from the top of the first A bead (fig 10).
These 30A beads form the foundation row for the first row of Brick stitch.

5 Thread on 2A and make a standard first stitch for a row of Brick stitch (fig 11).

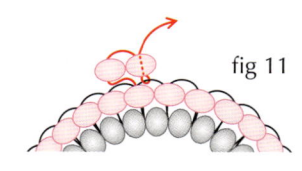

fig 11

Thread on 1B. Pick up the same thread loop along the foundation row and pass back through the B bead (fig 12). This is an increase Brick stitch.

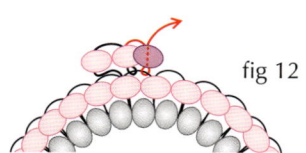

fig 12

Make two single Brick stitches attaching 1A to each of the next two thread loops.
Thread on 1B and make an increase stitch by picking up the same thread loop as the previous stitch.

Repeat the last three stitches to the end of the row and link the first bead of the row to the last to complete the ring (45 beads in total).

6 The colour sequence for the next row is 2B, 1A, 2B, 1A, 2B, 1A. Every fourth bead of the row is added as an increase stitch.

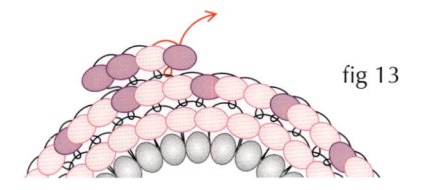

fig 13

Start the row with a 2B stitch.
Add a 1A Brick stitch on the next thread loop.
Thread on 1B and make an increase Brick stitch attaching it to the same thread loop as the previous 1A (fig 13).

Add 1B, 1A and 1B as single Brick stitches. Thread on 1B and Brick stitch to the same thread loop as the previous B bead to make the increase.

Maintaining this stitch order (three single / one increase) and the colour repeat of 2B and 1A, work to the end of the row (60 beads in total). Link the first bead to the last as before.

Make the next row in B beads only without adding any increase stitches and link the last bead to the first (60B).

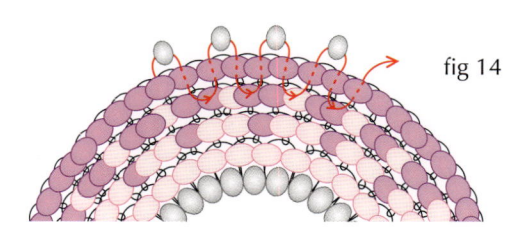

fig 14

The final row is made in G beads.
Thread on 1G pass down the next 1B along and up the following 1B. Repeat all around the edge of the tutu (fig 14).

Reverse the needle direction and repeat in the opposite direction to add 1G into each gap. The extra pass of thread will help to stiffen the edge of the tutu.

Finish off this thread end neatly and securely. Leave the other thread end attached and set the tutu aside.

7 The Arms - These are made using a modified version of Tubular Herringbone stitch. A Ladder-stitched foundation is required.

fig 15

Prepare the needle with 1.5m of single pink thread and tie a keeper bead 40cm from the end. Thread on 4D. Pass up the first 2D and down the second 2D to make a Ladder stitch (fig 15).

fig 16

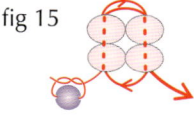

Make one 2D Ladder stitch (fig 16).

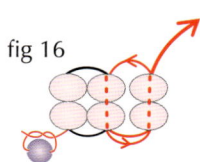

Link the first stitch to the last to make a small drum and reposition the needle to emerge from the top of the first column (fig 17).

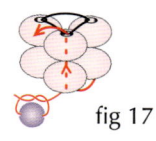

The foundation is complete.

fig 17

104

8 The needle is emerging from the top of column 1.

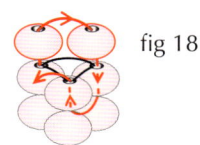

fig 18

Thread on 2D. Pass down the top 1D of column 2 and up the top 1D of column 3 (fig 18).

Thread on 1D. Pass down the top 1D of column 3 and up the top 2D of column 1. Make sure the new D bead sits horizontally across the top of column 3 (the elbow column, fig 19).

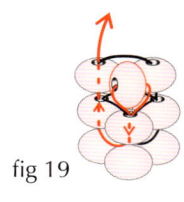

fig 19

9 Thread on 2D. Pass down the top 1D of column 2 and through the horizontal D of column 3 (fig 20).

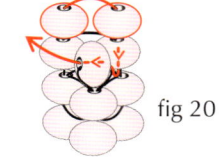

fig 20

Thread on 1D. Pass through the previous 1D again to bring the two beads parallel (a Square stitch)*. Pass up the top 2D of column 1 (fig 21).

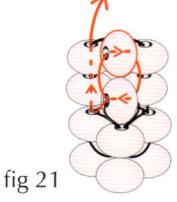

Repeat Step 9 four more times. Repeat Step 9 to *.

fig 21

10 The Elbow - Pass back through the new 1D and add a second D bead with a Square stitch to extend this column. Pass back through the previous two 1D stitches (fig 22).

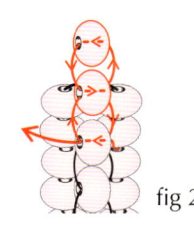

fig 22

Complete the row by passing up the top 2D of column 1.

Make the next row as Step 9 passing through the top horizontal D bead of column 3 - the previous 1D will stick out to form the elbow (fig 23).

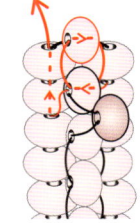

Add four more rows as Step 9.

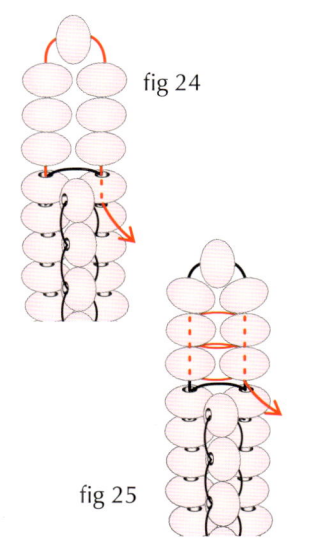

fig 23

fig 24

11 The Hand - Thread on 7D and pass down the top 1D of column 2 to make a long loop (fig 24).

Square stitch the bottom two pairs of D beads together (fig 25). Secure the last 1D from the elbow column to the bottom 2D of the hand to tuck it in neatly.

Finish off this thread end neatly and securely.

fig 25

12 Attaching the Arms to the Body - Remove the keeper bead at the start of the arm (the top of the arm) and attach the needle to this thread end.

The shoulder strap of the bodice is made from 5C beads. To ease the attachment of the arm to the main body block, the 5C shoulder strap beads are Square-stitched to the top of the arm first (see figs 26 and 27 showing the top and side views of the arm).

fig 26

Referring to fig 26 Square stitch three individual C beads to the top 1D bead on the elbow column of the arm. Square stitch 1C to each of the two remaining D beads on the top row of the arm.

Link these five C beads together with Square stitches to complete the band (fig 27).

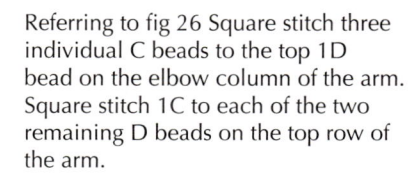

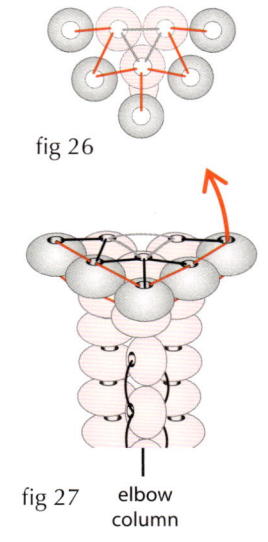

fig 27   elbow column

Fig 28 shows the attachment locations for the arm. The two ends of the C bead row just added at the top of the arm need to match up with the two C beads marked S and Q on the body grid.

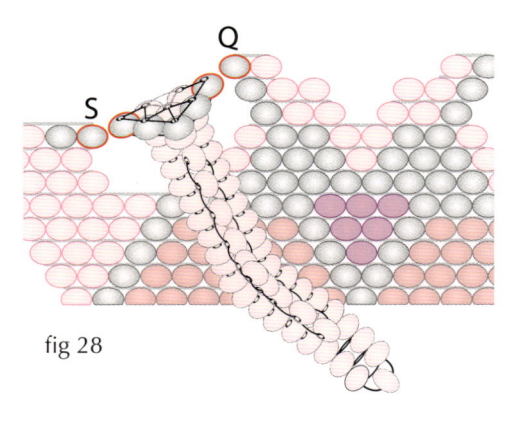

fig 28

Offer the arm up to the shoulder position on the body and line up the C beads as shown. The two connections are made using Square stitch. Make the required stitches so the holes in the connecting two C beads at each position are parallel and the arm is secure.

13 The Shoulders - Three D bead straps are added across the top of the shoulder and the arm. These straps neaten the shoulder and help to make the previous connections stronger. Fig 29 shows the top view of the straps required.

fig 29

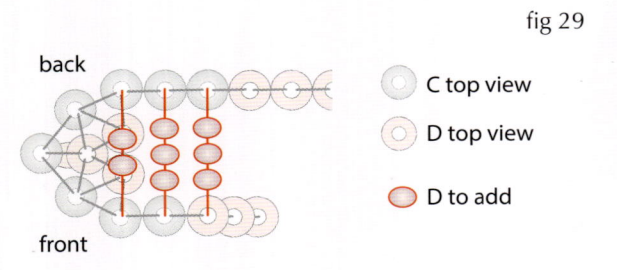

back

front

○ C top view
◎ D top view
● D to add

Line up the top of the shoulder as shown in fig 29 and add these parallel straps using straight stitches passing back and forth between the top beads of the weave.

To stabilise and neaten the two newly-added 3D stitches, Square stitch the middle 1D of both straps together.

Repeat from Step 7 to make and attach the second arm.

Leave the longest thread end attached and finish off all other ends neatly and securely.

14 The Legs - The legs are made in Tubular Herringbone stitch. A 6E deep foundation is required - this is made in Square stitch.

Prepare the needle with 1.5m of single pink thread and tie a keeper bead 15cm from the end. Thread on 6E for the first row.

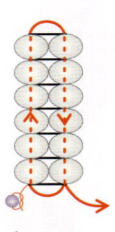

Square stitch a row of 6E to the first row and reinforce both rows by passing through the first row and back through the second (fig 30).

Add six more reinforced Square-stitched rows (columns) of 6E (eight columns in total) (fig 31).

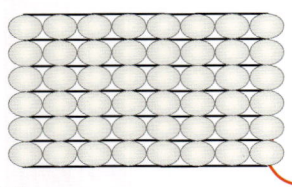

fig 30

fig 31

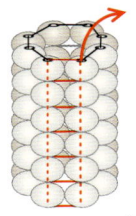

fig 32

Roll the work so the first row matches up with the eighth row and Square stitch the seam to complete a tube (fig 32).

Flatten the tube to make a block with four columns along each side and the needle emerging from the end of the second column from the corner (fig 33).

This block is divided into two sections of four columns - each section will support one leg (see fig 33).

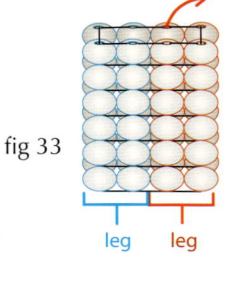

fig 33

leg   leg

15 The First Leg - The top of the leg is 6E beads in diameter so the first row of Tubular Herringbone stitch needs to be an increase row.

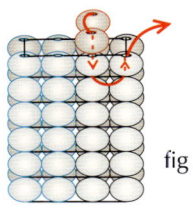

Thread on 2E. Pass the needle down the top 1E of the column on the opposite side of the block and up the adjacent 1E at the end (fig 34).

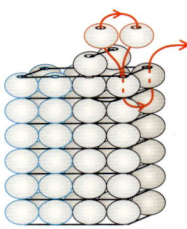

fig 34

Thread on 2E. Pass down the same 1E on the block and up the top 1E of the next column around (fig 35).

fig 35

Thread on 2E. Pass down the same 1E on the block and up the top 2E of the first column (fig 36).

The row has increased to 6E (six columns).

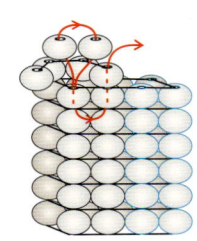

fig 36

16 Working on the new six columns only, nominate the current position as column 1 and thread on 2E. Pass down the top 1E of the second column and up the top 1E of the third (fig 37).

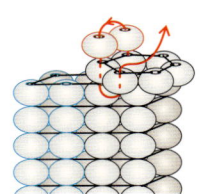

fig 37

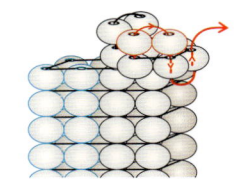

Thread on 2E. Pass down the top 1E of the fourth column and up the top 1E of the fifth (fig 38).

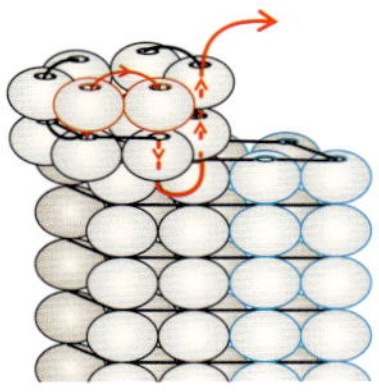

fig 38

Thread on 2E. Pass down the top 1E of the sixth column. Pass up the top 2E of the first column to complete the row and reposition the needle ready to start the next (fig 39). This is Tubular Herringbone stitch.

Repeat to add 13 more rows of 6E.

fig 39

Extra Info....
Thread colour is an important consideration in beadwork as it always peeks through at the edges and on shaping stitches.

Although white beads are used for the legs, a pink thread is chosen to impart a pinkish tinge.

The head is made with a white thread. This ensures that the white beads of the hair stay brilliant white and the face (made from pale pink beads) will be a little more luminous.

77 The Knee - The leg is narrowed and slightly bent to make the knee.

Knee Row 1 - The needle is emerging at the top of column 1. Thread on 1E, pass down the top 1E of column 2 and up the top 1E of column 3 (fig 40).

Thread on 3E to form the knee cap. Pass down the top 1E of column 4 and up the top 1E of column 5.

Referring to fig 41, thread on 1E and pass down column 6. Pass up column 1 and the single bead added in fig 40 (fig 41).

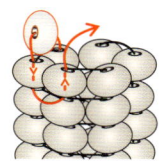

fig 40

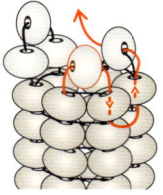

fig 41

Knee Row 2 - Thread on 2E. Referring to fig 42 pass through the single E bead at the top of columns 5 and 6 to point away from the knee cap. Pass up the 1E where this row started and the first 1E of the new 2E stitch (fig 42).

Two columns have been created from the two single E beads added on Knee Row 1.

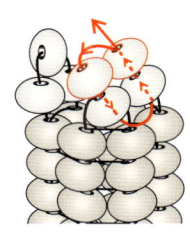

fig 42

Pass through the middle 1E of the 3E knee cap and thread on 2E. Pass through the middle E again to pull the 2E parallel to one another and establish two columns for the lower leg.

Pass down the top 1E of the following new column and up the top 1E of the next (fig 43).

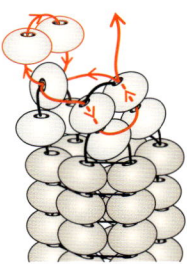

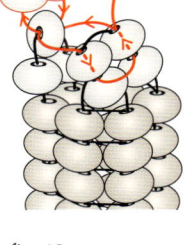

fig 43

Knee Row 3 - The direction of work now reverses with the first stitch being taken across the back of the knee.

Thread on 2E. Pass down the top 1E of the next (new) column and up the first 1E of the 2E at the knee cap (fig 44).

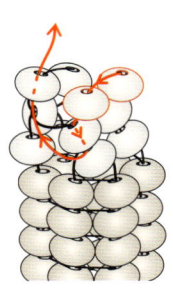

fig 44

Thread on 2E and pass down the following 1E and up the top 2E of the following column (fig 45).

The knee is complete and the six columns have been reduced to four.

Continue to work in this direction to add 14 rows of 2 x 2E stitches to make the lower leg.

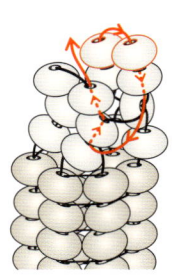

fig 45

78 The Foot - Continuing in Tubular Herringbone stitch make the next three rows with 2B for the first stitch (the sole) and 2E for the second (the top of the foot).

Foot Row 4 - Make one 2B stitch. Make the second stitch with 3E (as for the kneecap) and complete the row as before.

Foot Row 5 - Make one 2B stitch. The needle will to emerge from the first E bead of the 3E stitch on the previous row. Pass through the following 1E.
Thread on 3B. Pass through the same 1E and the last 1E of the previous row (fig 46).

Pass up the top 2B of the following column to complete Row 5 and to reposition the needle for Row 6.

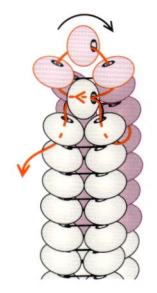

fig 46

Foot Row 6 - Thread on 3B. Pass down the top 1B of the following column and up the first 2B of the 3B stitch made on Row 5. Thread on 3B and complete this stitch as in Row 5 (fig 47).

Pass the needle up through the top 2B of the following column ready to make Row 7.

fig 47

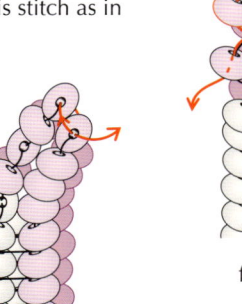

fig 48

Foot Row 7 - Square stitch the middle two B beads from the previous row together (fig 48).

Add 1B to make the tip of the point making a Square stitch connection to both previous single B beads (fig 49).

fig 49

19 Foot Row 8 - The Heel - Pass up and down the two columns of B beads along the sole, pulling the thread firmly to arch the instep.

Finish with the needle emerging from first row of B beads at the heel (fig 50).

fig 50

Thread on 2B. Pass through the first 3B of the same column along the sole to emerge at the heel. Pull firmly (fig 51). Repeat to add a 2B stitch to the adjacent B bead column of the sole. Square stitch these two 2B stitches together.

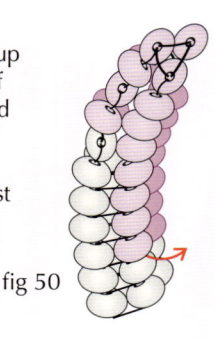

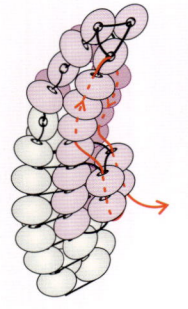

fig 51

Pass the needle down and up the heel and sole beads pulling firmly to secure the curve (fig 52).

Finish off the thread end neatly and securely.

fig 52

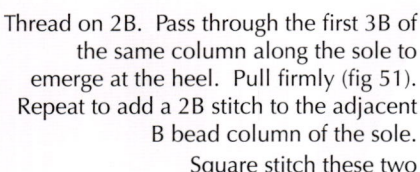

20 The Second Leg - Prepare the needle as in Step 14. You need to identify the start position on the block carefully to produce the second leg as a mirror image of the first.

Examine the first leg - trace the two columns at the front of the leg (the knee cap) back up to the foundation block and identify the bead supporting these two columns at the front of the leg. Call this bead X.

Referring to fig 54 bead X is at one corner. To make a mirror image the front of the second leg must attach to the opposite corner at bead Y.

Pass the needle through the beads of the block to emerge from the top of bead Z.

Referring to Steps 15 to 19 make a mirror image leg and foot. Note - The first stitch must pass across the depth of the block i.e. parallel to the first stitch of the first leg (see fig 54 which is a mirror image of fig 34). This means that you will be working the Tubular Herringbone stitch in the opposite direction to the first leg (figs 35 to 52 must also be reversed).

fig 53

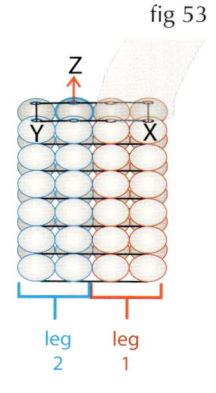

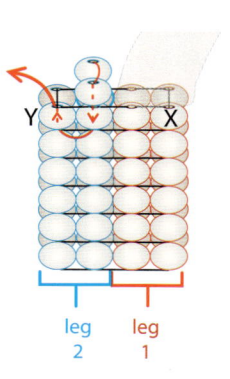

leg 2 | leg 1

fig 54

leg 2 | leg 1

21 The Head - Fig 55 shows a Brick stitch grid for the head.

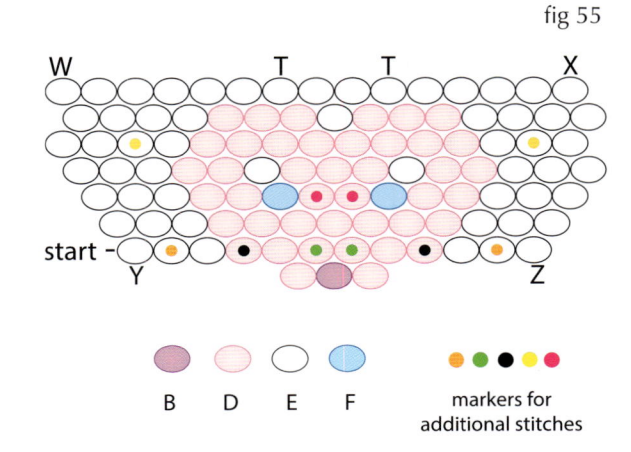

fig 55

W T T X

start - Y   Z

● ○ ○ ○   ● ● ● ● ●
B D E F   markers for additional stitches

Prepare the needle with 1.8m of white thread and tie a keeper bead 40cm from the end. Make the foundation row in Ladder stitch starting at the row indicated in fig 55 and work upwards to the top of the grid in Brick stitch.

Remove the needle and leave the thread end loose at X.

22 Remove the keeper bead and attach the needle to this thread end. Reposition the needle and add the last three beads below the foundation row as shown on the grid. Finish with the needle emerging downwards from the last D bead added.

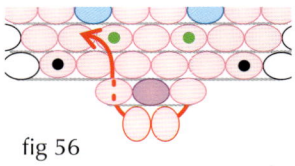

The Chin - Thread on 2D and pass up through the D bead at the other end of this short row to make the chin (fig 56).

fig 56

The Nose - Pass through the grid to emerge upwards from the closest bead marked in green. Thread on 1D and pass up one of the beads marked in cerise between the eyes. Pass down the adjacent marked bead, the new 1D and the other bead marked in green (fig 57).

fig 57

Pass through the work to emerge pointing downwards from the closest bead marked in black.

Thread on 3D. Square stitch the last 1D of the new 3D to the 2D chin beads added in fig 56 (fig 58).

Position the new 1D behind the 2D chin. Thread on 2D and pass up the bead marked in black on the other side of the chin.

Remove the needle leaving the thread end loose.

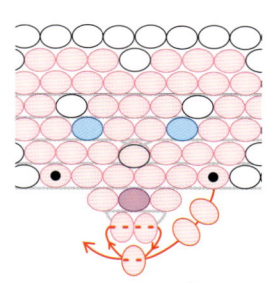

fig 58

108

23
Attach the needle to the thread end at X.

As in Step 2, roll the beadwork to match up X with W and Y with Z, interlock and stitch the stepped edges and Square stitch the remaining four rows of the centre back seam.

Pass the needle back up to the top edge of the seam.

Push the J bead into the head cavity so the wider end of the drop is just showing above the top of the hairline.

24
The top of the J bead needs to be concealed.

Add a series of parallel, front to back, E bead straps across the top of the head (see fig 59 for guidance) - six straps should suffice.

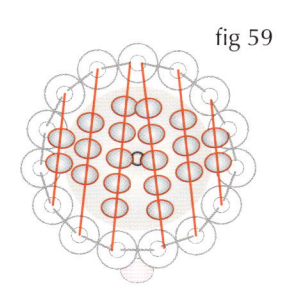

Finish with the needle emerging from the top of one of the beads marked T on the head grid (see fig 55).

fig 59

25
The Tiara - Thread on 9G.
Pass down the other bead marked T and up the adjacent E bead inside the new arch (fig 60).

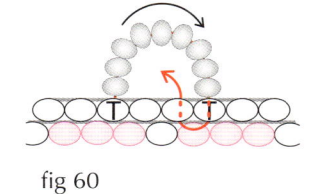

Thread on 2G.

Referring to fig 61 pass through beads 7 to 3 of the arch and thread on 1G.

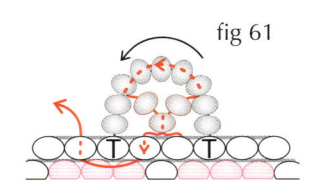

Pass down the first G just added and the other E bead inside the arch.

Reposition the needle to emerge upwards from the E bead adjacent to the outer edge of the arch (fig 61).

fig 60

fig 61

fig 62

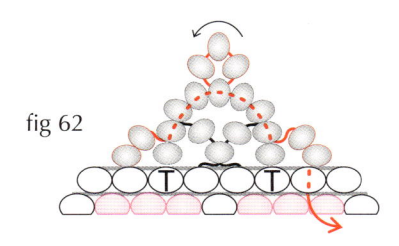

Referring to fig 62, thread on 2G. Pass through beads 2 to 5 of the arch and thread on 3G.

Pass through beads 5 to 8 of the arch and thread on 2G. Pass though the E bead adjacent to this edge of the tiara (fig 62).

26
The Hair - At present the hair is very flat. To add more texture and to create a hairstyle, a series of E bead stitches is added over top of the current surface.

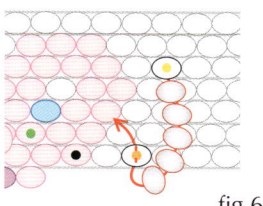

Reposition the needle to emerge downwards from the closest bead marked in yellow on fig 55. Thread on 5E and pass up the E bead marked in orange on the bottom edge of the grid (fig 63).

fig 63

Thread on 5E and make a stitch up to an E bead one or two rows above the bead marked in yellow to make a second strand (fig 64).

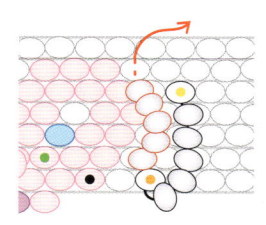

fig 64

Continue around the sides of the head to add vertical strands of between 3E and 6E covering the original plain E bead surface to create an effect of coiffed hair.

Repeat on the top of the head blending from the back of the tiara into the new strands around the sides (see photo below).
Finish off the thread end neatly and securely.

27
The neck is made from a D bead Peyote stitch tube - fig 65 shows the grid.

fig 65

start -   D

Prepare the needle with 80cm of pink thread and tie a keeper bead 15cm from the end. Thread on 6D for the first row.

Work to the top of the grid in Peyote stitch and roll the beading into a tube interlocking the first and last rows. Stitch the seam closed and finish off both thread ends neatly and securely. Set aside.

28 The Wings
Prepare the size 12 needle with 1.2m of single white thread and tie a keeper bead 15cm from the end. Thread on 3C.

*Thread on 7G. Pass up the last 1C to make a loop. Repeat on the other side of the same C bead (fig 66).

Pass through the first 2G of the first loop and thread on 9G. Pass through the last 3G of the previous loop and back up the same C bead (fig 67).

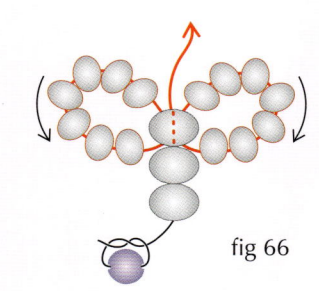

Repeat on the opposite 7G loop**.

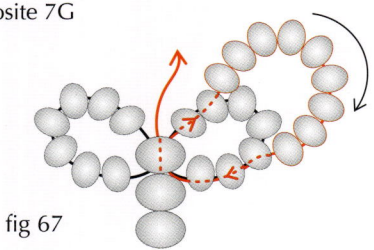

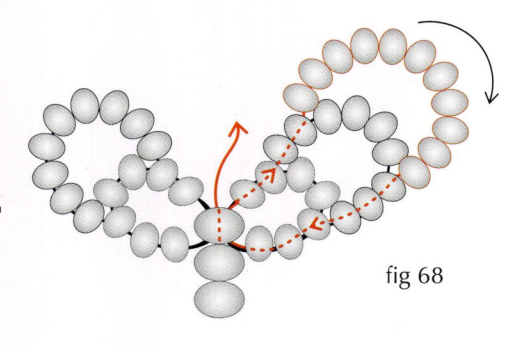

fig 66

fig 67

fig 68

Pass through the first 2G of both the 7G and the 9G loops and thread on 11G. Pass down the last 3G of both the 9G and 7G loops. Pass up the same C bead (fig 68).

Repeat on the opposite set of loops.

Pass through the first 2G of each of the 7G, 9G and 11G loops and thread on 15G. Pass down the last 3G of the previous three loops.
Pass up the same C bead (fig 69).

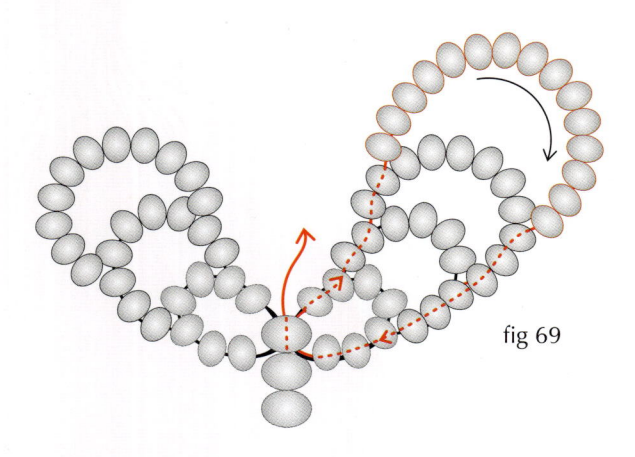

fig 69

Repeat on the opposite set of loops but do not pass up the C bead.

29
Pass down the first 2C to emerge at the keeper bead.

Turn the work so the keeper bead is at the top of the 3C central rib. Repeat Step 28 from * to ** to make a small pair of mirror image loops attached to this C bead.

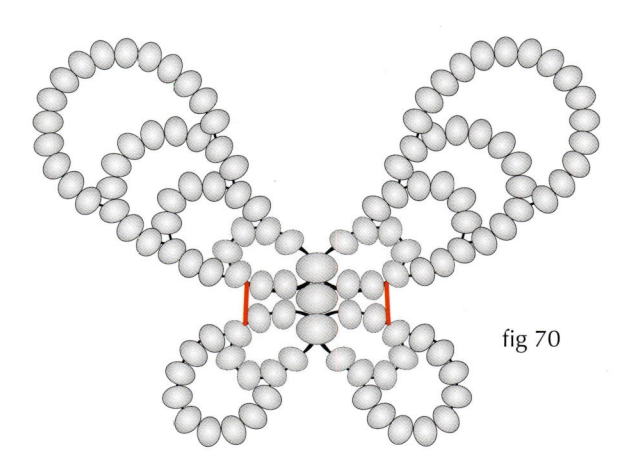

fig 70

Link the top and bottom wing loops into two pairs with two straight stitches where shown in fig 70.

30 Assembling the Fairy
A two-piece wire armature is made for the legs and the body.

The Legs - Cut 15cm of wire and straighten if necessary. Fold the wire in half.

Offer the wire up to the legs and foundation block.

Place the bend level with the top of the foundation block and gently smooth the beadwork to extend the legs. Trim the wire ends level with the point of the toes (fig 71).

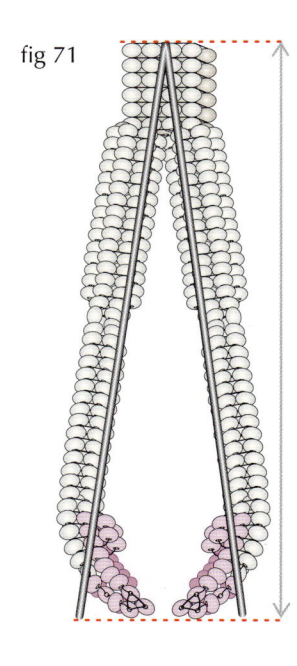

fig 71

Fold the last 6mm of each wire end into a flattened loop (fig 72).

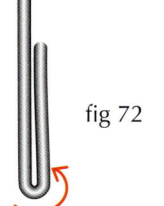

fig 72

Carefully thread both wire ends down through the foundation block. Separate the wire ends to travel down both central cavities of the legs to the feet. It will require patience and a bit of wiggling especially at the hips and knees.

The bend needs to finish level with the top of the foundation block and the flattened loops should push up against the inside of the toe point. Leave the legs straight.

31
Make a neat 3mm diameter loop at the end of the remaining length of wire. Attach this loop to the bend in the leg wire (fig 73).

Push the bend of the leg wire back inside the foundation block so it just disappears and the new loop touches the top of the block.

Stitch the <u>new loop</u> to the top of the block with several tight stitches and finish off any thread ends neatly and securely.

Thread this wire up through the body pulling the leg foundation block up into the bottom of the cavity (it's a tight fit) until the legs are positioned correctly for the body to be joined at the crotch.

Make sure the legs are the right way around, separate them to access the crotch and make a 1A stitch to join the front and back of the body between the legs.

Push the legs together and make sure the foundation block is pulled right down into the base of the body cavity against the stitch just made.

fig 73

32
Thread 1H onto the long wire end and push down into the body cavity.

The top of the body is now closed in a little to keep the H bead in place and to add a little stiffness.

Reattach the needle to the thread end at the top of the body (from Step 13).

Fig 74 shows the top rows of the body at the centre front. Two D beads are marked with blue dots.

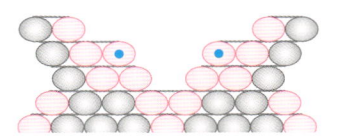

fig 74

Reposition the needle to emerge from the closest of these two marked beads.

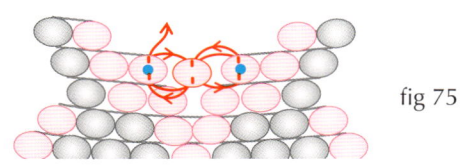

fig 75

Thread on 1D and Square stitch this bead to the current marked bead.

Square stitch the same new D bead to the other marked bead to close up the gap (fig 75). The front of the body will become very slightly domed.

33
Thread the neck tube onto the wire and push down to the H bead. Thread on the head through the hole in the J bead.

Check the length of the neck in proportion to the whole figure. A ballerina should have an elegantly long neck. If it is too short add 1D to the wire just below the head.

Trim the wire to 10mm above the top of the head and make a neat loop.

Repositioning the needle as necessary, stitch the back of the neck to the centre back seam of the body and the back of the head to the neck. Bend the head slightly to one side and raise the chin a little.

34
Slide the tutu up to the top of the legs.

Allowing tutu to fall a little lower at the front (so it tips up at the back), use the attached thread end and the size 12 needle to stitch the tutu into place. A few stitches at either side of the bodice at the tops of the legs and one or two stitches close to the centre front will suffice. Finish off the thread end neatly and securely.

Position the legs: bending one at the hip and knee. Curve each lower leg a little to emphasise the front of the foot and stitch the toe point into place to hold the pose.

Use the size 12 needle to stitch the 3C at the centre of the wings to the centre back seam of the body.

Finish off all remaining thread ends neatly and securely. Suspend your Sugar Plum Fairy on a length of clear thread to display.

Index & Suppliers

Anastasia Bauble, 64

beads, types of, 6-7
beading needles, 7
beading thread, 7

Brick stitch, 10
    Nutcracker Soldier, 89, 93-94
    Peacock Bauble, 77
    Sugar Plum Fairy, 103-104, 108

Candle Decoration, 48
    clip, 7, 54
    hanging, 55

Candy Canes, 12
Comet Bauble, 40

earrings, Twinkle Angel Earrings, 39
    Twinkle Tree Earrings, 39

findings, 7
Finlandia Tree, 28
filigree bead cups, 7

Hanging Candle Decoration, 55
Heavenly Bauble, 34
Herringbone stitch - see Tubular Herringbone stitch

Inspirations,
    Nubia Star, 63
    Twinkle Angel Earrings, 39
    Twinkle Tree Earrings, 39

keeper bead,
    attaching, 8

Ladder stitch, 10
    Candy Canes, 13
    Comet Bauble, 41-42
    Nutcracker Soldier, 91, 97
    Peacock Bauble, 80, 84
    Robin Bauble, 25-27
    Sugar Plum Fairy, 104, 108,
    Tin Drum, 100-101

Lotus Bauble, 56

materials, 6-7

Nib-Bit beads, 6, 58, 63
Nubia Star, 63
Nutcracker Soldier, 88

Peacock Bauble, 72

Peyote stitch, Even Count
    basic instructions, 11
    Candle Decorations, 49
    Nutcracker Soldier, 89-92
    Sugar Plum Fairy, 109
    Tin Drum, 99

Peyote stitch - Tubular
    Anastasia Bauble, 65, 70

Robin Bauble, 20

Snowdrop Bauble, 16

Square stitch, 11
    Anastasia Bauble, 66
    Candle Decoration, 51, 53-54
    Finlandia Tree, 32
    Nutcracker Soldier, 90-91, 93-97
    Peacock Bauble, 75, 82, 84, 86
    Robin Bauble, 21-22
    Sugar Plum Fairy, 103, 105-106, 108, 111

Sugar Plum Fairy, 102

threading materials, 7

Tin Drum, 98

tips and techniques, 8-9
tools, 7

Tubular Herringbone stitch, 11
    Candy Canes, 13-14
    Peacock Bauble, 80, 84
    Sugar Plum Fairy, 104-108

Twin beads, 9
    Anastasia Bauble, 66-69
    Lotus Bauble, 57-62
    Nubia Star, 63
    Snowdrop Bauble, 17-19

wire, types of, 7
    Candy Canes, 14-15
    Candle Decoration, 54-55
    Nutcracker Soldier, 97
    Peacock Bauble, 83-85
    Sugar Plum Fairy, 110-111

All of the materials used in this book should be available in any good bead shop or online. If you are new to beading, or need more supplies, the companies listed below run fast, efficient mail order services, hold large stocks of all of the materials you will need in their stores and give good, well-informed, friendly advice on all aspects of beading and beading needs.

In the UK

Spellbound Bead Co
47 Tamworth Street
Lichfield
Staffordshire
WS13 6JW
01543 417650

www.spellboundbead.co.uk

Spellbound Bead Co supplied all of the materials for the samples shown.

You can buy the beads for these projects loose (wholesale and retail), in counted bead packs or as fully illustrated kits.

In USA

Fire Mountain Gems
One Fire Mountain Way
Grants Pass
OR 97526 - 2373
Tel: + 800 355 2137
www.firemountaingems.com

Shipwreck Beads
8560 Commerce Place Dr.
NE Lacey
WA 98516
Tel: + 800 950 4232
www.shipwreckbeads.com